Studies in the Book of the Covenant in the Light of Cuneiform and Biblical Law

Studies in the Book of the Covenant in the Light of Cuneiform and Biblical Law

Shalom M. Paul

New Foreword by
Samuel Greengus

Wipf & Stock
PUBLISHERS
Eugene, Oregon

STUDIES IN THE BOOK OF THE COVENANT IN THE LIGHT OF CUNEIFORM AND BIBLICAL LAW

Wipf & Stock Publishers
199 W. 8th Ave., Suite 3
Eugene, OR 97401

ISBN: 1-59752-479-4

The Library of Congress cataloged the first edition of this book as follows:

Paul, Shalom M.

Studies in the book of the covenant in the light of cuneiform and biblical law / by Shalom M. Paul.

Supplements to Vetus Testamentum v. 18
xii, 149p. 25cm.
Bibliography p. [125]-142

1. Book of the Covenant—Criticism, interpretation, etc. 2. Law, Assyro-Babylonian. 3. Jewish law. I. Title.

BS410 V452 vol. 18 75568780

To Yona

אחת היא יונתי תמתי

Songs of Songs 6:9

and

To Michal, Yael, and Ben-Zion

והחוט המשולש לא במהרה ינתק

Koheleth 4:12

Contents

Acknowledgements *ix*
Abbreviations *xi*
Foreword by Samuel Greengus *xiii*

1. Introduction 1

2. Cuneiform Law 3

3. Cuneiform Prologues and Epilogues to Legal Collections 11

4. The Problem of Prologue and Epilogue to the Book of the Covenant and Leading Features of Biblical Law 27

5. Annotations to the Laws of the Book of the Covenant 43

6. Summary 99

Appendix I. Verse Arrangement of the Laws of the Book of the Covenant 106

Appendix II. Cuneiform and Biblical Legal Formulations 112

Bibliography 125

Index of Sources 143

ACKNOWLEDGMENTS

I am deeply indebted to my teacher, the late Professor E. A. Speiser, for having suggested this study and for his guidance and encouragement during the most critical period of his life. I would also like to express my gratitude to Professors Moshe Greenberg, Jacob J. Finkelstein, and Reuven Yaron for their helpful suggestions.

Jerusalem
July, 1970

Shalom M. Paul

ABBREVIATIONS

AASOR	Annual of the American Schools of Oriental Research
AfO	Archiv für Orientforschung
AHDO	Archives d'Histoire du Droit Oriental
AHw	Akkadisches Handwörterbuch (von Soden)
AJA	American Journal of Archaeology
AJSL	American Journal of Semitic Languages and Literature
ANEP	The Ancient Near East in Pictures Relating to the Old Testament
ANET	Ancient Near Eastern Texts Relating to the Old Testament
AO	Der Alte Orient
ARM	Archives Royales de Mari
ArOr	Archiv Orientální
BA	Biblical Archaeologist
BASOR	Bulletin of the American Schools of Oriental Research
BIES	Bulletin of the Israel Exploration Society
BiOr	Bibliotheca Orientalis
BJRL	Bulletin of the John Ryland's Library
BWAT	Beiträge zur Wissenschaft vom Alten Testament
BZ	Biblische Zeitschrift
BZAW	Beihefte zur Zeitschrift für die Alttestamentliche Wissenschaft
CAD	Chicago Assyrian Dictionary
CBQ	Catholic Biblical Quarterly
CBR	Canadian Bar Review
EvTh	Evangelische Theologie
FF	Forschungen und Fortschritte
GAG	Grundriss der Akkadischen Grammatik (von Soden)
HG	Hammurabi's Gesetz (Koschaker-Ungnad)
HL	Hittite Laws
HSS	Harvard Semitic Series
HTR	Harvard Theological Review
HUCA	Hebrew Union College Annual
IDB	Interpreter's Dictionary of the Bible
IEJ	Israel Exploration Journal
ILR	Israel Law Review
ITT	Inventaire des Tablettes de Tello
JA	Journal Asiatique
JAOS	Journal of the American Oriental Society
JBL	Journal of Biblical Literature
JCS	Journal of Cuneiform Studies
JEN	Joint Expedition with the Iraq Museum at Nuzi
JEOL	Jaarbericht Ex Oriente Lux
JJP	Journal of Juristic Papyrology
JNES	Journal of Near Eastern Studies
JQR	Jewish Quarterly Review
JSS	Journal of Semitic Studies
JTS	Journal of Theological Studies
KAR	Keilschrifttexte aus Assur Religiösen Inhalts
KB	Keilinschriftliche Bibliothek
KuD	Kerygma und Dogma

LE	Laws of Eshnunna
LH	Laws of Hammurabi
LI	Laws of Lipit-Ishtar
LU	Laws of Ur Nammu
MAL	Middle Assyrian Laws
MDP	Mémoires de la Mission Archéologique de Perse (Scheil)
MIO	Mitteilungen des Instituts für Orientforschung
MVAG	Mitteilungen der Vorderasiatisch-Aegyptischen Gesellschaft
NB	Neo-Babylonian Laws
NKRA	Neue Keilschriftliche Rechtsurkunden aus der el-Amarna-Zeit (Koschaker)
NRTh	Nouvelle Revue Théologique
OLZ	Orientalistische Literaturzeitung
Or	Orientalia
OTS	Oudtestamentische Studiën
PAPS	Proceedings of the American Philosophical Society
PEQ	Palestine Exploration Quarterly
PRU	Le Palais Royal d'Ugarit
RA	Revue d'Assyriologie
RB	Revue Biblique
RHD	Revue Historique de Droit Français et Étranger
RIDA	Revue Internationale des Droits de l'Antiquité
SDB	Supplément au Dictionnaire de la Bible (Pirot)
SDHI	Studia et Documenta Historiae et Iuris
SL	Sumerian Laws
StOr	Studia Orientalia
TB	Talmud Bavli
ThLZ	Theologische Literaturzeitung
ThR	Theologische Rundschau
ThRe	Theologische Revue
ThSt (USA)	Theological Studies, Woodstock (Md.)
ThSt (Z)	Theologische Studien, hrsg. von K. Barth (und M. Geiger), Zürich
ThZ	Theologische Zeitschrift
UM	University Museum of Pennsylvania
VAB	Vorderasiatische Bibliothek
VD	Verbum Domini
VT	Vetus Testamentum
WO	Die Welt des Orients
WZKM	Wiener Zeitschrift für die Kunde des Morgenlandes
ZA	Zeitschrift für Assyriologie
ZAW	Zeitschrift für Alttestamentliche Wissenschaft
ZDMG	Zeitschrift der Deutschen Morgenländischen Gesellschaft
ZDPV	Zeitschrift des Deutschen Palästina-Vereins
ZSS	Zeitschrift der Savigny-Stiftung, Romanistische Abteilung
ZSS. kanon.	Zeitschrift der Savigny-Stiftung, Kanonistische Abteilung
ZSTh	Zeitschrift für Systematische Theologie
ZTK	Zeitschrift für Theologie und Kirche
ZVRW	Zeitschrift für Vergleichende Rechtswissenschaft

Foreword

The publication of the ancient Laws of Hammurapi in 1902, emerging from excavations carried out in Susa and previously at Niniveh, ushered in a new era in the study of ancient Near Eastern laws. To begin with, there was a need to interpret these Babylonian laws in their cultural setting, to translate and relate them to the thousands of records and contracts already unearthed in the ancient cities of Sumer, Babylonia, and Assyria. The field of study widened further with the subsequent discovery, during the twentieth century, of other law collections, both older and younger than the Hammurapi Laws, written in Sumerian, Akkadian, and Hittite. Scholars eventually came to realize that these ancient law collections, which were written over a period of centuries, from c. 2100 to 560 B.C.E., were not "codes" in our modern sense of foundational legislation or regulation. They appear, rather, mostly to be corpora of existing norms presented in the form of cases, and compiled by palace and temple scribes, who comprised a small, literate minority among much larger bureaucracies working for such major institutions. Scholars have looked for but have so far been unable to identify operative links between these written laws and the judiciary; judges seem to have operated independently, although at the same time informed by an older and continuing oral tradition that, to varying degrees, is mirrored in the written laws that have been recovered. The exact purpose of writing down the laws thus remains unclear. The Laws of Hammurapi are unique in having been preserved, inscribed on several stone steles with royal prologue and epilogue. Paul (pp. 17–26) offers his views on this question of writing and, citing other scholars up to the time, suggests that these collections functioned as royal "apologia and testaments . . . primarily reports to the gods." But this issue is not settled even now and will bear revisiting.[1]

In the collections of ancient Near Eastern laws one finds many similarities to laws contained in the Bible; these similarities have attracted the notice of many scholars. Yet it is even now not easy to describe the lines of communication between ancient Israel and its neighbors. A major challenge, of course, is the lack of datable biblical manuscripts prior to the second or third centuries B.C.E. This gap in the archaeological record, while not addressed in this work, has in recent decades of scholarship taken on new importance and, as already mentioned, has emboldened scholars to wrestle anew with the dating of the Pentateuch and its literary components. But for Paul, writing when he did, the antiquity of our biblical text, i.e. its rootedness in the epoch that it describes, could be more readily assumed. His view is that the Book of the Covenant functioned as a "charter of laws for the new institution of statehood" and suggests (pp. 44–45) that pre-settlement, non-urban society may also be reflected in absence of laws dealing with commercial dealings and lack of class distinctions among free citizens. Similarly, he notes the absence of references to organs of centralized authority; instead we see self-help and role of next of kin. There is no reference to the land of Israel and we see the use of the term *nasî'* rather than king used to describe the leader in charge. Thus, according to Paul, we see evidence for the period before and following the conquest. Paul further quotes Walter Eichrodt who argued that Israelites would have been poorly served if Moses allowed them to enter with only an orally based law, for they needed a set of firmly implanted ideals to enable them to resist the social and moral "character of Canaan." Paul's comfortable assumption of early dating is a position shared by many scholars, although, to be sure, the early dating has been questioned in recent years by scholars who look to exilic and postexilic settings even for the Book of the Covenant.

Paul's approach proceeds on a number of other assumptions. He is impressed by the apparent cultural unity of the Near Eastern laws, i.e. the many similarities to be found among the Near Eastern law collections themselves, which had moved many scholars to speak of "cuneiform law" (p. 4) as an all-embracing term. He furthermore sees (p. 101) early Israelite

---

[1] For more recent discussion of laws written on steles in Babylonia and Assyria, see Klaas R. Veenhof, "In Accordance with the Words of the Stele: Evidence for Old Assyrian Legislation," *Chicago-Kent Law Review* 70 (1995) 1717–44 (see 1717–22).

society being "attracted by the magnetism and dynamism of Mesopotamian culture and institutions," and thus influenced by cuneiform law. To these Israel is indebted "for a profound respect for the law, for seeing it as the backbone of a society, for seeing man as the servant of the law, for legal terminology, for casuistic formulation," and for "many legal prescriptions which ultimately had an influence on the corresponding biblical laws." Paul asserts his belief that these connections are real even though one cannot easily explain how the two traditions came into contact with one another; he notes a number of theories (pp. 104–5) including possible mediation via a hypothetical "Canaanite law" which in turn itself drew upon more dominant Mesopotamian traditions; and he briefly mentions a less-likely idea that somehow the patriarchs brought these traditions with them.[2] Paul does not attempt to solve this problem; he relies here on the writings of number of important earlier scholars writing before 1970, especially his teacher Ephraim Speiser, who recognized the importance of these cultural connections. Paul acknowledges the hazards of comparing cultures (pp. 41–44) but does not feel deterred against doing so; and so he gives over the major part of his book to a careful comparative study of the Book of the Covenant itself, particularly Exod 21:2-22:16, which he believes to be the earliest biblical corpus of law. He considers this section of formal laws as offering the best links to pre-Mosaic and pre-Israelite traditions, even if they were then also modified by the "early Israelite jurisprudence."

A debate on the "comparability of laws" has continued over the years since Paul *Studies*. A notable "maximal" position has been stated by Raymond Westbrook who argues that biblical law, especially what one finds in the Covenant Code, is part of a single coherent literary-legal tradition. This is a challenging view and has generated much discussion.[3] There is actually

[2] For ideas about linkage in earlier periods, cf. also Samuel Greengus, "Biblical and Mesopotamian Law: An Amorite Connection?" in *Life and Culture in the Ancient Near East*, ed. Richard E. Averbeck et al. (Bethesda: CDL, 2003) 63–81. For linkage in later periods, compare W. F. Leemans, "Quelques considérations à propos d'une étude récente du droit du Proche-Orient ancien," *Biblica et orientalia* 43 (1991) 409–37 (see 411–12, 435); Greengus, "Filling Gaps: Laws Found in Babylonia and in the Mishna but Absent in the Hebrew Bible," *Maarav* 7 (1991) 149–71 and references cited there; and John Van Seters, who argues for exilic and postexilic periods in *A Law Book for the Diaspora: Revision in the Study of the Covenant Code* (New York: Oxford University Press, 2003).

[3] A collection of articles written in response to Westbrook's position appears in Bernard M. Levinson, ed., *Theory and Method in Biblical and Cuneiform Law: Revision, Interpolation, and Development*, JSOT Supplement Series 181 (Sheffield: Sheffield Academic, 1994).

no "minimal" position to be taken; what we find, rather, are degrees of "contrastive" treatments which attempt to highlight religious or cultural distance between the Bible and the Near East. Paul, *Studies* is, in a way, a landmark study touching on both directions in this debate. On the one hand he acknowledges the necessity of comparing literary, linguistic, and legal features. But, at the same time, he is also always on the alert for possible ways to distinguish the two cultures. One encounters this interest repeatedly in Paul, *Studies*.

One important distinction between the two cultures is that the Near Eastern law collections almost without exception deal only with secular rather than religious matters. Cultic or religious matters are typically contained in, "manuals of instruction" addressed to priests and cult specialists. In the Bible one finds an analogue of this type of literature in the detailed prescriptions for construction of the tabernacle (Exodus 24–39) and in the sacrificial rituals (Leviticus 1–16). Cultic and religious matters, however, are also found alongside of secular law in the Book of the Covenant. For example, Exod 20:22-26 precedes with commands concerning the altar; and Exod 23:10-19 follows the laws with discussion of the cultic calendar. It is a challenge to explain how these two genres come together. Paul finds his answer in the term "covenantal law" which he links it to Exod 19:3-6, where Israel is described as becoming " kingdom of priests and a holy nation." Paul sees the combination of genres as reasonable if one imagines a larger religious framework surrounding the laws. This framework, he argues, is present in Exodus and may be considered as an analogue to the addition of a prologue and epilogue which frame some of the Mesopotamian legal corpora, like the Laws of Urnamma (epilogue missing), Lipit-Ishtar, and especially the Laws of Hammurapi. The Mesopotamian frameworks do not contain any statement of the laws but are, rather, proud and inspirational statements about the gods, the king, his efforts to establish justice; and they conclude with blessings upon those who in the future, will protect and preserve the written record of the laws being proclaimed and curses directed against

More general works on the possibility of comparative studies involving the Bible have also appeared. See especially Meir Malul, *The Comparative Method in Ancient Near Eastern and Biblical Studies*, Alter Orient und Altes Testament 227 (Neukirchen-Vluyn: Neukirchener, 1990); and William W. Hallo, "Compare and Contrast: The Contextual Approach to Biblical Literature," in *The Bible in the Light of Cuneiform Literature*, ed. William W. Hallo et al., Ancient Near Eastern Texts and Studies 8 (Lewiston, N.Y.: Mellen, 1990) 1–30.

those who would deface or destroy it.

According to Paul, a biblical framework, albeit different in character, is likewise apparent. Paul points to elements like date and location (Exod 19:1-2) that he seeks to compare with the date formula at beginning of Eshnunna Laws (pp. 29–36). Exodus 19:3-6 proclaims purpose of legislation to follow. Exodus 19:7-25 describes people's preparation for theophany followed by the Decalogue in Exod 20:1-17. Exodus 20:18-21 describes reaction of the people. These elements constitute a kind of prologue, which is then followed by the actual collection of laws in Exod 20:22—23:19. The biblical counterpart to epilogue begins with promises and blessings in Exod 23:20-33 and a ratification ceremony in Exodus 24. Paul also draws analogies between the biblical components and the tradition of treaty and covenant found in the ancient Near East. Certainly Exod 23:20-33, speaking as it does about conquest of Canaan, creates a frame of redemptive history: just as God delivered Israel from Egypt, so would He aid them in conquest. This feature, together with the first part of the Decalogue, and the ratification ceremony in Exodus 24 bear clear resemblance to ancient treaties; and, using this mode, the laws themselves can likewise be pictured as analogues to paragraphs in the body of a treaty document. Paul thus states:

> The election of Israel is confirmed and ratified by means of a covenant whose stipulations are soon to be stated in the forthcoming Decalogue and legal corpus. Treaties and legal collections are common throughout the ancient Near East, but only in Israel does a legal collection embody the basis for the covenantal agreement between a deity and his elect. Only in Israel is there an inextricable relationship between covenant and law. (p. 31)

Paul does not in his exposition fully bring out and develop the "treaty framework" as a separate and distinct model from that of prologue and epilogue, which is his preferred reference. His analysis, would, I believe, be clearer for today's readers had he in fact done so. For, following his comments on treaty, he again states (p. 35): "The new constitution is intentionally inserted within a 'prologue-epilogue' frame which inextricably binds the history and destiny of Israel to the discipline of law." And similarly, "Thus, when all the heterogeneous components are viewed as one literary unit, the superstructure of the theophany at Sinai is seen to constitute the positional and functional analogue to the cuneiform prologues and epilogues" (p. 36).

To be sure, either framework–prologue and epilogue or treaty–offers an attractive model to which one could attach the concept of divine law in Israel. Through these models, the biblical laws can be seen as being presented to the ancient Israelites either in the fashion of royal laws or as treaty stipulations, both of which emanate from a sovereign God in the style of pronouncements made by ancient Near Eastern monarchs. Paul's position represents an important landmark in biblical scholarship because many, perhaps most, scholars have taken the Covenant Code to be an insertion into an earlier theophany narrative. Paul does not attempt to solve the many literary problems within the narrative framework; the unity he sees emerges out of his concept that law corpora were anciently embedded in larger frameworks which served to present them to the audience for whom they were intended.[4]

Another distinctive feature in the Book of the Covenant, not found in the Near Eastern laws, are injunctions for moral behavior; and these appear within the legal corpus itself. These injunctions are set in command form, i.e. in second person address, sometimes accompanied by "motive clauses" or explanatory comments, e.g. Exod. 23:9, "You shall not oppress a stranger, for you know the feelings of the stranger, having yourselves been strangers in the land of Egypt." The formulation of such second person statements has been called "apodictic" in contrast to the casuistically formulated laws that are the dominant form in ancient Near Eastern laws. Casuistic laws both in the Near East and in the Bible typically deal with secular affairs and are usually formulated in the third person, beginning with a description of events or actions followed by consequences or punishments. In apodictic laws, specific penalties following upon disobeying the individual commands are omitted. According to Paul (pp. 111–24), sanctions are omitted because their observance relies on the conscience of the individual and applies to every member of the community. This form of commandment is a categorical imperative, related to covenant. Unlike casuistic law, which deals with precedent, apodictic deals with what ought to be; they are prescriptive, absolute; observance relies on the conscience of the individual and

[4] It is interesting that Van Seters, *A Law Book*, 47–81, 172–75, argues for a similar unity between framework and laws but, at the same time, for a more direct literary dependence for the laws upon the Hammurapi Laws, which he attributes to contacts between Jews and their Babylonian neighbors during exilic times.

applies to every member of the community. Paul recognizes the use of apodictic law statements as a unique contribution of ancient Israel to "the theology of jurisprudence." Paul (pp. 118–19 note 1) also notes the presence of a number of legal formulation in "participial" style, like those found in Exod 21:12, 15-17; 22:17-19; these were likewise termed "apodictic" by Alt who first coined the term and saw them as uniquely Israelite. Paul does not attempt to explain them further or to link them with covenant. They are almost certainly Israelite; but some scholars in fact consider them to be a variation on the casuistic form.[5] Paul discusses the legal formulations in more detail in his Appendix II (pp. 112–24). Some scholars consider the apodictic laws to be later than the casuistic laws; but it is probably not possible to date them on the basis of formal character alone.

All parts of Paul *Studies* can still be read today with profit. But for many readers, Chapters Five and Six (pp. 43–111), which contain his comments on the laws in the Book of the Covenant followed by a summary, will be "required reading." It might, however, be useful to call current readers' attention to perspectives coming from other scholars writing since 1970; for, no doubt, Paul himself, with his careful reading of scholarly literature, would also be addressing some of these issues if he were re-writing this book today. I will only highlight a few of these issues, taking them up by chapter and verse, in keeping with the organization of the book.

Exodus 21:2-6. Paul (pp. 45–52) discusses the possible relationship between the terms *ʿibrî* and *ḫāpiru* and, at the same time, was also drawn to place strong emphasis on practices found in Nuzi contracts where much evidence about the *ḫāpiru* can be found. Accordingly, Paul was moved to observe (p. 47) that the six-year term of servitude for the Hebrew slave was an act of legal reform that had no parallel in the Nuzi slave contracts. But it is important to point out that evidence for this social class comes not only from Nuzi but from other places and period as well.[6] Because of his emphasis on Nuzi, Paul may have been led to give insufficient

---

[5] Cornelius Houtman, *Exodus*, 4 vols., trans. Sierd Woudstra, *Historical Commentary on the Old Testament* (Kampen: Kok, 2000) 3:84; Stanislav Segert, "Form and Function of Ancient Israelite, Greek, and Roman Legal Sentences," in *Orient and Occident: Essays Presented to Cyrus H. Gordon on the Occasion of his Sixty-fifth Birthday*, ed. Harry A. Hoffner Jr., Alter Orient und Altes Testament 22 (Neukirchen-Vluyn: Neukirchener, 1973) 151–65.

[6] Compare *CAD* Ḫ 84–85.

weight to Hammurapi Laws 117 where the term for slavery is only three years. This law paragraph offers a strong parallel to the biblical case and should be more highlighted, for its situation it presents is similar to what appears to have happened in biblical society. One finds the threatened foreclosure and seizure of persons, e.g., in 2 Kgs 4:1 "and now a creditor is coming to seize my two children as slaves." Rabbinic commentators on the Exodus law also saw the case in Exod 21:2-6 as one of foreclosure and seizure, linking it to the statement found later in Exod 22:2 where the impecunious thief will be sold into slavery for his debt.

Paul, displaying his keen sensitivity to language, frequently points out semantic parallels between expressions found in the Near Eastern (especially Akkadian) laws and those used in the Bible. Thus, for example, here he notes the functional equivalence between Akkadian *erēbu* : *yaṣô* and Hebrew *bō'* : *yṣ'* which are used to describe the entering into and leaving of servitude. There are many such insights scattered throughout his commentary.

He also presents in succinct and skillful fashion the essence of scholarly issues surrounding the ritual of permanent slavery described in Exod 21:5-6 and its parallel in Deut 15:15-16. The issues have indeed not changed over time, and it appears that the increased body of evidence more and more favors the position taken by Paul who was drawn to see the location of that ritual as taking place in the home and originally involving symbols of deity. He also allows for the possibility that images or symbols in temples might likewise have been the place of these rituals.[7]

Exodus 21:7-11. Paul here (pp. 52–61), like many other scholars, connects the sale of the free man's daughter with the institution of matrimonial adoption (Akkadian *kallūtu*/*kallatūtu* for which there are numerous examples to be found in the Nuzi documents. This is a useful comparison; but it must now also be pointed out that in Mesopotamia, unlike the Bible, the woman's adopter and guardian would not contemplate marrying her himself, as is suggested by the *Qerē* in Exod 21:8 and its traditional rabbinic understanding. Typically, the woman would be given in marriage to another person in his household although, in some cases, even to outsiders.[8] Exodus 21:8 is understood by Paul (p. 54) as prohibiting a match outside of the nuclear family, although

[7] See now the discussion with extensive review of literature given in C. Houtman, *Exodus*, 3:115–21.

[8] Cf. *CAD* K 85–86.

other interpretations are possible.[9] The requirement for a matrimonial bond is apparently designed to protect the young woman from sexual exploitation, as Paul (p. 55) notes.

In connection with the obligations for support in Exod. 21:10, Paul (pp. 56–61)) cites Near Eastern laws (Laws of Lipitishtar 28 and Hammurapi Laws 128) which require a husband to support his sick wife. He draws from them the idea that husband owes support for his wife and finds further details in Laws of Lipitishtar 27 which mentions the requirement to supply a wife with food, oil, and clothing. Paul adds still other contexts that mention these three items, e.g. in maintaining a wet-nurse, former owner of slave, upkeep of priestess, parents, abandoned wife, and the like. He thus comes to question the meaning of *'ônatâ*, which is a *hapax legomenon* that has been taken by many commentators to denote conjugal companionship (as in LXX). On the basis of the cuneiform triad, Paul suggests that it may here also refer to oil rations. This idea remains an attractive possibility; and Paul's exposition is its best and most complete statement to date.

Exodus 21:13-14. Paul sees the provision for asylum as unique in ancient Near East, which has no such institution to our knowledge. In note 2 (p. 63) he mentions *bīt napṭarim* which some scholars saw as possibly having some relation to asylum. Westbrook more recently has investigated this and concludes that the term is simply "visitor" to an inn or home and the *bīt napṭarim* is an inn or place of lodging for strangers. There is thus is no similarity as Paul intuits. However, Gaster does suggest the existence of possible parallels from Ugarit and prehistoric Arabia.[10]

Exodus 21:17. Paul links the severity of this penalty for cursing one's parents with "the biblical emphasis on the honor due to one's parents." In

---

[9] Differing views on the meaning of *'am nokrî* are found already in the LXX and the Targumim. The debate continued among the medieval rabbinic commentators; Nachmanides, for example, insists that the meaning of the biblical phrase is plainly that the woman is not to be sold to gentiles; and that the rabbinic use of this verse to support a ban on all second sales is only a midrashic interpretation; cf. further Houtman, *Exodus*, 3:128. In the ancient Near Eastern laws we also find laws prohibiting the sale of an originally free debt slave to a foreign country; we see this in Hammurapi Laws 280 and in Middle Assyrian Laws C+G 3 which, however, seems to make a distinction between a (temporary) debt hostage and one sold to satisfy the full amount of a debt.

[10] Raymond Westbrook, "The Old Babylonian Term *napṭarum*," *Journal of Cuneiform Studies* 46 (1994) 41–46. T. H. Gaster, *Myth, Legend, and Custom in the Old Testament* (New York: Harper Torchbooks, 1969) 490–91. Cf. also A. Rofé, "The History of Cities of Refuge," *Scripta Hierosolymitana* 31 (1986) 205–39.

ancient Near Eastern sources, the penalty for filial disrespect or neglect in old age was usually disinheritance but sometimes sale into slavery as in the Sumerian law preserved in YOS 28 4.[11] Akkadian documents usually use the term *palāḫu* which means both "serve" and "fear." In a second millennium testament document found at Emar, a father relates that he was excluding a previously disinherited son "who spoke insult(s) to his father's face" (*ana pāni abišu migirta idbub*).[12]

Exodus 21:18-19. Since Paul wrote, a new law paragraph has been discovered, Eshnunna Laws 47A, in which a man dies as a result of a brawl (*risbatu*); this case, like the biblical one, requires no oath, only monetary payment.[13]

Exodus 21:20-21. Paul (pp. 69–70) states that this protective law has no precedent among the ancient Near Eastern laws and in his discussion does not distinguish between debt slave and one who is born a slave. In this he follows Greenberg who believes that both kinds of slaves are intended.[14] But there is a longer history of discussion on this question of the slave's identity. The *Mekhilta* on this passage recognizes that the classification of slave in this passage is unclear, although they decide it refers to a chattel (Canaanite) slave. The rabbis thus taught that a Hebrew (debt) slave would not benefit from this law and be freed because of his injuries.[15] Ibn Ezra on these verses (and also in Exod. 21:26-27) notes that the Karaites, by contrast, taught that these laws actually concern Hebrew (debt) slaves. If so, then one must bring into the comparative discussion a number of Near Eastern laws dealing with the mistreatment of debt slaves, e.g. Hammurapi Laws 23-24, 115-116.[16]

---

[11] This collection of laws is presented in Martha T. Roth, *Law Collections from Mesopotamia and Asia Minor*, 2d ed., Writings from the Ancient World 6 (Atlanta: Scholars, 1997) 42–45.

[12] Akio Tsukimoto, "Akkadian Tablets in the Hirayama Collection," *Acta Sumerologica* 12 (1990) 275–333 (no. 28:19–20).

[13] Roth, *Law Collections,* 66.

[14] Moshe Greenberg, "Crimes and Punishments," in *Interpreter's Dictionary of the Bible,* ed. George A. Buttrick (Nashville: Abingdon, 1962) 1:738.

[15] See Rashi on Exod 21:26 and also comments on Exod 21:7, as well as the *Mekhilta* to these passages and to Exod 21:2.

[16] Gregory C. Chirichigno, *Debt Slavery in Israel and the Ancient Near East,* JSOT Supplement Series 141 (Sheffield: JSOT Press, 1993) 148–85; see also Houtman, *Exodus,* 3:156, 170, and Raymond Westbrook, *Studies in Biblical and Cuneiform Law,* Cahiers de la Revue Biblique 26 (Paris: Gabalda, 1988) 89–101.

Exodus 21:31. Paul (p. 83) explains the separate mention of minors as illustrating a conscious repudiation of vicarious talion which we find in some Near Eastern laws where, when minors are injured, the penalty falls on the son or daughter of the guilty party. An alternative interpretation for the mention of minors may simply be a requirement that their compensation was to be set at the same value as adults. For elsewhere in the Bible, difference in age does play a role in setting economic value, as in Lev 27:1-8 and most likely also in 2 Kgs 23:33-35. There is additional evidence from Mesopotamia for age and gender discrimination in the setting of compensation. An Old Babylonian treaty sets forth a series of compensations, presumably for the (accidental?) killing of citizens of Eshnunna or of its neighboring realm. The values are: two thirds of a mina (40 shekels) for the son of a freeman, fifteen shekels for a male slave, ten shekels for a female slave, and for an old man or woman like that of a child.[17] These sums appear to be set in a range that is identical to what we find in the paragraphs of the Eshnunna Laws 54 and 55 where compensations for deaths caused by a goring ox are 40 shekels for free person, 15 shekels for slave. The compensation for older adults is not stated in the Eshnunna treaty; it was probably well known and we may assume that it was in the range of 3-5 shekels as in Lev 27:1-8.

Exodus 21:35-36. Paul (p. 84 note 1) comments on the use of the verb *ngf* instead of *ngḥ* and suggests that it may reflect a different source. More recently, Malul has noted that this verb is remarkably similar to Akkadian *nakāpu*, the verb used in Old Babylonian sources to describe "goring." He sees it as a direct indication of relationship or even of borrowing for, as Paul also notes, that the disposition of the two cases is identical in Eshnunna Laws 53 and in the biblical law.[18]

Paul concludes his study of the Book of the Covenant with a summary chapter (pp. 99–105) and an appended chapter looking at the arrangements of laws in the Book of the Covenant. His bibliography, index, and list of citations add significant value to readers of this work. Of course, with the passage of years, literature has continued to appear on the Book of the Covenant; only some of these works have so far

[17] Samuel Greengus, *Old Babylonian Tablets for Ishchali and Vicinity,* Uitgaven van het Nederlands Historisch-Archaeologisch Institut te Istanbul 44 (Istanbul: Nederlands Historisch-Archaeologisch Institut, 1979) 74–77 (no. 326:4-8). The link to Lev 27:1-8 is also suggested by Houtman, *Exodus,* 3:176.

[18] Meir Malul, *The Comparative Method,* 106–7, 129.

been cited above. Houtman's commentary, which has been cited in the notes, perhaps offers current readers a good place to look for additional bibliography. The great virtue of Paul *Studies* is that it offers us a concise and focused look, a very impressive job within a little more than one hundred pages. As such it remains as an excellent introduction to the comparative study of biblical and ancient Near Eastern laws that can still provide great benefit both to students and scholars. It is an honor and privilege for me to play this small role in heralding its reprint which now makes this valuable book available to a new generation of serious Bible readers.

Samuel Greengus
Cincinnati, Ohio
Winter, 2005

CHAPTER ONE

INTRODUCTION

Law is an index of a civilization which reflects the underlying value concepts inherent within that civilization.[1] Thus an inquiry into a society's legal system affords an insight into its ideational pattern and helps to set into clearer focus the forces active within that society which served to mold it in the past and continue to motivate it for the present and the future. Nevertheless, in order to properly understand and interpret the concept of law in any given society, reference must constantly be made to the total framework and overall *Weltanschauung* which that society has evolved. Law then must be seen as an integral part of the entire structural complex of the society under study.

This book is devoted to such an investigation of biblical law in general and to the earliest biblical compilation, the Book of the Covenant, in particular. Since the contribution of early biblical law can be fully appreciated only against a backdrop of its own legal heritage, an analysis of the Mesopotamian concept of law is first undertaken. This is followed by a study of the early Mesopotamian legal collections, which are characterized by a manifest dichotomy of frame and corpus,[2] a temporal and personal container, so to speak, encasing traditional and impersonal case law, i.e., prologue-epilogue as against actual laws. From this clear distinction between two component parts, important data can be gleaned concerning the style, dialect, sources, and purpose of the literary frame as contrasted to the juridical corpus.

The question is then posed whether an analogous pattern, i.e., prologue-corpus-epilogue, comprising similar pertinent data, obtains in the Book of the Covenant, and this leads, in turn, to a listing of some of the unique characteristics of biblical law. The main

[1]) For the interpretation of law as a reflex of the values and postulates of a society, see E. A. Speiser, "Law and Civilization," *CBR* 31 (1953), p. 871, who calls law "the touchstone" (p. 871) and "the key" (p. 876) to a civilization; M. Greenberg, "Some Postulates of Biblical Criminal Law," *Yehezkel Kaufmann Jubilee Volume* (Jerusalem, 1960), p. 8; A. Goetze, "Mesopotamian Laws and the Historian," *JAOS* 69 (1949), p. 119; M. David, *Der Rechtshistoriker und seine Aufgabe* (Leiden, 1937), pp. 13-14, 17.

[2]) This applies to the legal collections of Ur Nammu (LU), Lipit-Ishtar (LI), and Hammurabi (LH).

portion of the study is reserved for annotations to the legal corpus of Ex. 21:2—22:16, which stress both its indebtedness to extra-biblical collections, and, at the same time, take note, wherever possible, of the unique Israelite aspects of these very same laws. Two appendices thereupon follow. The first is a structural analysis of the ordering of the laws in the legal corpus; the second is a study of cuneiform and biblical legal formulations.

CHAPTER TWO

CUNEIFORM LAW

A general survey of legal documents discovered in Mesopotamia and its cultural satellites reveals such a wealth of riches that it justly deserves the title *Ex Oriente Lex*.[1] The cradle of law is today no longer sought in Rome but rather in Mesopotamia.[2] Indeed a total structure of law governing a society is one of the major contributions made by that civilization to mankind.[3] The enormous fund of legal material from the middle of the third millennium to the end of the first century before the common era [4] ranges from scholastic texts and legal dictionaries to collections of laws,[5] special ordinances and decrees, deeds and letters, dockets and law suits.[6] The geographical

---

[1]) E. A. Speiser, "Cuneiform Law and the History of Civilization," *PAPS* 107 (1963), p. 541.

[2]) *Idem*, "Early Law and Civilization," *CBR* 31 (1953), pp. 863-864, 876-877, and esp. p. 877: "The really important thing is that the Mesopotamian had experienced more than two millenniums of notable legal progress before classical civilization began."

[3]) Witness its spread to and influence upon talmudic and Islamic law: *idem*, p. 876; M. San Nicolò, "Die Stellung der Keilschrifturkunden in der vorderasiatischen Rechtsentwicklung," *ZSS* 48 (1928), pp. 48-49; and Y. Muffs, *Studies in Aramaic Legal Papyri from Elephantine* (Leiden, 1969) = *Studia et Documenta ad Iura Orientis Antiqui Pertinentia*, Vol. 8, index to Arabic law, p. 257, and Talmudic law, p. 302. Cf. below, p. 4, n. 4.

[4]) See esp. San Nicolò, *Beiträge zur Rechtsgeschichte im Bereiche der keilschriftlichen Rechtsquellen* (Oslo, 1931).

[5]) Rather than call the legislative compilations "codes," this study follows the opinion of many scholars who identify the collections as the Laws of Ur Nammu, the Laws of Lipit-Ishtar, and the Laws of Hammurabi. (The etymological transliteration is most likely *Ḫammurapi*, but the spelling with *b* has been retained as the more familiar of the two. Cf. C. Virolleaud, "Sur le nom de Ḫammurabi," *JA* 243 [1955], pp. 133-134, and R. Borger, "Kleinigkeiten zur Textkritik des Kodex Ḫammurapi," *Or* 31 [1962], p. 364, n. 1.) Speiser, *op. cit.*, p. 866: "The handful of jurists . . . seem agreed that what we have before us is not properly a code or a digest but 'a series of amendments to the common law of Babylon' (Driver and Miles, *Babylonian Laws* I, p. 41). It is advisable, therefore, to speak here only of the 'Laws of Hammurabi.' The responsible authorities, then, were drafters rather than codifiers." Cf. P. Koschaker, *Rechtsvergleichende Studien zur Gesetzgebung Ḫammurapis, Königs von Babylon* (Leipzig, 1917), and his review of W. Eilers, "Die Gesetzesstele Chammurabis," (*AO* 31, 3/4 [1931]), in *ZSS* 53 (1933), p. 606. For a list of other opinions see p. 23, n. 2.

[6]) G. R. Driver and J. C. Miles, *The Babylonian Laws*, Vol. I (Oxford, 1960), pp. 5-26. P. Cruveilhier, *Introduction au code d'Ḫammourabi* (Paris, 1937), p. 141, stresses the importance of this rich fund of legal material for the understanding of that civilization.

borders encompassed by this huge fund of material extend from Sumer and Elam, to Assyria, Anatolia, and the Mediterranean coast.[1]) The entire Near East was virtually blanketed by a legal covering that bore the imprint of Mesopotamia. For law "bound up ultimately with the very fabric of the underlying society transcends regional, chronological, and interdisciplinary borders." [2]) This "spectacular cultural dynamism" [3]) of Mesopotamian law is one of the most important factors in accounting for the magnetic appeal of the Mesopotamian civilization that greatly attracted and influenced the Elamites, Hurrians, Syrians, Hittites, Canaanites, and Israelites.

A common legal tradition arose in the ancient Near East [4]) which amply justifies the use of the all-inclusive term "cuneiform law," [5]) a term characterized by several complementary features: first and foremost, the cuneiform script, the language, and the legal document; [6]) second, a common conception of the over-all character and content of the law,[7]) which, in turn, is highlighted by the use of similar juridical

---

[1]) A. Alt, "Eine neue Provinz des Keilschriftrechts," *WO* 1 (1947), pp. 78-92.

[2]) Speiser, "Cuneiform Law and the History of Civilization," *PAPS* 107 (1963), p. 536.

[3]) *Idem*, "Early Law and Civilization," *CBR* 31 (1953), p. 874.

[4]) R. de Vaux, *Ancient Israel: Its Life and Institutions*, trans. J. McHugh (New York, 1961), p. 146. Speiser, "Authority and Law in Mesopotamia," *JAOS*, Suppl. 17 (1954), p. 14, makes the same point: "The existing unifying factors outweigh the normally divisive differences of language, geography, and political boundaries and foremost among these unifying factors were the law and the concept of state." He further states on p. 15 that "the overwhelming importance of law as the key to a cherished way of life does not diminish with the end of the historic states of ancient Mesopotamia. The old tradition survives in the Babylonian Talmud and the Islamic legal schools."

[5]) This term was first coined by Koschaker, "Keilschriftrecht," *ZDMG* 89 (1935), p. 26; *idem*, "Forschungen und Ergebnisse in den keilschriftlichen Rechtsquellen," *ZSS* 49 (1929) pp. 188 ff. This one all-inclusive term encompasses Sumerian, Old Akkadian, Old Babylonian, Elamite, Old Assyrian, Middle Babylonian, Middle Assyrian, Hittite, Hurrian, Ugaritic, Neo-Assyrian, and Neo-Babylonian legal material. For the plural use of this term, see R. Haase, *Einführung in das Studium keilschriftlicher Rechtsquellen* (Wiesbaden, 1965), p. 2. For another complete survey of cuneiform law, see V. Korošec, "Keilschriftrecht," *Handbuch der Orientalistik*, 1. Abt., Ergänzungsband 3: *Orientalisches Recht* (Leiden, 1964), pp. 49-219, 466-478. Note that the title is "Keilschriftrecht" and not "Keilschriftrechte." Cf. on this point, J. Klíma's review of this study in *BiOr* 22 (1965), pp. 284-287, and *JJP* 15 (1965), p. 367.

[6]) Koschaker, "Keilschriftrecht," *ZDMG* 89 (1935), p. 27: "Was Babylon ihnen gab, war die Form des Rechtes: die Schrift, die Sprache, und die Urkunde."

[7]) Speiser, "Cuneiform Law and the History of Civilization," *PAPS* 107 (1963), p. 536.

principles; [1]) and last, but not least, a secular jurisprudence in which casuistic formulations predominate.[2])

Although the Mesopotamian civilization greatly prided itself on its extensive legal structure, a technical term for law itself did not exist, nor was there an expression for "by application of the law" or "in virtue of such and such a law." [3]) The basic underlying concept of law was expressed in two mutually complementary terms: *kittum* (Sum. n í g. g i. n a) and *mēšarum* (Sum. n í g . s i . s á). *Kittum* (pl. *kīnātu*) means "truth and right" and implies that which is firm and established. "The sum of cosmic and immutable truths was called *kittum*." [4]) *Mēšarum*, on the other hand, implies equity and justice. "It is the process whereby law is made to function equitably. This is one of the ruler's principal duties. It involves supervision, adjustment, amendments.... The ruler who has fulfilled these obligations, or claims to have done so, is described as a *šar mēšarim* 'the just king.' Together these two independent yet complementary terms mean impersonal and immutable order tempered with equity and fairness." [5])

Since the king's authority extended only to the institution of *mēšarum*, he was considered the agent of the law rather than its source. Hence, the origin of *kittum* is to be sought in another direction. An oft-repeated assumption is that the ultimate source of *kittum* is in the realm of the divine. The basis for this widely accepted opinion is most probably the statement found in the epilogue of LH, where the king

---

[1]) de Vaux, *loc. cit.* For the use of legal fictions in ancient Near Eastern law, see G. Boyer, "Sur quelques emplois de la fiction dans l'ancien droit oriental," *RIDA*, 3e série, 1 (1954), pp. 73-100.

[2]) See Appendix II.

[3]) B. Landsberger, "Die babylonischen Termini für Gesetz und Recht," *Symbolae ad iura orientis antiqui pertinentes Paulo Koschaker dedicatae* (Leiden, 1939), p. 220. Cf. Yaron, *Eshnunna*, pp. 77 ff.; Finkelstein, *JCS* 21 (1967), p. 42, n. 4.

[4]) Speiser, "Authority and Law," *JAOS*, Suppl. 17 (1954), p. 12.

[5]) *Idem*, "Early Law and Civilization," *CBR* 31 (1953), p. 874; and "Cuneiform Law and the History of Civilization," *PAPS* 107 (1963), p. 537: "*Kittum* and *mēšarum* combined express eternal verities. Jointly they spell law." For a further discussion of these two terms, see B. A. van Proosdij, "*Šar Mēšarim*," *Symbolae ad jus et historiam antiquitatis pertinentes Julio Christiano van Oven dedicatae* (Leiden, 1946), p. 35: "*Mēšaru* se trouve à côté de et en même temps en opposition à *kittu*; les deux mots se complètent mutuellement. *Kittu* est le droit qui fixé, c'est le droit avec le caractère inébranlable; ... mais *mēšaru* est une notion dynamique parce que c'est grâce à elle que le législateur est à même de corriger les iniquités, d'adapter les circonstances aux normes de la moralité et de l'équité." Cf. also J. Klíma, "La base religieuse et éthique de l'ordre social dans l'orient ancien," *ArOr* 16 (1947-1949), pp. 334-356, esp. p. 340, and Koschaker, "Cuneiform Law," *Encyclopedia of the Social Sciences*, Vol. 9 (New York, 1932), p. 213.

states, *Ḫa-am-mu-ra-pí šàr mi-ša-ri-im ša* ᵈ*Šamaš ki-na-tim iš-ru-ku-šum a-na-ku* "I, Hammurabi, am a righteous ruler, one to whom Shamash has granted the eternal truths" (XXVb:95-98). This clearly shows that Hammurabi was neither the author nor the source of the *kīnātu*, but that he had received them as a gift from Shamash, the sun-god.

The question now arises as to whether Shamash himself was the ultimate source of these eternal truths. Here the information gleaned from the introduction to the inscription of Yaḫdun-Lim is of the utmost importance: *a-na* ᵈ*Šamaš šàr ša-me-e ù er-ṣe-ti-im ša-pí-iṭ ili ù a-wi-lu-tim ša me-še-ru-um i-si-ik-šu-ma ki-na-tum a-na še-ri-ik-ti-im ša-ar-ka-šu-um* "To Shamash, the king of the heavens and the earth, the magistrate of gods and men, whose alloted portion is *mēšarum* and to whom *kīnātum* have been granted as a gift." [1]) Just as Hammurabi was given the *kīnātu* by the god Shamash, so Shamash himself had once received them as a gift from some higher source.[2]) Shamash, too, was the recipient of the *kīnātu*, and he, in turn, presented them to the duly elected mortal king. The sun-god, far from being the author or the ultimate source of these eternal truths, was "only their guardian, for that boon being eternal and universal could not originate with the gods, let alone mortals." [3])

The ultimate source of law in Mesopotamia, then, was independent of the deities and belonged to a sphere of existence that surpassed both the human and the divine. The nature of such a metadivine realm and the powers inherent within it have been thoroughly studied by Y. Kaufmann. He describes it as being a transcendent primordial force upon which the gods depend, and he assigns to this realm the powers of nature, fate, time, and magic—powers to which both the human and divine are subservient. [4]) To this transcendent impersonal realm may now be added *kittum*, the ultimate source of law.

---

[1]) G. Dossin, "L'inscription de fondation de Iaḫdun-Lim, roi de Mari," *Syria* 32 (1955), p. 4, lines 1-6.

[2]) Note that the same verb, *šarāku* "to present a gift," is employed in both the quoted lines from LH and the Yaḫdun-Lim inscription.

[3]) Speiser, "Cuneiform Law and the History of Civilization," *PAPS* 107 (1963), p. 536. Cf. also M. Greenberg, "Some Postulates of Biblical Criminal Law," *Yeheẓkel Kaufmann Jubilee Volume* (Jerusalem, 1960), p. 9: "In Mesopotamia the law was conceived of as the embodiment of cosmic truths (*kīnātum*, sing. *kittum*). Not the originator, but the divine custodian of justice was Shamash .... In theory, then, the final source of the law, was above the gods as well as man."

[4]) Y. Kaufmann, *The Religion of Israel*, trans. M. Greenberg, (Chicago, 1960), pp. 21-23.

In a society where *kittum* is metadivine, there can be no divine revelation of law.[1]) "What the god 'gives' the king is not 'laws' but the gift of the preception of *kittum*, by virtue of which the king, in distinction from any other individual, becomes capable of promulgating laws that are in accord or harmony with the cosmic principle of *kittum*." [2])

In view of this, a reinterpretation of the relief atop the stele of the laws of Hammurabi is called for. Handbooks as well as scholarly studies still state that Shamash is pictured here as presenting the laws directly to Hammurabi. However, upon closer examination, it will be seen that Shamash is not holding tablets of law in his outstretched hand but rather a rod and a ring. Moreover, this portrayal of a ruler standing before a deity is often found in the traditional presentation scenes of Mesopotamian art from the third dynasty of Ur onwards.[3]) It is an artistic device which is meant to convey a sense of confrontation and communication between the human and the divine.[4]) The rod and the ring in these presentation scenes have been interpreted as symbols of sovereignty, justice, and authority.[5]) Thus Shamash by stretching forth these two objects in the direction of Hammurabi would be symbolizing the transfer of his authority and responsibility to the king. This relief pictorially emphasizes and confirms the literary theme just cited in the epilogue to Hammurabi's laws.[6]) The king,

---

[1]) J. van der Ploeg, "Studies in Hebrew Law II," *CBQ* 12 (1950), p. 420.

[2]) J. J. Finkelstein in a note appended to Greenberg, *loc. cit.* Cf. H. Cazelles, *Études sur le code d'alliance* (Paris, 1946), p. 186.

[3]) T. Jacobsen in *City Invincible* (*An Oriental Institute Symposium*), eds. C. H. Kraeling and R. M. Adams (Chicago, 1960), p. 19. For a somewhat similar relief found at Mari, see A. Parrot, "Les peintures du palais de Mari," *Syria* 18 (1937), p. 336, pl. 39, who interprets it as an investiture scene. A ruler standing before a deity is typologically similar to scenes depicting a worshipper standing reverently before a god. See J. B. Pritchard, *ANEP* (Princeton, 1954), pp. 514-15, 529, 533, 535, 702; B. Meissner, *Die babylonisch-assyrische Literatur* (Wildpark-Potsdam, 1928), Table II.

[4]) H. Frankfort, *The Art and Architecture of the Ancient Orient* (Baltimore, 1955), p. 39.

[5]) Among the many studies that deal with the rod and ring motif, see E. Douglas van Buren, "The Rod and Ring," *ArOr* 17^2 (1949), pp. 434-450; T. Fish, "Law and Religion in Babylonia and Assyria," *Judaism and Christianity*, Vol. III, ed. E. J. J. Rosenthal (London, 1938), p. 43; Frankfort, *op. cit.*, p. 51 (Ur Nammu stele), p. 106, pl. 121 (Neo-Babylonian period); C. J. Gadd, *Ideas of Divine Rule in the Ancient East* (London, 1948), p. 90; E. Szlechter, "Les anciennes codifications en Mésopotamie," *RIDA*, 3e série 4, (1957), p. 83.

[6]) Fish, *loc. cit.* A leading motif in Mesopotamian literature is that kingship descended from heaven. This too would be symbolically represented on such a relief, for the king according to Frankfort was the "necessary bond between the

selected by the gods, was now being endowed with legislative authority.[1]) Inspired with the unique gift of perceiving the *kīnātu*, he alone was called upon to legislate laws "embodying the cosmic ideal in statutes of the realm." [2])

Since law is conceived as the embodiment of eternally valid truths (*kīnātu*), law in Mesopotamia is impersonal and timeless.[3]) The king himself is subjected to the discipline of law and may not put himself above it.

Whereas in theory the ultimate source of law is metadivine, its actual authorship is claimed by the king.[4]) Hammurabi expressly states this several times in his epilogue: *a-wa-ti-ia šu-qú-ra-tim i-na narî-ia aš-ṭur-ma* "I wrote my most precious laws on my stele" (XXIVb: 74-75); *a-wa-tu-ú-a na-ás-qá* "my words are choice" (XXIVb:81).[5]) Hence law in Mesopotamia is a strictly secular institution.[6]) Not only is LH—apart from its prologue-epilogue framework [7])—not a religious document or pronouncement,[8]) the religious motive is all but absent from this as well as from all other legislative compilations. Their major concern is the reparation of losses and damages and the safeguarding of property. An economic rather than a religious concern is all-pervasive; hence, laws dealing with matters of the cult are conspicuously absent in Mesopotamian legal collections. There is a complete separation of secular and religious law: *dīnu* (law), *kibsu* (moral rules), and *parṣu* (religious orders) are never combined in a single

---

people and the divine powers." (Frankfort, *Kingship and the Gods: A Study of Ancient Near Eastern Religion as Integration of Society and Nature* [Chicago, 1948], p. 339.) He was thus solely responsible for maintaining the economic, political, and social conditions of the land.

[1]) For the king's function as legislator, see R. Labat, *Le caractère religieux de la royauté assyro-babylonienne* (Paris, 1939), pp. 221-233.

[2]) Greenberg, "Postulates," *Kaufmann Vol.*, p. 9. Speiser, "Law and Civilization," *CBR* 31 (1953), p. 537: "The human ruler is but a temporary trustee who is responsible to the gods for the implementation of the cosmic design."

[3]) Speiser, "Cuneiform Law and the History of Civilization," *PAPS* 107 (1963), pp. 537-538, and "Authority and Law," *JAOS*, Suppl. 17 (1954), p. 13.

[4]) Cf. Szlechter, *loc. cit.*, and "Le code de Lipit Ishtar II," *RA* 51 (1957), p. 179; W. Kornfeld, *Studien zum Heiligkeitsgesetz* (Wien, 1952), p. 25; Greenberg, "Crimes and Punishments," *IDB*, Vol. I, p. 737.

[5]) See also XXVb:12 f., 64 ff., 78 ff., 99; XXVIb:3 f., 19 ff.

[6]) For a discussion of the secular realm of cuneiform law, see M. Weinfeld, "Israelite and Non-Israelite Concepts of Law," (Heb.), *Beth Mikra* 17 (1964), pp. 58-63.

[7]) See ch. III.

[8]) Driver and Miles, *Babylonian Laws*, Vol. I, p. 39.

corpus.[1]) Legal rules, moreover, have no didactic purpose; they do not serve as a goal for pedagogic instruction.[2])

The divine sanctions appended to the epilogue of Hammurabi's legal collection are to be understood as an admonitory appeal by that king to all future rulers to be guided by his *magnum opus*, since he, as well as the other legislators, was attempting to achieve some sort of permanence for his legal collection. A background of impermanence characteristic of divine sentences and commands [3]) had its natural counterpart in the human realm where laws were constantly subject to additions, deletions, changes, and reforms with the accession of new monarchs. One absolute, all-binding, normative law code never existed in Mesopotamia.[4]) Many kings, furthermore, at fairly regular intervals enacted their own *mēšarum*-acts ("rightings"), which were edicts normalizing the social and economic evils of their society.[5])

The presentation scene atop the Hammurabi stele may be viewed from yet another perspective. While the king is being favored with a boon from on high, he is at the same time presenting himself before the deity. The engraved image of the king places him perpetually within the presence of Shamash. This extension and representation of oneself is probably similar to other practices known from Mesopotamia, e.g., the brushing of the *kannu* or *sissiktu* "hem of one's garment" [6])

---

[1]) Landsberger, "Gesetz und Recht," *Symbolae Koschaker*, pp. 222-223. Certain religious laws found in Akkadian rituals, moreover, are not even disclosed to the laity, but are revealed only to the priests. See the colophon of the "Temple Program for the New Year's Festivals at Babylon," *ANET*, p. 331, which deals with the "secrets of the temple of Esagila. [Whoever rev]eres the god Bel shall show (them) to nobody except the *urigallu*-priest of the temple Ekua." (For a slightly different reading of the text, see *CAD*, Vol. 1, Part 1, p. 351, b, 1'.) Another example is found in *ANET*, p. 336, the first colophon. For the secrecy involved in the knowledge and teaching of certain priestly texts in Mesopotamia and Egypt, see the literature cited by Weinfeld, *op. cit.*, pp. 60-61.

[2]) Landsberger, *loc. cit.*

[3]) Fish, "Law and Religion," *Judaism and Christianity*, Vol. III, p. 35. Also Speiser, "Ancient Mesopotamia," *The Idea of History in the Ancient Near East*, ed. R. C. Dentan (New Haven, 1955), p. 43, and "Authority and Law," *JAOS*, Suppl. 17 (1954), pp. 10-11.

[4]) Frankfort, *Kingship and the Gods*, p. 278.

[5]) Both F. R. Kraus, *Ein Edikt des Königs Ammi-Ṣaduqa von Babylon* (Leiden, 1958), and J. J. Finkelstein's review of this important work, "Ammiṣaduqa's Edict and the Babylonian 'Law Codes'," *JCS* 15 (1961), pp. 91-104, thoroughly deal with the *mēšarum*-acts. See also the latter's study "Some New *Misharum* Material and Its Implications," *Studies in Honor of Benno Landsberger on His Seventy-Fifth Birthday* (Chicago, 1965), pp. 233-246.

[6]) On these terms and their juridical importance, see Koschaker, "*Neue keil-*

or the leaving of one's *ṣupru* "nail indentations" [1]) on a clay tablet. By means of the engraved relief, the deity has a tangible and concrete surrogate of the king always within his reach. The king would be held responsible under cosmic supervision to see that his laws are both just and justly enacted. The ruler is thus making a complete account of his legislative acts to the gods and would be rewarded accordingly. This he was obliged to do, for "on the one hand, the king had to satisfy the proper councils of his realm; and on the other hand, he must answer to the gods for the management of the affairs which they had entrusted to him." [2])

The presentation scene—also found atop the Ur Nammu stele—is followed in LH by a prologue, legal corpus, and epilogue. The prologue and epilogue represent the literary framework which encases the body of the legislation. This tripartite division is a traditional one, first occurring in the reforms of Urukagina and Gudea,[3]) and found later in legal collections,[4]) treaties,[5]) and even in late historical prisms.[6])

An investigation of the contents, literary genre, and purpose of the prologues and epilogues attached to legal compilations is now in order.

---

schriftliche Rechtsurkunden aus der el-Amarna-Zeit" (= *NKRA*), *Abhandlungen der Sächsischen Akademie der Wissenschaften; philologisch-historische Klasse* 39, Nr.5 (Leipzig, 1928), p. 20, and *Über einige griechische Rechtsurkunden aus den östlichen Randgebieten des Hellenismus, Ab. Sächs. Akad. d. Wiss.; philol.-hist.* 42, Nr. 1 (Leipzig, 1931), pp. 112, 115-117. On p. 116 he calls this symbolic action a "Persönlichkeitssymbol." San Nicolò, *Beiträge*, p. 141, similarly defines it as an "Identitätszeichen."

[1]) See Boyer, "*Ṣupur X kīma kunukkišu*," *Symbolae Koschaker*, pp. 208-218. For the image as a perpetual reminder to the deity, cf. van Buren, "The *ṣalmê* in Mesopotamian Art and Religion," *Or* 10 (1941), p. 70.

[2]) Speiser, "Authority," *JAOS*, Suppl. 17 (1954), p. 11.

[3]) For a study of these reforms, see M. Lambert, "Les 'réformes' d'Urukagina," *RA* 50 (1956), pp. 169-184; M. Lambert and R.-J. Tournay, O. P., "La statue B de Gudéa," *RA* 45 (1951), pp. 49-66.

[4]) See ch. III.

[5]) G. E. Mendenhall, *Law and Covenant in Israel and the Ancient Near East* (Pittsburgh, 1955). For a recent study of the content of prologues and epilogues appended to treaties, see D. J. McCarthy, *Treaty and Covenant* (Rome, 1963) = *Analecta Biblica* 21.

[6]) For the historical prism inscriptions of Ashurbanipal I, see A. C. Piepkorn, *Assurbanipal: King of Assyria* (Chicago, 1933).

CHAPTER THREE

CUNEIFORM PROLOGUES AND EPILOGUES TO LEGAL COLLECTIONS

Three legal collections earlier than the laws of Hammurabi (LH) [1]) have already been brought to light: the laws of Ur Nammu (LU),[2]) Lipit-Ishtar (LI),[3]) and Eshnunna (LE).[4]) Apparently these compilations of laws—LU and LI composed in Sumerian and LE and LH in Akkadian—were originally encased within a literary framework consisting of prologue and epilogue sections. While this framework has fortunately survived *in toto* in LH, in the earlier legal compilations it has been only partially preserved. LI still has a good part of its prologue and epilogue intact, but LU and LE have suffered considerably—the former has only small portions of its prologue preserved, while the latter has only the end of a broken date formula preceding the corpus of law. This sharp dichotomy between frame and corpus [5])

---

[1]) For translation and commentary see G. R. Driver and J. C. Miles *The Babylonian Laws*, 2 Vols. (Oxford, 1960). Also T. J. Meek, *ANET*, pp. 163-180. LH dates *ca.* 1690 B.C.E.

[2]) S. N. Kramer and A. Falkenstein, "Ur Nammu Law Code," *Or* 23 (1954), pp. 40-51; E. Szlechter, "Le code d'Ur-Nammu," *RA* 49 (1955), pp. 169-177; O. R. Gurney and S. N. Kramer, "Two Fragments of Sumerian Laws," *Studies in Honor of Benno Landsberger on his Seventy-Fifth Birthday, April 21, 1965* (Chicago, 1965), pp. 13-19. LU dates *ca.* 2050 B.C.E.

[3]) F. R. Steele, "Lipit-Ishtar Law Code," *AJA* 52 (1948), pp. 425-450; Szlechter, "Le code de Lipit-Ishtar," *RA* 51 (1957), pp. 57-82, 177-196, and *RA* 52 (1958), pp. 74-90; Kramer, *ANET*, pp. 159-161. M. Civil, "New Sumerian Law Fragments," *Studies in Honor of Benno Landsberger*, pp. 1-12. LI dates *ca.* 1870 B.C.E.

[4]) A. Goetze, *The Laws of Eshnuna* (New Haven, 1956), and *ANET*, pp. 161-163; Szlechter, *Les lois d'Eshnunna* (Paris, 1954); R. Yaron, *The Laws of Eshnunna* (Jerusalem, 1969). LE was originally dated *ca.* 1930 B.C.E. This dating presupposed that the laws were given during the reign of Bilalama. For a later dating of the laws—almost contemporary with LH, see D.O. Edzard, *Die "zweite Zwischenzeit" Babyloniens* (Wiesbaden, 1957), p.106.This view is now the accepted one. Cf. R.Haase, *Einführung in das Studium keilschriftlicher Rechtsquellen* (Wiesbaden, 1965), p. 22; V. Korošec, "Keilschriftrecht," *Handbuch der Orientalistik*, 1 Abt., Ergänzungsband 3: *Orientalisches Recht* (Leiden, 1964), p. 86; B. Landsberger, "Jungfräulichkeit: Ein Beitrag zum Thema 'Beiləger und Eheschliessung' (mit einem Anhang: Neue Lesungen und Deutungen im Gesetzbuch von Ešnunna)," *Symbolae Juridicae et Historicae Martino David Dedicatae*, Vol. 2 (Leiden, 1968), pp. 65-67; and Yaron, *op. cit.*, pp. 1-8.

[5]) The legal collections subsequent to LH—Middle Assyrian (MAL), Hittite (HL), and Neo-Babylonian (NB)—no longer continue this traditional literary pattern. LE too is highly questionable. For other examples, see p. 10.

yields important data relating to the style, content, sources, and purpose of the prologue-epilogue frame as contrasted to the juridical corpus.[1]) For whereas the non-juridical, temporal, and personal frame composed in hymnic language [2]) presents the religious setting of law along with the main achievements and attributes of the king, and thereby embodies the historical-poetical-religious contribution, the corpus, drafted in formulaic legal terminology, contains traditional and current impersonal case law reflecting societal norms.

The prologue and epilogue to LH is the longest and best preserved example of such a literary arrangement. The prologue has been called "a religious introduction in the form of an encomium, written in the language of poetry." [3]) It first recounts Anu's and Enlil's selection of Hammurabi to be king over Babylon. He is charged by these gods to promote the welfare of the people entrusted to his care by "causing justice to shine forth in the land and by destroying the wicked and evil so that the strong might not oppress the weak" (I:32-39). A long list of his principal military, economic, political, social, and cultic achievements then follows, whereupon he declares, "When Marduk commissioned me to guide the people of the land aright, I set forth truth and justice in the language of the land, thereby making the mood of the people happy" (V:14-24). Hammurabi's catalogue of personal accomplishments, a testimonal to his successful execution of a divine commission, constitutes the literary prelude and background for his legal promulgation.

The epilogue, immediately following the legal corpus, commences with the statement that the laws which Hammurabi established were just and equitable. In this poetic panegyric,[4]) the king declares, "In order that the mighty not harm the underprivileged, that justice might be dealt the orphan and widow (XXIVb:59-62)...(and) to judge the cases of the land, to render legal decisions for the country,

---

[1]) Cf. P. Cruveilhier, *Introduction au code d'Hammourabi* (Paris, 1937), pp. 11, 83 ff. For an important study of prologues and epilogues, see J. Klíma, "Einige Bemerkungen zur Bedeutung der 'nichtjuristischen' Bestandteile der altbabylonischen Gesetzeswerke," *JJP* 5 (1951), pp. 161-186. Further relevant points are found in J. Leroy, *Introduction à l'étude des anciens codes orientaux* (Paris, 1944); R. Labat, *Le caractère religieux de la royauté assyro-babylonienne* (Paris, 1939), pp. 228 ff.; M. San Nicolò, "Nuove fonte prehammurapiche di diritto," *SDHI* 15 (1949), pp. 29 ff.

[2]) W. von Soden, "Der hymnisch-epische Dialekt des Akkadischen," *ZA* 40 (1931), pp. 163-227, and *ZA* 41 (1933) pp. 90-183. See Driver and Miles *Babylonian Laws*, Vol. I, pp. 39-40, for several illustrative examples.

[3]) Driver and Miles, *op. cit.*, p. 36.

[4]) *Ibid.*, p. 37.

to do right by him who has been wronged, I wrote my most precious words on my stele and set it up before my statue (named) 'The King of Justice' (XXIVb:70-78).... Let any wronged person go before my statue (named) 'The King of Justice' and then read carefully my inscribed stele and give heed to my most precious words, and let my stele point out to him the verdict; let him see the law which applies to him; let his mind find relief" (XXVb:3-19). He later reiterates the religious setting of his promulgation when he states that "I, Hammurabi, am a righteous ruler, one to whom Shamash has granted the eternal truths" (XXVb:95-98). Hammurabi then exhorts all future kings not to alter his laws or remove his reliefs. For those who heed his words, he invokes the blessing: "May Shamash perpetuate his sceptre [i.e., lengthen his rule] as long as mine, the just king, that he may shepherd his people in justice" (XXVIb:11-17). The stele concludes with a lengthy catalogue of curses invoking the gods to punish those who fail to comply with his words and disregard his wishes.

Several of the salient features of the literary frame to LH can now be traced back to the earlier collection of LI. The following is a list of many of the striking similiarities between these two prologues and epilogues: [1])

A. LI I:1-19—LH I:1-26

1. Neither Hammurabi nor Lipit-Ishtar records his name at the beginning of his legal collection.

2. Both prologues commence with a "when...then" protasis-apodosis construction common to epic style (e.g., *Enuma Elish*):

LI: [u_4.an.] gal "[when] the great [Anu] ..." u_4.ba "then I ..." (l. 38).

LH: *i-nu Anum ṣi-ru-um* "when lofty Anu ..." *i-nu-mi-šu* "then..." (l. 27).

3. Anu is mentioned first in both prologues with a corresponding epithet:

---

[1]) Comparative studies have been made by Klíma, *loc. cit.*, and "New Discoveries of Legal Documents from Pre-Hammurapian Times," *ArOr* 19^{1-2} (1951), pp. 37-59; Szlechter, "Les anciennes codifications en Mésopotamie," *RIDA*, 3e série, 4 (1957), pp. 73-92. F. R. Steele, "The Lipit-Ishtar Law Code," *AJA* 52 (1948), pp. 446, 449, was the first to call attention to several of the analogues. Cf. also J. van Dijk, "L'hymne à Marduk avec intercession pour le roi Abīʾešuḫ," *MIO* 12 (1966), pp. 57-74, esp. pp. 58-63.

Translations of the passages cited are taken, as a rule, from Steele, *op. cit.*, for LI, and from Meek, *ANET*, for LH.

LI: [a.a.dingir.ri].ne.ke$_4$ "the great [Anu father of the go]ds."

LH: *Anum ṣi-ru-um šàr* d*A-nun-na-ki* "lofty Anu king of the Anunnaki."

4. The name of Enlil then follows with his proper epithet:

LI: [den].lil [lugal.kur.kur].ra.ke$_4$ ["En]lil, [the king of all the lan]ds."

LH: d*Ellil be-el ša-me-e ù er-ṣe-tim* "Enlil the lord of heaven and earth."

5. Enlil is called in both the determiner of destinies:

LI: [en.nam.tar].ri.de "[the lord who determines destin]ies."

LI: *ša-i-im ši-ma-at mātim* "he who allots the destinies of the land."

6. In the Sumerian text Anu and Enlil empower Ninisinna, the tutelary deity of Isin, to rule over Sumer and Akkad, while in the Babylonian text they empower Marduk, the tutelary deity of Babyon, to be the ruler of the world:

LI: [dnin.in.] si.na [dumu.an.]na.ra...ra... [gá]l.la.ni.šè...ḫúl.la [sag.ki.]zalag.ga.ni.šè mu.un.ši.in...[.a] ì.si.inki in.dub.ba an.nì.gar.ra.na bal.sag$_5$.ga nam.lugal ki.en.gi ki.uri im.m[a.n]a.sì.mu.uš.a "(When Anu and Enlil had ...d to [Nini]sinna, [the daughter of A]nu the ... for her ... (and) the rejoicing ... for her bright [forehead]; when they had giv[en h]er the kingship of Sumer (and) Akkad (and) a favorable reign in her (city) Isin, the ... established by Anu."

LH: *a-na* d*Marduk mārim re-eš-ti-im ša* d*Ea* d*ellilu-ut kiššat ni-šì i-ši-mu-šum* "(When Anu and Enlil) determined for Marduk, the first-born of Enki, the Enlil functions [i.e., supreme power] over all mankind." The text continues, "(and) made him great among the Igigi, called Babylon by its exalted name, made it supreme in the world, established for him in its midst an everlasting kingship whose foundations are as firm as heaven and earth...."

B. LI I:20-37—LH I:27-49, 50-53

1. The divine election, in the one case, of Lipit-Ishtar, and, in the other, of Hammurabi is asserted:

LI: an.ni den.lil.li dli.pí.it.iš$_4$.tár...mu.un.pàd.dè.eš.a.ba "Anu and Enlil had called Lipit-Ishtar."

LH: *Anum ù* ᵈ*Ellil... šu-mi ib-bu-ú* "Anu and Enlil named me."

2. The epithet of shepherd is applied to both kings:
   LI: sipad.giš.tuku "The wise shepherd" (l. 22).
   LH: *Ḫa-am-mu-ra-pí re-iu-um* "Hammurabi, the shepherd" (l. 51).
3. There follows another mention of their election by Enlil:
   LI: mu.pàd.da ᵈnu.na[m].n[i]r.ra "whose name had been pronounced by Nunamnir" (another name for Enlil).
   LH: *Ḫa-am-mu-ra-pí re-iu-um ni-bi-it* ᵈ*Ellil a-na-ku* "Hammurabi the shepherd, called by Enlil, am I" (lines 50-53).
4. In both the legislators set a similar task for themselves:
   LI: "in order to establish justice in the land, to banish complaints, to turn back enmity and rebellion by the force of arms, and to bring well-being to the Sumerians and Akkadians."
   LH: "to cause justice to prevail in the land, to destroy the wicked and evil, that the strong may not oppress the weak, to rise like the sun over the black-headed (people) and to light up the land... to promote the welfare of the people [lit. 'to make their mood happy']." [1]

In announcing their care and concern for the public welfare, two phrases are strikingly similar:

(1) "to make justice appear in the land"
  LI: níg.si.sá kalam.ma gá.gá.dè (I:25-26).
  LH: *mi-ša-ra-am i-na ma-tim a-na šu-pí-i-im* (I:32-34).[2]

(2) "to better the mood of the people"
  LI: kuš.ba dùg.gi.dè (I:32).
  LH: *a-na ši-ir ni-ši ṭú-ub-bi-im* (I:47-48) [3]

C. LI I:38-51—LH I:50-V:13

This section consists of a panegyric, extremely long in LH, [4] in which both kings pride themselves on their many feats and accomplishments. In the list of cities recorded here, Nippur—though no

[1] LI: níg.si.sá kalam.ma gá.gá.dè I.AN.UTU ka.ta ku_6.lam.e. dè níg.erím níg.á.zi giš.tukul $gi_4.gi_4$.dè ki.en.gi ki.uri kuš. ba dùg.gi.dè.
LH: *mi-ša-ra-am i-na ma-tim a-na šu-pí-i-im ra-ga-am ù ṣe-nam a-na ḫu-ul-lu-qí-im dan-nu-um en-ša-am a-na la ḫa-ba-li-im ki-ma* ᵈ*Šamaš a-na ṣalmāt qaqqādim wa-ṣe-e-em-ma ma-tim nu-wu-ri-im . . . a-na ši-ir ni-ši ṭú-ub-bi-im.*

[2] For the important role of the king in seeing that justice prevails in his land, see Driver and Miler, *op. cit.*, Vol. 2, pp. 21-23.

[3] This is most probably a translation from the Sumerian into Akkadian.

[4] Cruveilhier, *Introduction au code d'Hammourabi*, p. 95.

longer of any political importance in the age of Hammurabi [1])—is mentioned first by both kings, while Eridu occupies second place in LH and third place in LI. The three other cities listed in the prologue to LI, Ur, Erech, and Isin, are also found in LH.

D. LI I:52-55—LH V:14-24

Here both kings state the establishing of justice as their primary mission:

LI: [níg].si.sá [ki].en.gi ki.uri [i.ni.i]n.gar.ra.aš "I... [estab]lished [jus]tice in [Su]mer and Akkad."

LH: *ki-it-tam ù mi-ša-ra-am ... aš-ku-un* "(When Marduk commissioned me to guide the people aright, to direct the land), I set forth law and justice (in the language of the land, thereby promoting the welfare of the people)."

The corresponding features in both epilogues now follow:

1. LI XIX:6-8—LH XXIVb:84-88 attribute the kings' establishing of justice to the command of the sun god:

LI: [inim.gi].na.^{d}utu.ta [ki].en.gi ki.uri di.gi.na ḫé. bí.díb "Verily in accordance with the tr[ue word] of Utu, I caused [Su]mer and Akkad to hold to true justice."

LH: *i-na qí-bí-it* ^{d}*Šamaš da-a-a-nim ra-bi-im ša šamê ù erṣetim mi-ša-ri i-na mātim li-iš-te-pí* "By the order of Shamash, the great judge of heaven and earth, may my justice shine forth in the land."

2. LI XIX:9-17—LH XXIVb:8-58 reiterate the accomplishments of both kings, especially the bringing of well-being to the land:

LI: XIX:17 kuš.ki.en.gi.ki.uri ḫu.mu.dùg "I brought well being to the Sumerians and Akkadians."

LH: XXIVb:33-34 *ši-ir ma-tim ú-ṭì-ib* "I have made happy the mood of the land."

3. LI XIX:36-37—LH XXIVb:53-54 mention the land's prosperity:

LI: u_4 níg.gál.ki.en.gi.ki.uri i.ni.in.gar.ra.a "Verily when I had established the wealth of Sumer and Akkad."

LH: *i-na la-ma-sí-i-a iḫ-ḫi-ša* "They prospered under my protective deity."

4. LI XIX:38—LH XXIVb:74-75 record the erection of their stelae:

[1]) Klíma, "Einige Bemerkungen," *JJP* 5 (1951), p. 171.

LI: na$_4$.bi ki ḫé.im.ma.ni.tag$_4$ "I erected this stele."
LH: *a-wa-ti-ia šu-qú-ra-tim i-na narî-ia aš-ṭur-ma* "I wrote my most precious words on my stele."

Both epilogues conclude with sanctions—with the blessings preceding the curses (LI XIX:39-48—LH XXVIb:2-17), and the latter far outnumbering the former (LI XIX:49-XX:51—LH XXVIb: 18-XXVIIIb:91). The blessings are invoked upon those who obey and respect the laws; the curses—upon those who alter or abolish them.[1])

These formal elements can now be traced as far back as two centuries prior to LI. For LU, adorned with a presentation scene atop the stele similar to the one found on LH, also commences with a prologue,[2]) which, in turn, can be divided into three separate sections: theological, historical, and ethical-moral.[3]) The theological section records, along with several cultic practices, the divine selection of Ur and its god Nanna by Anu and Enlil—analogous to Anu's and Enlil's selection of Isin and Ninisinna in LI and Babylon and Marduk in LH.[4]) The historical achievements of Ur Nammu which led to the consolidation

---

[1]) Blessings and curses at the end of inscriptions are found as early as the Vulture Stele of Eannatum and Statue B of Gudea. Cf. F. Thureau-Dangin, *Die sumerischen und akkadischen Königsinschriften* (Leipzig, 1907), pp. 11 ff., 66 ff., and G. A. Barton, *The Royal Inscriptions of Sumer and Akkad* (New Haven, 1929). For the common literary genre of blessings and curses attached to codes, covenants, treaties, and *kudurru* ("boundary stone") inscriptions, see M. Noth, "Die mit des Gesetzes Werken umgehen, die sind unter dem Fluch," *Gesammelte Studien zum Alten Testament* (Munich, 1960), pp. 160 ff.; F. C. Fensham, "Maledictions and Benedictions in Ancient Near Eastern Vassal-Treaties and the Old Testament," *ZAW* 74 (1962), pp. 1-9, and "Common Trends in Curses of the Near Eastern Treaties and *Kudurru*-Inscriptions with Maledictions of Amos and Isaiah," *ZAW* 75 (1963), pp. 155-175; D. J. McCarthy, *Treaty and Covenant* (Rome, 1963), pp. 69-70. Similarly in hymns and royal inscriptions, see F. R. Kraus, "Altmesopotamisches Lebensgefühl," *JNES* 19 (1960), p. 127, and McCarthy, *op. cit.*, p. 123, n. 30. Cf. also S. Gevirtz, "West Semitic Curses and the Problem of the Origins of Hebrew Law," *VT* 11 (1961), pp. 137-158, and M. Mühl, *Untersuchungen zur altorientalischen und althellenischen Gesetzgebung* (Leipzig, 1933), pp. 88-95.

[2]) Klíma, "Zu den neuentdeckten Gesetzesfragmenten von Ur-Nammu," *ArOr* 21 (1953), pp. 444-447. Unfortunately the bulk of the legal corpus and its epilogue are no longer preserved.

[3]) Kramer, "Ur Nammu Law Code," *Or* 23 (1954), p. 41. His translation is adopted in the footnotes. Cf. J. J. Finkelstein, *JCS* 22 (1968-69), pp. 66-82.

[4]) Lines 1-30: ". . . there was established for him . . . of the [la]nd . . . monthly 90 *kor* barley . . . . 30 sheep, 30 *sila* butter, as a regular offering."

Lines 43-72: "After Anu and Enlil had given the kingship of Ur to Nanna, then did Ur-Nammu, the son born of Ninsun, for the beloved mother (?) who gave birth to him in accordance with his straight forwardness (and) [uprightness (?)]."

of his rule over Sumer and Akkad are next mentioned.[1]) There then follows a list of social and economic reforms instituted by the king in order to establish justice in the land—[níg.si].sá [kalam.ma hu].mu.ni.gar (lines 112-113).[2]) LU can thus be viewed as an important link between the earlier bureaucratic reforms of Urukagina and Gudea, on the one hand,[3]) and the later prologues to LI and LH (i.e., theological, historical, and ethical motifs), on the other.[4])

Two phrases found in the prologue to LU are of particular interest. The first is paralleled in the reforms of Urukagina and Gudea:

a) LU:162-165: (162) nu.síg lú.níg.tuku.ra (163) ba.ra.an.gar [or read ba.ra.na.an.gar] (164) mu.un.su [or read <nu> mu.un.su] lú.á.tuku.ra (165) ba.ra.na.an.gar "The orphan was not handed over to the rich man; the widow was not handed over to the powerful man." [5])

1) Lines 73-86: "He . . . d the seven . . ., killed Namhani, the governor of Lagash, (and) by the power of Nanna, the city's king, he returned Nanna's Magan-boat on the boundary (canal). He (thus) became celebrated (?) in Ur."

2) Lines 97-103: "At that time there were the, . . . there were the duties (?) (and) the big sailors, there were those who [forceful]lly [seized the oxen], seized the [sheep], seized [the donkeys]."

. . . .

Lines 104-116: "[Then did Ur-]Nammu [the mighty-man, the king] of [Ur, the king of Sumer] (and) Akkad, by [the power] of Nanna, [the ci]ty's king, (and) by the . . . established justice in the land, (and) [by force of ar]ms, did he turn back [evil (and) violence]." Cf. lines 112 ff. with LI lines 25 ff.

. . . .

Lines 117-123: "He did away with (?) the duties, the 'big' sailors, those who forcefully seized the oxen, seized the sheep, seized the donkeys . . . of [Sumer] (and) Akkad."

. . . .

Lines 143-149: "He fashioned 1 bronze sila, regulated 1 mina, regulated 1 shekel of silver (and) stone . . . one mina."

. . . .

Lines 162-165: "The orphan was not given over to the rich; the widow was not given over to the powerful; the man of one shekel was not given over to the man of one mina."

3) Kramer, *op. cit.*, p. 46. Cf. T. Jacobsen, "Early Political Development in Mesopotamia," *ZA* 52 (1957), p. 128, and "An Ancient Mesopotamian Trial for Homicide," *Studia Biblica et Orientalia*, Vol. 3, p. 132.

For the text of Urukagina, see Thureau-Dangin, *Königsinschriften*, pp. 44-94; P. Deimel, "Die Reformtexte Urukaginas," *Or* 2 (1920), pp. 3-31; M. Lambert "Les 'réformes' d'Urukagina," *RA* 50 (1956), pp. 169-184.

For a study of Gudea, see M. Lambert and R.-J. Tournay, "La statue B de Gudéa," *RA* 45 (1951), pp. 49-66.

4) Similarly, Szlechter, "À propos du code d'Ur Nammu," *RA* 47 (1953), p. 6.

5) The bracketed readings are those of A. Falkenstein, "Ur Nammu Law Code," *Or* 23 (1954), pp. 49-51. The comparisons were already noted by P. Koschaker, *Rechtsvergleichende Studien zur Gesetzgebung Ḫammurapis, Königs von Babylon* (Leipzig, 1917), p. 4, n. 8.

b) Urukagina, Cones B and C, XII:23-25: (23) nu.síg nu.ma.su (24) lú.á.tug (25) nu.na.gá.gá. [a] "The orphan and the widow were not handed over to the powerful man."
c) Gudea, Statue B, VII:42-43: (42) nu.síg lú.níg.tug nu.ma. na.gar (43) nu.ma.su lú.á.tug nu.na.gar "The orphan was not handed over to the rich man; the widow was not handed over to the powerful man."

The second is echoed in LH:

a) LU:166-167: (166) lú.1.gín.e (167) lú.1.ma.na.ra [ba.ra. na.]an.gar "The man of one shekel was not given over to the man of one mina."
b) LH Ia:37-39: (37) *dan-nu-um* (38) *en-ša-am* (39) *a-na la ḫa-ba-li-im* "That the strong (privileged) might not harm the underprivileged." (Cf. also LH XXIVb:59-62.) [1]

Though it has been shown that the prologue and epilogue to LH draw upon earlier literary motifs, the historical references are to the age and accomplishments of the king himself. Thus he mentions both the foundation of the great wall at Sippar (IIa:24-25), which is cited in the dates of his 23rd, 25th, and 43rd years, and the restoration of the temple Emeteursag and the tower of Ilbaba at Kish (IIa:56-65), known from his 36th year. He refers to a number of places whose dates of conquest are independently known from other sources: Uruk (IIa:37-38), Isin (IIa:49-51), Malgum (IVa:11-16), Larsa (IIa:32-33), Mari (IVa:29-30), etc. Based on these and other historical allusions found in the prologue, scholars have concluded that the promulgation took place in its final form toward the end of Hammurabi's long reign of forty-three years.[2]

The literary genre of this traditional frame found in the reforms of Urukagina and Gudea,[3] in legal collections, in treaties,[4] and even in

---

[1]) For the use of the same phrase in a *mēšarum*-act, see J. J. Finkelstein, "Some New *Misharum* Material and Its Implications," *Studies in Honor of Benno Landsberger on His Seventy-Fifth Birthday* (Chicago, 1965), pp. 234, lines 50-54. Cf. also, W. G. Lambert, "Nebuchadnezzar King of Justice," *Iraq* 27 (1965), pp. 1-11, where the king remarks that in former times (l. 3) *dan-nu en-šú i-ḫab-bil*.

[2]) Driver and Miles, *Babylonian Laws*, Vol. I, pp. 34-36.

[3]) Cf. above p. 18, n. 3.

[4]) G. E. Mendenhall, *Law and Covenant in Israel and the Ancient Near East* (Pittsburgh, 1955). A recent study of treaties is by D. J. McCarthy, *Treaty and Covenant*. In ch. 2 he traces the treaty form back to Old Babylonian times. V. Korošec, *Hethitische Staatsverträge. Ein Beitrag zu ihrer juristischen Wertung* (Leipzig, 1931), also thinks that the treaty-form antedates the Hittites.

late historical prism inscriptions [1]) remains to be studied. Scholars have already noted stylistic and linguistic similarities to hymnal literature [2]) and to building, dedicatory, and royal inscriptions. [3]) It is reasonable to infer that the boastful and bombastic tone of the first-person panegyric—so well exemplified by the frame to LH—is the common link between the inscriptional literature and the prologue-epilogue genre. A review of several of the characteristic features of inscriptional literature [4]) reveals that here, too, there exists a dichotomy between frame and corpus. An introductory section (or "prologue") commences with the name of the king along with his many epithets and continues with a temporal clause (beginning with Akk. *enū/enūma*, Sum. ud) which records his being selected by the gods to be king and shepherd of the land. The corpus proper (beginning with Akk. *ina ūmišu/inūmišu*, Sum. ud.ba—similarly LI u_4 ... u_4 . ba and LH *inū* ... *inūmišu*) then lists those events which have led to the composition and erection of the monument, and it, in turn, is followed by a

---

[1]) See A. C. Piepkorn, *Assurbanipal: King of Assyria* (Chicago, 1933), for the historical prisms of Ashurbanipal I. First comes an introduction which records both his titulary and genealogy, calls him the favorite of the gods, and adds an account of temple restoration. The bulk of the inscription proper describes his campaigns. The prism concludes with an account of the erection of a memorial in his honor and a traditional catalogue of blessings and curses.

[2]) von Soden, "Der hymnisch-epische Dialekt," *ZA* 40 (1931), pp. 163-227, and *ZA* 41 (1933), pp. 90-183; Driver and Miles, *Babylonian Laws*, Vol. I, p. 40. For a collection of hymns and prayers, see A. Falkenstein and W. von Soden, *Sumerische und akkadische Hymnen und Gebete* (Zurich, 1953).

[3]) Driver and Miles, *op. cit.*, p. xxxi, note to pp. 36-41; Klíma, "Über neuere Studien auf dem Gebiete des Keilschriftrechtes III," *ArOr* 20 (1952), p. 544; H. Schmökel, "Ḫammurabi und Marduk," *RA* 53 (1959), p. 186. Similarities to royal inscriptions were already noted by San Nicolò, *Beiträge zur Rechtsgeschichte im Bereiche der keilschriftlichen Rechtsquellen* (Oslo, 1931), p. 71. For the inscriptions from Ur, see W. W. Hallo, "The Royal Inscriptions of Ur: A Typology," *HUCA* 33 (1962) pp. 1-43. The article also contains many bibliographical references to former studies of the subject.

An important literary relationship between building inscriptions and letters to the gods has been established by E. A. Speiser in "Ancient Mesopotamia," *The Idea of History in the Ancient Near East*, ed. R. C. Dentan (New Haven, 1955), p. 65.

[4]) The most comprehensive study of royal inscriptions was made by S. Mowinckel, "Die vorderasiatischen Königs- und Fürsteninschriften—Eine stilistische Studie," *Eucharisterion: Studien zum Religion und Literatur des alten und neuen Testaments. Hermann Gunkel zum 60. Geburtstage* (Göttingen, 1923), pp. 278-322, from whose work the following comments are drawn.

Note the similar remarks of R. Lacqueur, "Formen geschichtlichen Denkens im alten Orient und Okzident," *Neue Jahrbücher für Wissenschaft und Jugendbildung* 7 (1931), p. 495.

See above, n. 3.

concluding section (or "epilogue") which invokes a traditional catalogue of blessings upon those who preserve the stele and curses upon those who destroy it. The royal inscriptions, in sum, exhibit exactly the same literary pattern characteristic of the prologue and epilogue sections to LH and LI. An additional stylistic feature of many of these inscriptions is their extensive use of participles—a style familiar to the prologue to LH. (There exists such a remarkable similarity in form, style, and content between these inscriptions and the hymns to the gods that were it not for the name of the king or the god being placed at the beginning of the inscription, it would be very difficult to determine whether it was dedicated to a human or to a deity.) [1])

Since the stylistic features and literary pattern of both the frame of early legal collections and inscriptional literature are identical, it is now all the more necessary to examine and compare the purpose and the aim of the latter with the former. The following are some of the conclusions of Mowinckel's study of royal inscriptions: It is incorrect to call these inscriptions "historical," since they merely describe the deeds and achievements of the king without paying attention to points of chronology. Their aim is twofold: to achieve everlasting posthumous fame for the king,[2]) and, primarily, to ensure for him the favor of the gods to whom he has dedicated his life's work.[3]) Hence from the very beginning these inscriptions were meant to be read by the gods so that upon learning of the ruler's exemplary behaviour and his accomplishment of those tasks which they had entrusted to him, they would amply compensate him and his posterity. [4])

In the light of the foregoing, a re-examination of the aim of the contents of the literary frame to LH is in order. The prologue, similar

---

[1]) This is the opinion of Mowinckel, *loc. cit.*

[2]) Hallo, *op. cit.*, p. 10: "All building inscriptions served the same purpose: they were to be read by future kings and other potential rebuilders of the structure. It was a matter of indifference to their royal author whether his contemporary subjects could read them, i.e., whether they formed a visible, exposed part of the building. Even their decorative value was incidental."

[3]) Cf. Klíma, "Einige Bemerkungen," *JJP* 5 (1951), p. 176.

[4]) Further evidence that the royal inscriptions were not addressed to the populace in general might be deduced from the fact that many stelae were erected in or before the temple—access to which was most probably not readily available to the laity. Foundation deposits were even buried in and under walls and thus were never seen by the people. Cf. C. J. Gadd, *Ideas of Divine Rule in the Ancient East* (London, 1948), pp. 60-61, and Hallo, *op. cit.*, pp. 10 ff.

to royal inscriptions, merely describes—in as laudatory a fashion as possible—the manifold accomplishments of the king irrespective of chronological accuracy. In the epilogue Hammurabi declares that he set up his laws in order to establish justice, promote good government, and protect the rights of the underprivileged. He magnanimously offers the "wronged person who has a legal case to go before my statue (named) 'King of Justice', and then read carefully my inscribed stele and give heed to my most precious words; let my stele point out to him the verdict, and let him see the law which applies to him; let his mind find relief" (XXVb:3-19). He then advises all future kings to abide by the words of his stele so that they, too, may promote the welfare of their people (XXVb:59-94). If they do, he prays to Shamash that he lengthen their reign (XXVIb:2-17); if, however, they rescind his laws, he invokes the gods to rain down upon them multiple curses (XXVIb:18-XXVIIIb:91).

Hammurabi is obviously interested in ensuring just and equitable government for the present and the future. That he was very much concerned with the welfare of his empire and its inhabitants is also clearly revealed in his letters.[1]) Nevertheless, his desire to gain the favor of the gods is not to be gainsaid. He prays, "May my name be spoken in reverence forever in Esagila which I love" (XXIVb:93-XXVb:2). And after making the wonderful offer of allowing all to come and read his stele in order to clarify their individual cases—a unique offer whose practicality must be questioned in the light of the following considerations: was the laity given free access to enter that part of the Esagila where his stele was erected; if so, how many could actually read the stele; and finally, would they be competent to interpret the laws and apply them accordingly [2])—he says that they should pray for him with their whole heart in the presence of Marduk and Ṣarpanitum, his consort (XXVb:41-47). He then adds, "May the guardian spirit, the protecting genius, the gods who enter Esagila, (and) Lebettum [the god of brickmaking] of Esagila, give me daily a good report before Marduk, my lord, (and) Ṣarpanitum,

---

[1]) Cf. Driver and Miler, *Babylonian Laws*, Vol. 1, pp. 23-24, and W. F. Leemans, "King Ḫammurapi as Judge," *Symbolae Juridicae et Historicae Martino David Dedicatae*, Vol. 2 (Leiden, 1968), pp. 107-129.

[2]) Cf. Klíma, *op. cit.*, p. 180; D. J. Wiseman, "The Laws of Hammurabi Again," *JSS* 7 (1962), p. 166; H. G. Güterbock, "Authority and Law in the Hittite Kingdom," *JAOS*, Supp. 17 (1954), p. 22. Finkelstein, "Ammiṣaduqa's Edict and the Babylonian 'Law Codes'," *JCS* 15 (1961), p. 103, is of the opinion that the appeal of a litigant would carry only moral rather than legal force.

my lady" (XXVb:48-58). Thus Hammurabi, too, was very much concerned about his own everlasting fame and the favor of the gods.

Just as the engraved relief of the king in the presentation scene atop the stele has been interpreted as a means by which Hammurabi's image would permanently be in the presence of Shamash,[1]) so, too, the prologue and epilogue to LH may be understood as one grand auto-panegyric to bring the attention of that deity to bear upon the deeds and accomplishments of the king. By dedicating his life to the service of his people and his gods, he would thereby justify his divine election as king and legislator.

Once it is realized that the prologue and epilogue are written essentially to gain the attention of the gods, a reinvestigation of the ultimate purpose of the legal corpus itself is in order. Controversy has raged over this point ever since the discovery of LH. Is this a codification, a series of reforms and amendments, or merely a guide to judges? [2])

---

[1]) See pp. 9-10, and p. 10, n. 1.

[2]) Cf. p. 3, n. 5, for references to the views expressed by Koschaker, Driver and Miles, and Speiser. Other representative opinions concerning LH are: San Nicolò, *Beiträge*, p. 76 (following Koschaker and recently discussed by Korošec, "Le code de Hammurabi et les droits antérieurs," *RIDA*, 3e série, 8 [1961], pp. 12-27)—a harmonization of the differences between two legal systems, Sumerian and Akkadian; (for a comprehensive study of the traditions underlying cuneiform law, i.e., the problem of Sumerian versus Akkadian law, see Y. Muffs, *Studies in Aramaic Legal Papyri from Elephantine* [Leiden, 1969], pp. 90 ff.); W. Eilers, "Die Gesetzesstele Chammurabis," *AO* 31, 3/4 (1932), pp. 7, 9—a codification and reform but of a utopian nature; T. Fish, "Law and Religion in Babylonia and Assyria," *Judaism and Christianity*, Vol. III (London, 1938), p. 40—an attempt to conserve precedent; (cf. also Meek, *Hebrew Origins* [New York, 1960], p. 54); Szlechter, "Les anciennes codifications," *RIDA*, 3e série, 4 (1957), p. 77—a unification of the norms of both written and customary law; Jacobsen, "An Ancient Mesopotamian Trial for Homicide," *Studia Biblica et Orientalia*, Vol. III, p. 132, "statements of desirable modifications and changes in the law meant to compete with and supersede it with the help of royal authority;" M. Greenberg, "Some Postulates of Biblical Criminal Law," *Yehezkel Kaufmann Jubilee Volume* (Jerusalem, 1960), p. 7—a consistent guide to the judges; (cf. also Klíma, "Zu einigen Problemen der altmesopotamischen Gesetzgebung," *Festschrift für Wilhelm Eilers* [Wiesbaden, 1967], p. 117); H. Tadmor, "Hammurabi and His Period," (Heb.), האישיות ודורה (Jerusalem, 1963), p. 51, and Haase, *Einführung in das Studium keilschriftlicher Rechtsquellen* (Wiesbaden, 1965) p.19—exemplary decisions and models of just and equitable laws (the latter also calls them reforms, on p. 25); L. Oppenheim, *Ancient Mesopotamia: Portrait of a Dead Civilization* (Chicago, 1964), p. 158, "a traditional literary expression of the king's social responsibility and . . . his awareness of the discrepancies between existing and desirable conditions. Ultimately . . . a formulation of social critism (which) should not be taken as normative directions;" W. G. Lambert, "Morals in Ancient Mesopotamia," *JEOL* 15 (1957-1958), p. 187—the collections of laws incorporate "precise regulations for specific needs of society . . . (and) offer an ideal of legal decisions to be taken as a pattern rather than a working manual,"

Were these prescriptions actually carried out, or were they merely theoretical and academic? [1]) Discovery of additional legal compilations further complicated the issue: Are they to be considered law books or actual codes? [2])

Although a scholarly consensus has not yet been reached, it is possible to infer that LH is a legal compilation of customary law,

---

For the problem of codification in general, see F. Pringsheim, "Some Causes of Codification," *RIDA*, 3e série, 4 (1951), pp. 301-311. Cf. also the remarks of Mendenhall, *Law and Covenant*, pp. 9-11.

For the possible existence of two different legal compilations at approximately the same time, see G. Cardascia, "La transmission des sources juridiques cunéiformes," *RIDA*, 3e série, 7 (1960), pp. 31-50. The copy of LU from Nippur dates *ca.* 1700, and thus must have been copied, according to Cardascia, at about the same time that Hammurabi was collecting his laws. He concludes (p. 42) that LU preserves traditional Sumerian law. Cf. above, p. 11, n. 3, for the dating of LE at approximately the same time as LH. See also Klíma, *op. cit.*, p. 110.

[1]) Cf. F. R. Kraus, "Ein zentrales Problem des altmesopotamischen Rechts: Was ist der Codex Ḫammu-rabi," *Genava* 8 (1960), pp. 283-296. On pp. 288-290, he states that the question is not whether the laws are a codification or a reform but whether they are a "Praxis oder literarisch-schematische Konstruktion." On p. 291, he calls the laws "Musterentscheidungen, Vorbilder guter Rechtssprechung," and on p. 293, he uses the term "Rechtsangleichung." He thinks that they are a collection of laws—not a law code—and are an example of Babylonian academic literature couched in phraseology typical of hypothetical scribal propositions. Finkelstein, *loc. cit.*, thinks that the purpose of the collections was not legislative; they are to be viewed as "royal apologia and testaments." For a slightly different view, see Wiseman, *loc. cit.*, who considers LH as the means whereby law and order was preserved as a living and continuing tradition. For another recent discussion of the subject, see Leemans, *loc. cit.*

As regards the problem of whether LH was ever put into practice in Old Babylonian times, see Leemans, "Some Aspects of Theft and Robbery in Old Babylonian Documents," *Rivista degli Studi Orientali* 32 (1957) = *Scritti in Onore di Giuseppe Furlani*, p. 666, who finds an incongruity between the laws of Hammurabi dealing with the consequences of cases of theft and the legal records that reflect the common law as actually applied. A similar conclusion is reached by G. Boyer, "Articles 7 et 12 du code de Ḫammurabi," *Publications de l'institut de droit romain* 6 (1950), p. 157, who says that there is no evidence in the Babylonian deeds or state correspondence during the reign of Hammurabi that a death sentence was ever passed for an act of theft. Cf. also the remarks of Driver and Miles, *Babylonian Laws*, Vol. 2, p. 53.

For a case of kidnapping and murder during this period, see B. Landsberger, "Gerichtsprotokoll über einen Mordprozess," *ZA* 43 (1936), pp. 315-316.

[2]) For a discussion of MAL, see Cardascia, "La codification en Assyrie," *RIDA*, 3e série, 4 (1957), pp. 53-71. Cardascia is opposed to Koschaker's view in *NKRA*, p. 2, n.1, that MAL constitutes "nicht einen gesetzgeberischen Akt, sondern eine Privatarbeit darstellte, also ein Rechtsbuch sei." The following hold an opinion similar to Koschaker: E. Jacob, "Die altassyrischen Gesetze und ihr Verhältnis zu den Gesetzen des Pentateuch," *ZVRW* 41 (1925), p. 321; A. F. Pukko, *Die altassyrischen und hethitischen Gesetze und das Alte Testament* (= *StOr* 1 [1925]), p. 164 ff.; E. Ring, *Israels Rechtsleben im Lichte der neuentdeckten assyrischen*

which incorporates reforms and amendments, and which, in addition, selects from several extant traditions the one legal prescription that is to become authoritative. That it might have had some impact on the populace is evidenced by its attested popularity and constant recopying.[1])

However, the ultimate goal of the law collections was to give tangible evidence to the gods that the king was a *šar mēšarim*. This could best be done by compiling a corpus to which he added his own reforms and amendments, thereby furnishing justice and equity to the four corners of the earth. Hammurabi vindicates and justifies his divine election through his legislative action which fulfills one of the main tasks for which he was chosen. This would delight the gods who, in turn, would reward the king and his posterity. As Finkelstein has said, "These 'law codes' with their stylized prologues and epilogues of purely 'historical' and religious import must be viewed in the first instance as royal apologia and testaments. Their primary purpose was to lay before the public, posterity, future kings, and, above all, the gods, evidence of the king's execution of his divinely ordained mandate to have been 'the Faithful Shepherd' and

---

und hethitischen Gesetzesurkunden (Stockholm, 1926), pp. 2 ff.; San Nicolò, "Die Stellung der Keilschrifturkunden in der vorderasiatischen Rechtsentwicklung," *ZSS* 48 (1928), p. 35, and *Beiträge*, p. 87. Cardascia, however, thinks that MAL has a "gesetzlichen Charakter" and is not to be considered a private work. Cf. also Landsberger, "Die babylonischen Termini für Gesetz und Recht," *Symbolae ad iura orientis antiqui pertinentes Paulo Koschaker dedicatae* (Leiden, 1939), p. 233, and Driver and Miles, *The Assyrian Laws* (Oxford, 1935), pp. 12-15.

For HL, see Korošec, "Le problème de la codification dans la domaine du droit hittite," *RIDA*, 3e série, 4 (1957), pp. 93-105. For the non-uniform enforcement of HL, see Güterbock, "Authority and Law in the Hittite Kingdom," *JAOS*, Suppl. 17 (1954), p. 22.

[1]) Cf. Eilers, *op. cit.*, p. 5. For a quotation from LH in a treaty, see R. Borger, "Marduk-zākir-šumi I und der Kodex Ḫammurapi," *Or* 34 (1965), pp. 168-169. Hammurabi claimed to establish justice, protect the rights of the under-privileged, give good government, abolish enmity and rebellion, and prosper the people. For a much later text extolling the king's virtues of lawgiver and judge and claiming accomplishments similar to those recorded here, see Lambert, "Nebuchadnezzar King of Justice," *Iraq* 27 (1965), pp. 1-11.

For the reason behind the variant readings in the later versions of LH, see J. Laessøe, "Literacy and Oral Tradition in Ancient Mesopotamia," *Studia Orientalia Ioanni Pedersen Septuagenario* (Copenhagen, 1953), pp. 205-218. On p. 216 he states that the differences are due to the existence of several editions of LH already in the time of Hammurabi. The variants then are due to faithful reproductions of these editions and are not scribal alterations. This of course would attest to the popularity of LH even in Old Babylonian times. For the problem of graphic variants, see Cardascia, "La transmission," *RIDA*, 3e série, 7 (1960), pp. 31-50, esp. p. 35. Cf. also J. Nougayrol, "Le prologue du code Hammourabien d'après

the *šar mēšarim*." [1]) LH is a royal inscription directed to the gods; [2]) it is representative of a literary 'law code' genre that developed a kind of canonicity." [3])

Thus Mesopotamian legal corpora, with their personal prologue and epilogue frames, are primarily reports to the gods delivered by the king in order to vindicate his royal office of *šar mēšarim*.

---

une tablette inédite du Louvre," *RA* 45 (1951), pp. 66-79, and "Les fragments en pierre du code Hammourabien," *JA* 245 (1957), pp. 339-366.

[1]) Finkelstein, "Ammiṣaduqa's Edict," *JCS* 15 (1961), p. 103, and "Ancient Near Eastern Law," (Heb.), *Encyclopaedia Biblica*, Vol. 5 (Jerusalem, 1968), pp. 611-612.

[2]) *Idem*, "Ammiṣaduqa's Edict," *JCS* 15 (1961), p. 103. Cf. Wiseman, "The Laws of Hammurabi Again," *JSS* 7 (1962), p. 166.

[3]) Finkelstein, *loc. cit.*

CHAPTER FOUR

THE PROBLEM OF PROLOGUE AND EPILOGUE TO THE BOOK OF THE COVENANT AND LEADING FEATURES OF BIBLICAL LAW

Since some early Mesopotamian legal compilations are encased within a prologue-epilogue frame, the question arises whether a similar literary device is found in the corresponding biblical collections of law. A striking parallel to such a tripartite division is present in the book of Deuteronomy, where the legal corpus (Dt. 12—26:15) is introduced by a lengthy hortatory prologue section [1]) replete with historical references and parenetic material (Dt. 1—11), and is followed by an epilogue section (Dt. 26:16—31:30) which consists, in part, of a traditional collection of blessings and curses.[2]) And, in true Mesopotamian fashion, the legal corpus of Leviticus, known as the Laws of Holiness, also concludes with a catalogue listing of sanctions (Lev. 26).[3])

It is the suggestion of the present study that the earliest collection of biblical law, the Book of the Covenant, as it is now presented in Exodus, also betrays the influence of a threefold structure, even though it deviates from the traditional pattern as studied above. The point to be emphasized is the *present* collocation of the various literary units included within Ex. 19—24. For although several of these sections might well have had an originally different *Sitz im*

[1]) Or, better, sections: 1:1—4:40 and 4:44—11:32. Cf. O. Eissfeldt, *The Old Testament: An Introduction*, trans. P. R. Ackroyd (New York, 1965), pp. 221 ff.

[2]) For the literary genre of blessings and curses found in epilogues, cf. above p. 17, n. 1. The latest study of the similarity between a series of imprecations in Deuteronomy and in Assyrian treaties was made by M. Weinfeld, "Traces of Assyrian Treaty Formulae in Deuteronomy," *Biblica* 46 (1965), pp. 417-427. Cf. R. Frankena, "The Vassal-Treaties of Esarhaddon and the Dating of Deuteronomy," *OTS* 14 (1965), pp. 122-154; F. C. Fensham, "Maledictions and Benedictions in Ancient Near Eastern Vassal-Treaties and the Old Testament," *ZAW* 74 (1962), pp. 1-9; D. J. McCarthy, *Treaty and Covenant* (= *Analecta Biblica* 21 [Rome, 1963]), pp. 122-123; and D. R. Hillers, *Treaty Curses and the Old Testament Prophets* (= *Biblica et Orientalia* 16 [Rome, 1964]), pp. 30-42.

[3]) See above, n. 2. The "Laws of Holiness" in Leviticus actually consist of small independent blocks of law combined into one formal legal corpus. Thus the sanctions of Lev. 26 are meant to apply to the entire collection even though the individual units themselves may still preserve their own codas, e.g., 18:1-5, 24-30; 19:37; 20:26; and others.

Leben and thus are to be studied as independent units,[1]) when once arranged in their present literary complex, they exhibit an overall structure which must be subject to further investigation.[2]) Here, then, the whole may consist of more than its component parts.

The mosaic of Ex. 19—24 presents a number of difficult literary-critical problems: How does one separate the various strands of tradition that have been woven together to form the fabric of the account of the preparations for the theophany in Ex. 19? Does the term "Book of the Covenant" (Ex. 24:7) refer originally to the legal corpus of Ex. 20:22—23:30 or merely to the Decalogue, Ex. 20:2-17? What is the relationship of the legal corpus to the Decalogue—is it original or a secondary insertion? How does the pericope of Ex. 20:18-21 (describing the people's reaction to the theophany) relate to the sequence of events? Furthermore, what is the explanation for the heterogeneous combination of cultic, legal, and moral injunctions within the juridical corpus: (1) 20:22-26, cultic prescriptions, (2) 21:2—22:16, legal precepts casuistically formulated (together with a block of participially formulated laws, 21:12, 15-17), (3) 22:17—23:13, moral instructions interspersed with additional religious obligations, e.g., 22:19, 28-30; 23:10-13, (4) 23:14-19, cultic calendar? What, in turn, is the relationship between this cultic calendar and the almost identical one found in Ex. 34:14-26? Finally, what is the nature of the concluding section, Ex. 23:20-33, which itself is most likely a composite of two separate units, vss. 20-25 and vss. 26-33, and is analogous, in turn, to Ex. 34:9-13?

While it is not within the scope of this study to attempt to answer all these questions, several of them do relate directly to our thesis and thus must be carefully analyzed. To help clarify the general structure of these chapters, the following pattern of events should be kept in mind:

---

[1]) Eissfeldt, *op. cit.*, pp. 212-219, and "Die Komposition der Sinai-Erzählung Ex. 19-34," *FF* 40 (1966), pp. 213-215 = *Kleine Schriften*, Vol. 4 (Tübingen, 1968), pp. 231-237.

[2]) *Idem*, *The Old Testament*, p. 241: "The important point is indeed, in the last analysis, not this or that individual dissection of the material, but the total outlook." In Rosenzweig's letter to Rosenheim wherein he identifies the assumed final redactor of the Torah "not as redactor but as *rabbenu*—for he is our teacher," he comments in a postcript on the importance of "a preoccupation with the new (R) formulation of the question alongside of the old (J, E, and P) formulation of the question." F. Rosenzweig, "Die Einheit der Bibel," *Kleinere Schriften* (Berlin, 1937), pp. 129, 133, respectively. The role of R in the final juxtaposition of the various heterogeneous literary units must not be overlooked.

(1)	19:1-2	date formula and geographical location [1]
(2)	19:3-6	proclamation of the purpose of the forthcoming legislation
(3)	19:7-25	preparations for the theophany
(4)	20:1-17	Decalogue
(5)	20:18-21	reaction of the people
(6)	20:22—23:19	legal corpus
(7)	23:20-33	promises and blessings
(8)	24	ratification ceremonies

The two sections preceding the legal corpus which are set forth as a formal declaration of YHWH are 19:3-6 and 20:1-17; both of these will now be commented upon:

(1) 19:3-6 [2]

"Thus shall you say to the house of Jacob and declare to the children of Israel:
'You have seen what I did to the Egyptians,
How I bore you on eagles' wings and brought you to me.
Now, then, if you will obey me faithfully and keep my covenant,
You shall be my treasured possession among all the peoples.
Indeed, all the earth is mine,
But you shall be to me a kingdom of priests and a holy nation'." [3]

A stylistic and contextual study of this pericope reveals an oracular

[1] Cf. the date formula at the beginning of LE; B. Landsberger, "Jungfräulichkeit: Ein Beitrag zum Thema 'Beilager und Eheschliessung' (mit einem Anhang: Neue Lesungen und Deutungen im Gesetzbuch von Ešnunna)," *Symbolae Juridicae et Historicae Martino David Dedicatae*, Vol. 2 (Leiden, 1968), pp. 66-67.

[2] M. Haelvoet, "La théophanie du Sinai. Analyse littéraire des récits d'Ex. XIX-XXIV," *Ephemerides Theologicae Lovanienses* 29 (1953), pp. 375-382, thinks that this pericope is (post-)Deuteronomic. Similar views are expressed by J. L'Hour, "L'alliance de Sichem," *RB* 69 (1962), pp. 350 ff., and M. Noth, *Exodus*, trans. J. S. Bowden (Philadelphia, 1962), p. 157. However, W. Beyerlin, *Origins and History of the Oldest Sinaitic Traditions*, trans. S. Rudman (Oxford, 1965), pp. 66-77, esp. p. 70, n. 229, has pointed out that the points of contact between this pericope and the language and style of Deuteronomy do not necessarily imply dependence on Deuteronomy. Unnoticed by all these scholars is the specific use of several terms found here that are unprecedented in the Bible. These will be commented upon in this chapter. For the influence of the motifs of the Sinaitic theophany on Deuteronomy, see J. Muilenburg, "The 'Office' of the Prophet in Ancient Israel," *The Bible in Modern Scholarship*, ed. J. Philip Hyatt (Nashville, 1965), p. 83.

For doubts expressed as to whether these verses were originally part of the Sinai narrative, cf. McCarthy, *op. cit.*, p. 175.

[3] Cf. A. B. Ehrlich, *Randglossen zur hebräischen Bibel*, Vol. I (Leipzig, 1908), p. 337.

introduction (19:3b), a proclamation of the mighty acts of God (19:4), and the covenant condition (19:5-6).[1] In an elevated and hymnic style [2] marked by parallelism, this section proclaims in historical terms the basis of God's claim upon Israel.[3] Vss. 3-6, furthermore, clearly and unequivocably state the purpose of the forthcoming covenant: Israel, by observing the covenant laws, shall become the Lord's סגולה "treasured possession," [4] a ממלכת כהנים "kingdom of priests," i.e., a people who will occupy among the nations of the world the sanctified position that the priests enjoy in each individual nation,[5] and a גוי קדוש "holy nation" set apart and dedicated to the service of YHWH. Israel, then, has only to be faithful to the covenant in order to remain a spiritual aristocracy.[6] The covenant, a well known political institution, is here adapted to a unique theological concept, the election of Israel.[7] The election of Israel is confirmed and ratified by means of a covenant [8] whose stipulations are soon to be stated in the forthcoming Decalogue and legal corpus. Treaties

---

1) This study was made by Muilenburg, "The Form and Structure of the Covenantal Formulations," *VT* 9 (1959), pp. 347-365, and is now followed by K. Baltzer, *Das Bundesformular*, 2. Auflage (Neukirchen, 1964), pp. 37-38, and Beyerlin, *loc. cit.* Muilenburg, *op. cit.*, p. 352, thinks that this is the *fons et origo* of covenantal pericopes. McCarthy, *op. cit.*, pp. 155 ff., on the other hand, correctly voices a dissenting opinion when he states that there is nothing present here to take the place of the stipulations which are always to be found in covenants; there is merely a demand for obedience which, in turn, will be properly rewarded. The stipulations, according to our view, are first mentioned in the forthcoming sections.

2) Cf. McCarthy, *op. cit.*, p. 156, (who calls it "hieratic"); Haelvoet, *op. cit.*, pp. 375-381, and L'Hour, *op. cit.*, p. 356, n. 280.

3) Muilenburg, *loc. cit.*

4) For a study of this term, see M. Greenberg, "Hebrew *s^e^gullā*: Akkadian *sikiltu*," *JAOS* 71 (1951), pp. 172-174. The word now appears in a letter from the Hittite king to 'Ammurapi, king of Ugarit (*PRU* V, No. 60, l. 12): ʿ[ ] [*s*]*glth. at* "You are [his servant] (?) his property." See H.B. Huffmond and S. B. Parker, "A Further Note on the Treaty Background of Hebrew *Yādaʿ*," *BASOR* 184 (1966), pp. 36-38.

5) For a collection of the various translations offered for this expression, see R. B. Y. Scott, "A Kingdom of Priests (Ex. XIX:6)," *OTS* 8 (1950), pp. 213-219; J. B. Bauer, "Könige und Priester, ein heiliges Volk (Exodus XIX, 6)," *BZ* 2 (1958), pp. 283-286; and W. Moran, "A Kingdom of Priests," *The Bible in Current Catholic Thought*, ed. J. L. McKenzie (New York, 1962), pp. 7-20.

6) Cf. U. Cassuto, *A Commentary on the Book of Exodus*, Heb. (Jerusalem, 1951), p. 156.

7) Cf. G. E. Wright, *The Old Testament Against Its Environment* (= *Studies in Biblical Theology*, No. 2 [Naperville, 1957]), pp. 54 f. Cf. also McCarthy, *op. cit.*, p. 174.

8) For the importance of covenant in Israel, see W. Eichrodt, *Theology of the Old Testament*, Vol. I, trans. J. A. Baker (Philadelphia, 1961).

and legal collections are common throughout the ancient Near East,[1]) but only in Israel does a legal collection embody the basis for the covenantal agreement between a deity and his elect. Only in Israel is there an inextricable relationship between covenant and law.[2]) The future of this nation now becomes predicated upon the observance of covenantal law.

The unique status conferred upon the corporate body of Israel is expressed in two poetic images unprecedented in the rest of the Bible: ממלכת כהנים and גוי קדוש. While the term עם קדוש is found several times in Deuteronomy,[3]) the expression גוי קדוש is a *hapax legomenon*. The intended emphasis upon גוי and its corresponding synonym ממלכה—both political terms meaning "nation/state"—rather than עם— a familial term meaning "kinsmen/family" [4])— is fundamental to a correct understanding of the historical setting of the forthcoming legal collection. For this body of law is an integral part of the transformation of the divine promise to Abraham, "I will make of you a great nation" (Gen. 12:2), into a reality during the time of Moses.

> "The term in question [in Gen. 12:2] is *goy* not *ʿam*, and rightly so. For Abraham was an *ʿam* to begin with.... The reason, then, behind the patriarch's departure from Mesopotamia and the Israelite liberation from Egypt was that Israel might become a nation.... Israel was his [God's] *ʿam*. It was chosen and treated as such. But to carry out God's purpose, the *ʿam* was not enough; what was needed was the added status and stability of nationhood in a land specifically designated for that purpose." [5])

However, Israel lacked not only a land, but a constitution as well. This, then, is the importance of the unique term גוי קדוש: Israel is about to become a polity (גוי/ממלכה) based on law. The future institution of statehood is presently granted an official charter. First Israel is told what its mission is to be: it was elected for the purpose of becoming a "holy nation" devoted to God. Then the means to achieve and maintain this consecrated status are fully expounded in

---

[1]) For recent studies, see McCarthy, *Treaty and Covenant*, and "Covenant in the Old Testament: The Present State of Inquiry," *CBQ* 27 (1965), pp. 217-240.

[2]) Weinfeld, *Deuteronomy and the Deuteronomic School* (Oxford, 1970), ch. 2, correctly emphasizes the convergence of treaty and law-corpus forms in Deuteronomy.

[3]) Dt. 7:6; 14:2, 21; 26:19; 28:9; cf. also Num. 16:3 and Isa. 62:12.

[4]) E. A. Speiser, " 'People' and 'Nation' of Israel," *JBL* 79 (1960), pp. 157-163. For another view, see A. Cody, "When is the Chosen People Called a *Gôy*," *VT* 14 (1964), pp. 1-6.

[5]) Speiser, *op. cit.*, p. 163.

the Decalogue and legal corpus which together form the constitution of this newly created nation. The epithets "kingdom of priests" and "holy nation" are more than mere attributes; they are an ideal which can only be realized when and if Israel fulfills the will of God as expressed in his covenant.[1])

This covenant is founded upon the historical experience of Israel: "You have seen what I did to the Egyptians, how I bore you on eagles' wings and brought you to me" (Ex. 19:4). The deliverance from Egypt, the house of spiritual and physical bondage, was the first major feat performed by God for Israel and, as such, inaugurated the history of that nation. The purpose of this historical prelude is not so much identification as motivation: God's redemptive intervention into history demands a corresponding act on the part of the redeemed;[2]) their response now becomes obedience to God's will as revealed in the covenant. (The rest of this chapter, Ex. 19:7-25, dramatizes the preparations for the theophany and describes the awesome natural phenomena accompanying the manifestation of God.)

This motif of redemptive history is heard once again in the introduction to the Decalogue: "Since I the Lord am your God who brought you out of the land of Egypt, the house of bondage, therefore..." (Ex. 20:2). The children of Israel, individually addressed as members of the chosen community, owe their fidelity to the Lord who has redeemed them from bondage. Whatever might have been the original *Sitz im Leben* of the Decalogue,[3]) in its present context it

---

[1]) Cf. the remarks of M. J. O'Connell, "The Concept of Commandment in the Old Testament," *ThSt* 21 (1960), pp. 370-373.

[2]) An analogue to this motif is found in the historical introduction ("prologue") to Hittite vassal treaties where the suzerain states the basis of his claim upon the vassal in historical terms. It must be remembered, however, that the relationship in the Bible between God and Israel is not portrayed so much as that of a suzerain to a vassal, but rather as a more personal one, i.e., Israel is God's "treasured possession."

[3]) For a sampling of the enormous literature on the Decalogue, cf. H. Rowley, "Moses and the Decalogue," *BJRL* 34 (1951), pp. 81-118; J. J. Stamm, *Der Dekalog im Lichte der neueren Forschung* (Bern, 1958), and "Dreissig Jahre Dekalogforschung," *ThR* 27 (1961), pp. 189-239, 281-305; H. G. Reventlow, *Gebot und Predigt im Dekalog* (Gütersloh, 1962); W. J. Harrelson, "Ten Commandments," *IDB*, Vol. IV (New York, 1962), pp. 569-573; Noth, *op. cit.*, pp. 160-168; L'Hour, *op. cit.*, pp. 353 ff.; E. Nielsen, *Die zehn Gebote* (Copenhagen, 1965); J. J. Stamm and M. E. Andrew, *The Ten Commandments in Recent Research* (Naperville, 1967); A. Jepsen, "Beiträge zur Auslegung und Geschichte des Dekalogs," *ZAW* 79 (1967), pp. 277-304; and W. F. Albright's reference in *Yahweh and the Gods of Canaan* (New York, 1968), p. 174, n. 56, to his forthcoming *History of the Religion of Israel*, where he will present his evidence for a date of no later than the thirteenth century for the Decalogue.

comes to delineate the principal obligations imposed upon this newly formed "holy nation." It is thus the initial elaboration of the fundamental religious and moral requirements [1]) alluded to in the former pericope. This summary of exemplary rules together with the ensuing legal corpus form the "text of the covenant"between God and Israel.[2])

(The next section, Ex. 20:18-21, may have originally belonged to the narrative introduction preceding the Decalogue; if such is the case, it would have been transposed to its present setting with the

---

[1]) Cf. S. R. Driver, *The Book of Exodus* (Cambridge, 1918), *in situ*; Cassuto, *op. cit.*, p. 165; G. Fohrer, "Das sogenannte apodiktisch formulierte Recht und der Dekalog," *KuD* 11 (1965), pp. 52, 67, 73; E. Gerstenberger, "Covenant and Commandment," *JBL* 84 (1965), p. 51. G. E. Mendenhall, *Law and Covenant in Israel and the Ancient Near East* (Pittsburgh, 1955 [= *BA* 17 (1954), pp. 26-46, 50-76]), p. 15, states that "the Decalogue is the statement of religious obligation which the law protected." Cf. Harrelson, *op. cit.*, p. 161, and "Law in the Old Testament," *IDB*, Vol. III, p. 80.

According to Eichrodt, *op. cit.*, p. 76, "The really remarkable feature of the Decalogue is rather the definite connection of the moral precepts with the basic religious commands."

[2]) However, the Decalogue itself is not the "text of the covenant," *contra* Mendenhall, *op. cit.*, p. 5. Mendelhall in this study first gives a brief résumé of Korošec's juristic analysis of the Hittite covenant form (V. Korošec, *Hethitische Staatsverträge. Ein Beitrag zu ihrer juristischen Wertung* [Leipzig, 1931]): (1) preamble, (2) historical prologue, (3) stipulations, (4) provision for deposit in temple and periodic public reading, (5) list of gods as witnesses, (6) curses and blessings formula. He then attempts to show that the Decalogue falls into this same pattern (p. 36). However, as he himself points out (pp. 39-40), the last three elements of the Hittite treaty pattern are lacking in the Decalogue. Though the structure of Hittite treaties is somewhat more flexible than Mendenhall first posited—cf. McCarthy, *op. cit.*, p. 41, for a revised version of Korošec's study, and pp. 158-161, for his objections to Mendenhall; cf. also Gerstenberger, *op. cit.*, pp. 46 ff.—the Decalogue, nevertheless, should not be forced to conform to this preconceived pattern. It is unfortunate, then, that Beyerlin, *op. cit.*, pp. 59-67, goes one step beyond Mendenhall in attempting to find all the elements of the formal structure of Hittite treaties present in the Decalogue. See the cautious remarks of W. Zimmerli, "Das Gesetz im Alten Testament," *ThLZ* 85 (1960), p. 493. (The book of Deuteronomy, on the other hand, is a very good example of the treaty pattern as outlined above.) See Weinfeld, *op. cit.*, ch. 2. Following Baltzer, *Das Bundesformular*, pp. 22-33, he designates point (3) above as the basic stipulation of allegiance and (4) as the covenant clauses.

While Mendenhall compared both the Decalogue and Jos. 24 to Hittite treaties, Beyerlin examined only the former. Baltzer, *loc. cit.*, in turn, broadened the scope of investigation to include other sections of the Bible and post-biblical literature by his distinction between covenant forms and renewals of covenant. For the latest review of the problem, see McCarthy, "Covenant in the Old Testament: the Present State of Inquiry," *CBQ* 27 (1965), pp. 217-240.

For the similarity of Ex. 20:3-6 with the motif of absolute faithfulness in treaties, cf. Beyerlin, *op. cit.*, p. 63, and F. C. Fensham, "Clauses of Protection in Hittite Vassal-Treaties and the Old Testament," *VT* 13 (1963), pp. 133-143.

incorporation of the legal corpus, thus forming a bridge between the Decalogue and the Book of the Covenant.)[1])

The legal collection of Exodus, commonly referred to as the Book of the Covenant, then follows with its distinctive blending of legal, moral, and cultic prescriptions (Ex. 20:22—23:19).[2]) It is interesting to note that this legal corpus commences (Ex. 20:22-26—law of the altar and sacrifices) and concludes (Ex. 23:10-19—cultic calendar) with matters pertaining to the cult. This cultic framework to a legal corpus is not unique to the Book of the Covenant, for both the Laws of Holiness in Leviticus (Lev. 17:1 ff. and 26:1-2) and the Deuteronomic collection (Dt. 12:1 ff. and 26) share this analogous feature. It is particularly blatant at the conclusion of the laws of Leviticus, Lev. 26:1-2, where the coda dedicated to the injunction against idolatry and the admonition to observe the Sabbath is an obvious appendix unrelated to the preceding section which deals with various stages and consequences of indebtedness.[3]) Nonetheless, the addition of this appendix is not accidental but intentional, in line with the preplanned internal pattern of biblical legal corpora.

Two further points of interest may be noted in this connection. First, the prime position in all three legal corpora is assigned to the correct site of the cult, for all three begin with laws concerning the place of sacrifice. Second, there is a frequent juxtaposition to be found between the description of correct cultic rites and the commandment to avoid incorrect and pagan rites.[4]) Thus, Ex. 23:20-33 (esp. vs. 24) following Ex. 23:10-19, Lev. 17:7 ff. after Lev. 17:1-6, and Dt. 12:1-3 preceding Dt. 12:4-28 and Dt. 12:29-31 concluding the chapter, all fall within a similar pattern. This same juxtaposition is also mani-

---

[1]) Cf. Beyerlin, *op. cit.*, pp. 4-5, and L'Hour, *op. cit.*, pp. 352 ff., for the various views. That the people's reaction to the theophany does not presuppose the Decalogue was already noted by Moses ben Nachman in his commentary to Exodus, *in situ*. Since according to Dt. 5:20 ff. the people are reported to have asked for the aid of a mediator after they heard the Decalogue, this pericope, which may have originally stood between Ex. 19:18-19, might have been transposed to its present position in order to harmonize the two accounts.

[2]) B. Landsberger, "Die babylonischen Termini für Gesetz und Recht," *Symbolae Koschaker* (Leiden, 1939), p. 223, compares these three types of prescriptions to *dīnu*, *kibsu*, and *parṣu*—the Akkadian terms for legal, social, and religious injunctions. The amalgam of these three realms in one collection, however, is unique to biblical jurisprudence and will be discussed further on.

[3]) For a study of this section, see Speiser, "Leviticus and the Critics," *Yeheẓkel Kaufmann Jubilee Volume* (Jerusalem, 1960), pp. 36-39, 43-45.

[4]) Cf. Ex. 23:24; Lev. 18:3, 26; Dt. 12:31.

fest in Ex. 34 where vss. 11-17 (cf. Ex. 23:20-33),[1]) exhorting the people to eradicate all traces of idolatry when they enter the land of Canaan, are followed by a reiteration of correct cultic procedure in vss. 18-26 (cf. Ex. 23:10-19). The order found in the parallel section of Ex. 23:10-33,[2]) i.e., proper cultic procedure followed by the abolishing of all improper ritual (vs. 24) when they enter the promised land, is intentionally reversed in Ex. 34:11-26 because of the preceding narrative of the Golden Calf incident, which serves as a warning to Israel not to fall prey to idolatry again.

The explanation for the coda of Ex. 23:20-33 (probably composed of two independent literary traditions—vss. 20-25 and vss. 26-33) is now perfectly clear: in accordance with the pattern described above it naturally follows the cultic prescriptions of Ex. 23:10-19. The emphasis upon the impending conquest is also precisely in place here, for the imposed sojourn of forty years in the wilderness had not yet been decreed for Israel.

That and more. From a structural point of view this pericope serves to terminate the legal corpus with the promise of God's presence and protection in the imminent conquest of Canaan. Hence, the mosaic of Ex. 19 ff. concludes on the same note on which it began: the role of God in the history of Israel. The covenant is encased within a literary frame of redemptive history: just as God delivered Israel from Egypt, so he would aid them in the conquest of Canaan. The new constitution is intentionally inserted within a "prologue-epilogue" frame which inextricably binds the history and destiny of Israel to the discipline of law.

The rhythm of this epilogue section borders on the poetic with the employment of parallelism and one definite poetical form.[3]) The formula for divine protection found in vs. 22, "I shall be an enemy to your enemies and a foe to your foes," is similar to a well-known phrase found in documents from Ugarit: *it-ti* ^*amēl*^*nakri ša bēli-ia na-ak-ra*[*ku ù*] *it-ti ša-la-mi ša bēli-ia šal-ma-ku* "To the enemy of my lord, I am hostile; with the friend of my lord, I am friendly."[4])

---

[1]) Cf. Ex. 23:32-33; 34:12; Dt. 12:29-30.

[2]) For a discussion of the relationship between these two parallel sections, see Beyerlin, *op. cit.*, pp. 82-90. They are most likely two independent rescensions of one common source.

[3]) וגרשתמו ("and you shall drive them out"), Ex. 23:31. Cf. Cassuto, *op. cit.*, pp. 213-216, who makes a similar point and compares this coda to the Mesopotamian epilogues (pp. 213, 216).

[4]) J. Nougaryol, *PRU*, Vol. IV (Paris, 1956), p. 49, document 17.340, lines

Thus, when all the heterogeneous components are viewed as one literary unit, the superstructure of the theophany at Sinai is seen to constitute the positional and functional analogue to cuneiform prologues and epilogues. However, the uniqueness of this event—a revelation before the entire body of Israel and the declaration of the divine will as embodied in the Decalogue and the legal corpus, i.e., a covenant relationship which stressed the observance of law—produced a novel prologue-epilogue frame. The prologue states the purpose: to fashion a "holy nation;" the Decalogue and legal corpus stipulate the means to realize this ideal; the epilogue promises further divine protection for all those who remain faithful to the covenant.

The object of this legal corpus, as has been seen, is to form a "holy nation." Law, moreover, is presented here not as a secular instruction but as a divine pronouncement.[1]) The biblical frame to the corpus refers law directly to God; hence, it derives its validity from being a revelation of the divine will.[2]) This is the decisive feature of biblical law and is the key to the understanding of its unique characteristics. For although the Israelite society was greatly indebted to its Mesopotamian predecessors for its deep respect for law, for the view of man not as the ultimate source, but rather as the servant of the law,[3]) and for many legal prescriptions which eventually were adapted into biblical legal corpora, the basic concept of law in Israel was radically opposed to all other systems of jurisprudence.

Law in Israel has a divine authorship; it is not a "humanly authored safeguard of cosmic truth."[4]) Since there is no metadivine sphere present in biblical thought, God does not receive any *kīnātu* from a higher power for future dispensation. God alone is the ultimate source and sanction of law. The entire law is ascribed directly to him.

12-13; cf. also p. 36, document 17.132, lines 11-13. Cf. Fensham, *op. cit.*, pp. 140-141. See also F. R. Kraus, Review of *Baghdader Mitteilungen*, Vol. 2 (Berlin, 1963) in *BiOr* 22 (1965), p. 289. The roles, however, are reversed.

[1]) Cf. J. Leroy, *Introduction à l'étude des anciens codes orientaux* (Paris, 1944), p. 108; Cassuto, *op. cit.*, p. 180; and Weinfeld, "Israelite and Non-Israelite Concepts of Law," (Heb.), *Beth Mikra* 17 (1964), p. 64. Weinfeld, *Deuteronomy and the Deuteronomic School*, ch. 2, make the further distinction between treaties which serve a political need in the ancient Near East and a religious need in Israel. Loyalty to God is the conceptual analogue to loyalty to the king.

[2]) Cf. J. van der Ploeg, "Studies in Hebrew Law II," *CBQ* 12 (1950), p. 423, and Eichrodt, *op. cit.*, pp. 74-75.

[3]) Speiser, "Cuneiform Law and the History of Civilization," *PAPS* 107 (1963), p. 539.

[4]) Greenberg, "Some Postulates of Biblical Criminal Law," *Yehezkel Kaufmann Jubilee Volume* (Jerusalem, 1960), p. 12.

"Here God is not merely the custodian of justice or the dispenser of 'truths' to man, he is the fountainhead of the law; the law is a statement of his will.... The only legislator the Bible knows of is God." [1]) God, furthermore, is not merely the guarantor of the covenant, as the deities are in the epilogues to Mesopotamian legal collections and treaties; he is the author of the covenant who directly addresses his people.[2])

In light of this, several characteristic traits of biblical law may now be singled out: [3])

1. Since law is an expression of the divine will, all crimes are considered sins,[4]) and certain offenses become absolute wrongs incapable of pardon by human agency.[5])

2. The whole of one's life is now directly related to the will of God. The distinction between *jus* and *fas* known to Roman law is non-existent. Man's civil, moral and religious obligations all ultimately stem from God, and hence are interwoven within a single corpus of divinely given law. These three realms, which in extra-biblical societies would be incorporated respectively in law collections, wisdom literature, and priestly handbooks, are here combined into one body of prescriptions.[6])

---

[1]) *Ibid.*, p. 11.

[2]) Only in biblical legal corpora are there to be found prescriptions by the deity addressed in the first person.

[3]) It must be remembered that these features pertain primarily to the theory of biblical law rather than to its actual practice about which there is a paucity of information.

[4]) Cf. Eichrodt, *op. cit.*, p. 75, and Greenberg, *op. cit.*, pp. 11-12.

[5]) This according to Greenberg, *loc. cit.*, is the reason behind the refusal of biblical law to admit of pardon or mitigation of punishment in certain cases where cuneiform law allows it, i.e., adultery and homicide. For the laws of adultery, contrast Lev. 20:10 and Dt. 22:23-24 with LH 129, MAL A 14-16, 23, and HL 198; for the laws of homicide, contrast Ex. 21:12 ff. and Num. 35:31 with HL 1-4. The laws concerning the goring ox exemplify the latter point and will be fully discussed in the next chapter. Cf. also the discussion of both Weinfeld, "Israelite and Non-Israelite Concepts of Law," (Heb.), *Beth Mikra* 17 (1964), pp. 58-63, and S. E. Loewenstamm, "The Laws of Adultery and Homicide in Biblical and Mesopotamian Law Corpora," (Heb.), *Beth Mikra* 13 (1962), pp. 55-59, and 19 (1964), pp. 77-78.

[6]) This distinctive feature—absent from extra-biblical legal corpora—of the commingling of religious and civil laws together with moral exhortations has been emphasized in the works of Eichrodt, *loc. cit.*; Greenberg, *loc. cit.*; Leroy, *op. cit.*, p. 107; W. Kornfeld, *Studien zum Heiligkeitsgesetz* (Wien, 1952), p. 15; and R. de Vaux, *Ancient Israel: Its Life and Institutions*, trans. J. McHugh (New York, 1961), p. 149. Cf. also Jepsen, "Israel und das Gesetz," *ThLZ* 93 (1968), pp. 85-94.

3. Since God is the sole legislator, Israel is held responsible to him and not to any human ruler or legislative body.[1])

4. Unlike Mesopotamia where the king alone was chosen by the gods and granted the gift of the perception of the *kīnātu*, God selects the entire corporate body of Israel to be the recipients of his law. His care and concern extend to all members of this community and not merely to one chosen individual. Thus everyone is held personally responsible for the observance of the law. This leads, in turn, to the concept of individual and joint responsibility. No longer is it the sole concern of the leader of the community (e.g., the king in Mesopotamia) to maintain justice and to protect the rights of his community. This responsibility is now shared by every member of the society; since the law was communicated to all, the responsibility for its observance rests on the people *in toto*. Each member of this community, then, has a dual responsibility: to observe the law personally and to see that the law is observed by the group. Each must see that justice is executed and that all crimes are punished—otherwise the community and its members are threatened with dire consequences. [2]) Faithful observance of the law, on the other hand, grants divine protection and reward to both the individual and the group. Law becomes the single most important factor in the life and destiny of Israel.

5. Publicity, not secrecy, is the hallmark of the law, which is proclaimed openly to the entire society and is not restricted to any professional class of jurists, lawyers, or judges. Ex. 21:1 makes this patently clear: "These are the norms that you shall set before them." Law publicly promulgated in advance is to be contrasted with the epilogue to LH (LH XXVb:3-19), where the aggrieved party learns of the law pertaining to his case only after the crime has been committed. Law in Israel is prospective and prescriptive not retrospective and descriptive. Though LH was frequently copied in scribal circles, there is no mention in the collection itself of making the law part of the public domain. In the Israelite society, on the other hand, law was not only proclaimed publicly at the very outset, but, in addition, a renewed proclamation was required once every seven years.[3])

---

[1]) Muilenberg, *The Way of Israel: Biblical Faith and Ethics* (New York, 1961), p. 64.

[2]) Cf. the remarks of G. E. Wright, *The Old Testament Against Its Environment* (= *Studies in Biblical Theology*, No. 2 [Naperville, 1957]), p. 69, and D. N. Freedman, "Divine Commitment and Human Obligation: The Covenant Theme," *Interpretation* (1964), pp. 11-12.

[3]) Dt. 31:10-13. Cf. also Neh. 8:1-8, and Saadiah Gaon's comment to Ex. 21:1

6. Law, then, becomes a body of teaching directed to the entire community. Each member of the community knows prospectively of his individual and communal obligations. Since law serves as an instrument of education, a didactic aim is to be found only in biblical legislation.[1] Thus, unlike most other ancient legal corpora, motive clauses are occasionally appended to both apodictic and casuistic injunctions. These explanatory, ethical, religious, and historical comments appeal to the conscience of the people and pedagogically aid and motivate them to observe the law.[2] God desires "men who confirm them inwardly." [3]

7. Since man is conceived as being created in the divine image, the sacredness of a human being becomes a primary concern of the law. Thus whoever destroys a human life must give a reckoning for it. Monetary compensation and property settlement, characteristic of extra-biblical legal corpora, are absent from biblical legislation. "Life and property are incommensurable" in the Israelite system of law, where religious rather than economic values predominate.[4] As a correlate the death penalty is now abolished for all crimes against property.[5]

8. Whereas biblical legislation demands a "life for a life," brutal and multiple punishments frequently found in several extra-biblical legal collections are all but absent from Israelite law.[6] The principle of

---

in M. Zucker, *Rav Saadya Gaon's Translation of the Torah* (New York, 1959), pp. 332-333, where he states that the law should be made public so that no one can later complain that he was unaware of the correct legal procedure. The laws are publicized before the people are judged by them.

Since Israel was to become a "kingdom of priests" all the laws—even those pertaining to the cult—were publicly proclaimed. Contrast the publication of the cultic prescriptions in the biblical legal corpora with the secrecy of such laws outside of Israel, p. 9, n. 1.

1) Cf. de Vaux, *loc. cit.*, and Muilenberg, *op. cit.*, pp. 66-67.

2) See B. Gemser, "The Importance of the Motive Clause in Old Testament Law," *Supplements to VT* 1 (1953), pp. 50-66. For an early dating of the motive clauses in the Book of the Covenant, see W. Beyerlin, "Die Paränese im Bundesbuch und ihre Herkunft," *Gottes Wort und Gottes Land*: *Festschrift für H. W. Hertzberg* (Göttingen, 1965), pp. 9-29. Cf. Yaron, *Eshnunna*, p. 75, n. 20.

3) G. von Rad, *Old Testament Theology*, trans. D. M. G. Stalker, Vol. I (Edinburgh, 1962), p. 198.

4) See the important study by Greenberg, *loc. cit.*, who clarifies several of the unique features of biblical criminal law by means of this principle. The quotation is taken from p. 18. For the emphasis placed upon human life and dignity in Deuteronomy, see Weinfeld, *Deuteronomy and the Deuteronomic School*, Part 3.

5) Contrast, e.g., LH 6-11, 21, 22, 25.

6) Cf. Eichrodt, *op. cit.*, pp. 78-79. Examples of multiple punishments are MAL A 4, 7, 9, 18-21, 40, 44. For examples of brutal punishments (primarily

individual culpability, moreover, predominates throughout the biblical legal corpora proper and leads eventually to the abrogation of vicarious punishment. Secular offenses are punished on the actual offender, not collectively or vicariously.[1])

9. Since all men are created by God and thus stand equal before him, class distinction is rejected in the meting out of justice.[2]) This feature of Israelite law, absent from other legal compilations, is exemplified in the biblical version of *lex talionis*. Rather than being a primitive residuum, it restricts retaliation to the person of the offender, while at the same time limiting it to the exact measure of the injury—thereby according equal justice to all.[3])

10. The sole exception to the principle of equal justice as exemplified in *lex talionis* is the slave. Nevertheless, all the laws pertaining to slaves are concerned with furthering his protection and preserving his human dignity, e.g., his status is temporary, his physical being must be guarded against abuse, and he is considered a human being in his own right and not merely his owner's chattel.[4])

Whereas these leading features [5]) characterize the legal corpora in general and thereby embody the biblical concept of law, several of them will be elaborated upon in the forthcoming annotations to the legal section of the Book of the Covenant.

The leading motifs of early biblical literature, election, redemption, covenant, and law, are closely interconnected: God elected the children of Israel to be his treasured possession; his redemptive intervention into history liberated an enslaved people who became bound to God through a pact whose stipulations demand the utmost

---

mutilation), cf. LH 192-195, 205, 218, 226, 253, 282; MAL A 4, 5, 8, 9, 15, 20, 24, 40; HL 92, 166 (both subsequently abolished). For a complete list of such penalties, see R. Haase, "Körperliche Strafen im altorientalischen Recht," *RIDA*, 3e série, 10 (1963), pp. 61-63. (In the Bible the only example of mutilation occurs in Dt. 25:11-12.)

[1]) Cf. Greenberg, *op. cit.*, p. 23. Examples of vicarious punishment are LH 116, 210, 230; MAL 50, 55. In biblical law, on the other hand, cases of murder, negligent homicide, and seduction are punished solely on the actual offender.

[2]) Eichrodt, *op. cit.*, p. 79. Some doubt the existence of classes all together in early Israel.

[3]) Cf. the remarks of Albright, *History, Archaeology and Christian Humanism* (New York, 1964), pp. 74, 98-99. A further elaboration of this principle in LH and Exodus will be found in the next chapter; cf. comments to Ex. 21:23-25.

[4]) This feature will be examined in the next chapter in those laws pertaining to slaves, e.g., Ex. 21:2-6, 20, 26-27.

[5]) For several other dominant motifs, cf. Eichrodt, *op. cit.*, pp. 75-77, and Muilenberg, *op. cit.*, pp. 98-99.

obedience; the continued existence of this religious community is completely predicated upon the observance and performance of those principles and injunctions that constitute the charter of its covenant with God. The will of God expressed through law is the basis of the covenant relationship between God and Israel.

In the prologue and epilogue to LH constant stress is placed upon political and economic benefits: establishment of justice, abolishment of rebellion, prosperity of the people, establishment of good government.[1]) The biblical frame, on the other hand, is marked by its explicit religious tone: "Indeed, all the earth is mine, but you shall be to me a kingdom of priests and a holy nation" (Ex. 19:5-6). The prime purpose of biblical compilations is sanctification.[2]) Ruth Benedict has demonstrated that the unique beliefs and customs of a people are determined by certain overwhelming preoccupations dominant in their respective cultures; these features form a coherent and comprehensive whole that she called a "pattern."[3]) One may, on the basis of this term, which implies order and coherence, refer to the "religious pattern" of biblical law.[4]) The religion of Israel had an overriding influence upon law. The theocentric theme of the frame to the Book of the Covenant has echoes in the corpus proper, where certain legal prescriptions are unique to Israel, while others slightly, yet noticeably, diverge from otherwise clearly attestable cuneiform precedents. These innovations, modifications, and changes help one to gain a further insight into the value concepts of the early Israelite society.

However, Israel was not an island unto itself, well-insulated from other societies; the strong appeal of cuneiform law was deeply felt in Israel.[5]) Though the narratives in Genesis are a monumental witness to the protest and revolt of the patriarchs against the religious solution of Mesopotamia, those very same stories shed much light on the influence of that environment upon the newly born society.[6])

---

1) Greenberg, *op. cit.*, p. 11. Cf. also P. Cruveilhier, *Introduction au code d'Ḫammourabi* (Paris, 1937), p. 44.

2) See H. Cazelles, "Loi israélite," *Supplément au dictionnaire de la Bible*, Vol. V, ed. Pirot (Paris, 1952-1953), p. 513, who states that the redaction of biblical laws is inspired by theological concepts.

3) R. Benedict, *Patterns of Culture* (New York, 1960).

4) Greenberg, "Crimes and Punishments," *IDB*, Vol. I, p. 734, refers to the "religious cast of biblical law."

5) Cf. E. Ring, *Israels Rechtsleben im Lichte der neuentdeckten assyrischen und hethitischen Gesetzesurkunden* (Stockholm, 1926), p. 202.

6) For the latest collection and explication of the patriarchal narratives in the

Israel did not renounce everything that bore the "Mesopotamian" imprint. Indeed it drew heavily—as did so many other cultures—from the fountain of law that constituted the backbone of the parent civilization. Law, "the force that held the world together [and] made the essential difference between order and chaos, civilization and barbarism," [1]) became the focal point of the Israelite society. Thus biblical law is part and parcel of the cultural correspondence between Israel and Mesopotamia. Though one must maintain utmost caution before drawing parallels from one civilization to another,[2]) biblical legislation clearly bears the telltale marks of its cuneiform predecessors. Hence, "the ultimate achievement that is the Bible cannot be properly understood, still less appreciated, except in terms of the setting in which the work originated, and of the initial values which it went on to transfigure and transcend." [3]) With such a twofold focus in mind, this study now turns to an investigation of the earliest biblical legal corpus, the Book of the Covenant.

---

light of the common law of the Near East, esp. Nuzi, see Speiser, *Genesis* (New York, 1964), and N. M. Sarna, *Understanding Genesis* (New York, 1966).

[1]) Speiser, "The Ancient Near East and Modern Philosophies of History," *PAPS* 95 (1951), p. 586.

[2]) See the important remarks of P. Koschaker, "Was vermag die vergleichende Rechtswissenschaft zur Indogermanenfrage beizusteuern," *Germanen und Indogermanen: Volkstum, Sprache, Heimat, Kultur. Festschrift für Hermann Hirt*, Vol. I., ed. Helmuth Arntz (Heidelberg, 1936), pp. 145-153. On pp. 149-150 he cautions, "Die Rechtsvergleichung ist ein empfindliches Instrument, bei dessen Gebrauch Fingerspitzengefühl notwendig ist und die Persönlichkeit des Forschers stets eine entscheidende Rolle spielen wird. Schlechte Rechtsvergleichung ist schlimmer als keine."

[3]) Speiser, "The Biblical Idea of History in its Common Near Eastern Setting," *IEJ* 7 (1957), p. 202.

CHAPTER FIVE

ANNOTATIONS TO THE LAWS OF THE BOOK OF THE COVENANT

The laws of the Book of the Covenant, in common with those of cuneiform legal compilations, are the end result of a long process of development, and thus were influenced by many legal antecedents. The various echoes of more than one substratum, which the following annotations to the formal legal corpus (Ex. 21:2—22:16) highlight, show that much of the material was originally pre-Mosaic and even pre-Israelite. However, this customary law was supplemented, in turn, by certain significant additions and modifications which mark the early Israelite contribution to jurisprudence.

The moral and sapiential exhortations and the cultic calendar that follow the juridical corpus proper (Ex. 22:17—23:19)— though an integral part of the charter of this newly organized nation— constitute an appendix to the preceding section and, as such, will not be studied here. It is precisely at this point (Ex. 22:16-17) that the associative ordering of the formal legal corpus terminates,[1]) the analogues to cuneiform laws become very few, and the characteristic Israelite apodictic declarations and motive clauses begin to appear. It must be remembered, however, that only in biblical compilations are moral exhortations and religious injunctions combined with legal prescriptions; elsewhere, as noted above (p. 37), these three distinct spheres are found in separate independent collections.

The Book of the Covenant, when studied as a literary unit,[2]) is characterized by several salient features.[3]) There is a noticeable ab-

---

[1]) Cf. Appendix I.

[2]) Many scholars today are of the opinion that this entire legal collection is a secondary insertion: cf. M. Noth, *Exodus*, trans. J. S. Bowden (Philadelphia, 1962), p. 173; O. Eissfeldt, *The Old Testament: An Introduction*, trans. P. R. Ackroyd (New York, 1965), pp. 212-219; and W. Beyerlin, *Origins and History of the Oldest Sinaitic Traditions*, trans. S. Rudman (Oxford, 1965), pp. 4-6, for representative views. However, one must not confuse the date of insertion, even if late—a still unproved assumption—with the date of composition. All the characteristic elements of this corpus, as will be shown in this chapter, point to a very early dating.

[3]) For a comprehensive discussion of many of the social, political, economic, and religious features of the Book of the Covenant together with a commentary and study of legal formulations, *hapax legomena*, and form-critical problems, see

sence of family law—only two verses in the entire legal section (Ex. 22:15-16) pertain to this subject—in contrast to a substantial number of such laws in LH and MAL.[1]) Since the specific aim of this juridical corpus is to provide a charter of laws for the new institution of statehood, family law per se is not incorporated here. The corpus is geared to a new political entity, a nation that is about to settle in its own land. Hence, a new kind of legislation adapted to the needs of a settled rather than a seminomadic society (which surely possessed family law ever since its presettlement days) is given prime importance.

A societal framework of a non-monarchic tribal polity is indicated in several ways: the corpus reflects a pastoral-agricultural non-urban society; [2]) laws pertaining to commercial dealings are completely absent; there are no class distinctions characteristic of a monarchic bureaucratic society; the basic nuclear unit is the family—with no mention of any other ouside central organization; laws punishing secular offenses are addressed to the injured party or next of kin, rather than to judges and courts; the right of self-help is recognized; new categories of crimes present under the monarchy are absent; [3]) there is no reference to Israel; [4]) and a נשיא "elected chieftain," rather than a מלך "king," is the only official mentioned.[5]) In sum,

H. Cazelles, *Études sur le code d'alliance* (Paris, 1946), and "Loi israélite," *Supplément au dictionnaire de la Bible*, Vol. V, ed. Pirot (Paris, 1952-1953), pp. 501 ff. Cazelles concludes that the Book of the Covenant was presented by Moses to the tribes that settled in Transjordan prior to the Israelite conquest of Canaan. B. D. Eerdmans, *The Religion of Israel* (Leiden, 1947), p. 40, and W. Eichrodt, *Theology of the Old Testament*, Vol. I, trans. J. A. Baker (Philadelphia, 1960), pp. 83-84, also argue for a Mosaic authorship.

[1]) See G. R. Driver and J. C. Miles, *The Babylonian Laws*, Vol. I (Oxford, 1960), pp. 245-358, and *The Assyrian Laws* (Oxford, 1935), pp. 126-271, for a discussion of the Mesopotamian family laws that appear in the respective legal collections.

[2]) Cazelles, *Études*, pp. 131-145.

[3]) M. Greenberg, "Crimes and Punishments," *IDB*, Vol. I, p. 735.

[4]) M. Noth, *Die Gesetze im Pentateuch: Ihre Voraussetzungen und ihr Sinn* (Halle, 1940), p. 21 = *Gesammelte Studien zum Alten Testament* (Munich, 1960), p. 40.

[5]) *Ibid., Die Gesetze*, p. 27, n. 79 = *Gesammelte Studien*, p. 49, n. 79.

The verse in which נשיא appears, Ex. 22:27, has been interpreted by H. C. Brichto, *The Problem of "Curse" in the Hebrew Bible = Journal of Biblical Literature Monograph Series*, Vol. 13 (Philadelphia, 1963), pp. 150-159, in the light of material found at Mari. The Akk. expression *asakka(m) akālu(m)* "to eat the *asakku*" (of a king or god) metaphorically expresses that he who disobeys a royal decree is considered guilty of a serious offense against the king or the divinity. (Cf. the remarks of G. Boyer, *ARM*, Vol. 8 [Paris, 1958], pp. 116 ff. and *CAD*, Vol. 1, p. 255, 7a.) According to Brichto (and first suggested by E. A. Speiser, "An Angelic 'Curse': Exodus 14:20," *JAOS* 80 [1960], p. 199), something of the force of "eating the *asakku*" of a king or a god still inheres in the biblical verse. He translates as follows: "Do not act in disrespect of God nor bring under a ban an

these features all point to the period immediately before and following the conquest.[1])

TEXTUAL ANNOTATIONS

21:2-6. Ḫāpiru documents have been fully discussed in several studies.[2]) However, the evidence for a possible interconnection between Heb. עברי "Hebrew" and cuneiform *Ḫāpiru* still remains ambiguous and is further complicated by the legal phrase "Hebrew slave"—a phrase without parallel in cuneiform sources. Though it is difficult to determine whether עברי (vs. 2) is a gentilic,[3]) i.e., a fellow Israelite, or an appellative,[4]) i.e., a slave of the Ḫāpiru-type status, it is most probable that both later references, Dt. 15:12 ff. and Jer. 34:8 ff., interpret the term as a gentilic: the former adds אחיך "your brother"

---

elected chieftain of your people." This translation, in turn, is based upon his study of the two Hebrew terms which appear in the verse, קלל and ארר.

For a study of the institution of נשיא, see Speiser, "Background and Function of the Biblical *Nāśī*," *CBQ* 25 (1963), pp. 111-117.

[1]) Eichrodt, *loc. cit.*, contends, "how vital it is for our understanding of the period of Israel's settlement in Canaan to assume that the associated tribes were able to enter the strange country with a law of their own. The history of Israel in the time of the Judges becomes extremely hard to comprehend, indeed, almost a complete enigma, if the incoming migrants be supposed to have possessed nothing but an orally transmitted prescriptive law of a primitive kind" (p. 83). "If Moses is to be credited with no more than merely oral instruction in, and promulgation of, the law—and that in any case limited to the Decalogue—then there cannot be any solid reason for a comparative strong Israelite resistance to the character of Canaan" (p. 84).

For a pre-monarchial background for biblical law in general, see S. E. Loewenstamm, "Biblical Law," (Heb.), *Encyclopaedia Biblica*, Vol. 5 (Jerusalem, 1968), pp. 622-623.

[2]) Greenberg, *The Ḫab/piru* (New Haven, 1955), and J. Bottéro, *Le problème des Ḫabiru à la 4e rencontre assyriologique internationale* (= *Cahiers de la société asiatique* 12), Paris, 1954. For later discussions of the Ḫāpiru and their relation to the Hebrews, see M. P. Gray, "The Ḫâbirū-Hebrew Problem," *HUCA* 29 (1958), pp. 135-202, and R. de Vaux, "Le problème des Ḫāpiru après quinze années," *JNES* 27 (1968), pp. 221-228. All future references to Ḫāpiru documents follow Greenberg's enumeration. For the original form, *ʿApiru*, see de Vaux, *op. cit.*, p. 222, and R. Borger, "Das Problem der *ʿapiru* ("Ḫabiru")," *ZDPV* 74 (1958), pp. 121-132.

[3]) Greenberg, *op. cit.*, pp. 91-93. Cf. S. R. Driver, *The Book of Exodus* (Cambridge, 1918), p. 14, and now de Vaux, *op. cit.*, esp. pp. 225-228.

[4]) Among others, A. Alt, *Die Ursprünge des israelitischen Rechts* (Leipzig, 1934) = *Kleine Schriften*, Vol. I (Munich, 1959), pp. 278-322, esp. pp. 291 ff.; J. Lewy, "Ḫābirū and the Hebrews," *HUCA* 14 (1939), p. 609; Cazelles, *op. cit.*, pp. 44-45; U. Cassuto, *A Commentary on the Book of Exodus*, Heb. (Jerusalem, 1951), pp. 184-185; Gray, *op. cit.*, pp. 173-174; and M. Noth, *op. cit.*, p. 177, ". . . a legal and social status . . . . People of different nationality who belonged to the under-privileged or even unprivileged classes and who undertook, indeed had to undertake, subordinate service . . . ." Cf. also *CAD*, Vol. 6, pp. 84-85.

(vs. 12), while the latter adds אחיו "his brother" (vs. 14; cf. vs. 9), and alternates עברי with יהודי "Jew" (vs. 9). The analogues, however, which will be shown to exist between the legal terminology and stipulations of the verses in Exodus and the Ḫāpiru slave documents from Nuzi, tend to favor the interpretation of עברי in Ex. 21:2 as an appellative. This pericope, then, with its own unique features, is most likely a later reflex of these Ḫāpiru documents.

The Ḫāpiru at Nuzi were self-enslaved individuals who, occasionally with their families, served their patrons in return for food and raiment.[1]) No time limit was placed upon the length of their service. Should they infringe their agreement, they would have to make either a payment of silver or gold to their patron,[2]) incur a severe penalty,[3]) or provide a substitute in their stead.[4])

2. "When [כי] [5]) you acquire [תקנה] a Hebrew (?) slave [עבד עברי], he shall serve six years; in the seventh year he shall go free [יצא לחפשי] without payment." [6])

תקנה juridically means to acquire as one's own property.[7]) At Nuzi no price is mentioned nor is any money exchanged when the master acquires a Ḫāpiru slave.

---

[1]) Greenberg, *op. cit.*, p. 67. An indication of the difference in treatment between a Ḫāpiru and an ordinary slave may be found in No. 41:13-15: *šum-ma* [Id]*Adad-rabī* [*mi-im-ma* (?) *iš-tu bīti*[ti]] *i-šar-ri-iq* [*be-el*]-*šu ša ki-i wardi* [*ippus-su* (?)] "If A. steals [anything from the house], his [master shall treat him] like a slave." The bracketed readings are those of Bottéro. If his restored reading is correct, the penalty clause threatens treatment "like a slave" for a Ḫāpiru who is caught stealing. This comparison would indicate that his status quo prior to the offense was superior to that of a slave. However, the reading is completely conjectural.

[2]) Nos. 44, 48, 60, 62. [3]) Nos. 45, 58, 61, 63. [4]) Nos. 41, 42, 43, 59, 60.

[5]) In the biblical casuistic formulation, כי introduces the general law in the main clause, and אם or או precedes the specific conditions or circumstances that follow. For a discussion of various legal formulations, see Appendix II.

[6]) The translation of the verses are taken essentially from *The Torah: The Five Books of Moses*, Jewish Publication Society (Philadelphia, 1962, 1967). This does not imply, however, total agreement with this translation.

[7]) Cf. Cazelles, *op. cit.*, p. 44. Alt, *op. cit.*, p. 291, n. 2, following A. Jepsen, *Untersuchungen zum Bundesbuch* (Stuttgart, 1927), p. 56, who emends this verb to the third-person singular (יקנה) so as to conform to the regular grammatical construction of casuistically formulated laws, suggests that originally the reading must have been יִמָּכֵר. This emendation, however, is incorrect, for not only is a grammatical change of person a well known stylistic feature in the Bible as well as in West Semitic inscriptions—cf. S. Gevirtz, "West Semitic Curses and the Problem of the Origins of Hebrew Law," *VT* 11 (1961), p. 157—but the protasis of the first law was most likely influenced by the second-person grammatical construction of the previous verse, Ex. 21:1, and hence, constitutes a direct link between the personal superscription to the legal corpus and the ensuing impersonally constructed laws.

עבד עברי. Even though the Ḫāpiru at Nuzi enjoy certain privileges not accorded the ordinary slave,[1]) they nevertheless are *wardū* "slaves," and their status is called *wardūtu.* The usual formula is *ramanšu ana wardūti ana X uš(t)ēribšu* "He made himself enter into the service of X." עבד עברי, when interpreted as an appellative denoting a member of a particular class of the population, would be a slave of the Ḫāpiru-type status. Upon termination of his service he would then enter the state of חפשי, i.e., "belonging to the class of freedmen." [2])

A major reform of this institution is at once evident: the law in Exodus states the terms of emancipation. Unlike the practice at Nuzi, a time limit of six years is placed upon the Ḫāpiru's service.[3]) At the end of this period he incurs no penalty upon leaving his master. He departs "without payment" (חנם); he neither has to pay for his release nor provide a replacement to work on his behalf.

3. "If he came [יבא] single [בגפו],[4]) he shall leave [יצא] single [בגפו]."

יבא and יצא are legal terms for "entering" and "leaving" (one's authority), i.e., the slave status. Akk. *erēbu* and *waṣû* are similarly

---

[1]) Greenberg, *op. cit.*, p. 67.

[2]) See Cazelles, *op. cit.*, p. 45, and "Hébreu, Ubru, Ḫapiru," *Syria* 35 (1958), p. 200; Alt, *op. cit.*, p. 293; and Noth, *op. cit.*, pp. 177-178, who emphasize the social significance of the term. Note also the *nisbe* (relative adjectival) construction of the word. For a possible correspondence to the social class of *ḫupšu* "free born persons primarily engaged in agricultural work as day-laborers, share croppers, or tenant farmers," see I. Mendelsohn, "The Canaanite Term for Free Proletarian," *BASOR* 83 (1941), pp. 36-39, and "New Light on the *Ḫupšu*," *BASOR* 139 (1955), pp. 9-11. For the meaning of *ḫupšu* as "a member of one of the lower social orders" together with further references, see *CAD*, Vol. 6, pp. 241-242. For linguistic analogues to Heb. ישלחנו חפשי, see Y. Muffs, *Studies in Aramaic Legal Papyri from Elephantine* (= *Studia et Documenta ad Iura Orientes Antiqui Pertinentae* 8 [Leiden, 1969]), p. 40, n. 1.

[3]) LH 117, which provides for the release of the debtor at the end of three years, is only seemingly the same. This law deals with a specific debt to a specific creditor, where the debtor or his family is bound as collateral.

In the Deuteronomic version of the law, Dt. 15:12-18, the "Hebrew" slave departs with gifts. Abarbanel in his commentary to Exodus (Tel Aviv, 1960) compares the liberation of the slave in the seventh year to the institutions of the Sabbath and the Jubilee.

[4]) This word appears only in this section, twice in vs. 3 and once in vs. 4. Though its etymology is unclear, contextually it means "single, by himself." If the word is in any way connected with Heb. גוף "body," cf. ibn Ezra and Cazelles, *Études*, p. 46, the corresponding semantic analogue in Akkadian would be *pagru*, which also develops the meaning "himself" (*pagrišu*), cf. F. R. Kraus, *Ein Edikt des Königs Ammi-Ṣaduqa von Babylon* (Leiden, 1958), p. 169.

employed in Nuzi Ḫāpiru [1]) and *ditennūtu* documents.[2]) The former, *erēbu*, is the interdialectal functional equivalent of Heb. בוא; the latter, *waṣû*, is the etymological and functional equivalent of Heb. יצא.

"If he had a wife, his wife shall leave with him."

At Nuzi a Ḫāpiru occasionally took his family with him into servitude.[3]) They all then would be held responsible for any infringement of the agreement.

4. "If his master gave him a wife, and she has borne him children, the wife and her children [האשה וילדיה] shall belong to the master, and he shall leave alone."

Contracts stipulating the provision of a wife for the Ḫāpiru are also found at Nuzi.[4]) An exact parallel to this verse is found in one document where a Ḫāpiru slave, who was given a wife by his master, is not permitted to take her or his offspring with him when he terminates his period of servitude: [*šum*]-*ma* *^{I}Zi-ni ibbalakkatu^{tu_4} ù uš-tu bīt ^{I}Ta-ak-ku ú-uṣ-ṣí aš-ša*-[*as*]-*su ù še-er-ri-šu*... *^{I}Zi-ni* [*a-na*] *^{I}Ta-ak-ku i-na-an-din-ma ú-uṣ-ṣí* "If Zini infringes (the agreement) and leaves the house of Takku, his wife and his offspring... Zini must give (back) [to] Takku; then he may leave." [5])

---

1) Although the IV/1, *ušērib*, is the usual form in such agreements, the I/1 *īrub*, is also found: Nos. 49:10 *e-ru-um-me*, 60:4 *i-ru-ub*, 65:4 *i-te-ru-ub*. For *waṣû*, see Nos. 64:16 *ú-uṣ-ṣí*, 65:8, and many others. *rêqu*, the functional variant of *waṣû*, is found in Nos. 59:19 and 60:16.

2) The usual formula is *ramanšu* ... *uš*(*t*)*ēribšu* "he made himself enter." The same legal phraseology is current in Nuzi *ditennūtu* texts. Speiser, "New Kirkuk Documents Relating to Security Transactions," *JAOS* 53 (1933), pp. 36-37, lines 6-10: *ù ra-ma-ni-a a-na ti-te-en-nu-ti i-na bīt*^{meš}*-it ša A.* ... *uš-te-ri-ib* "and myself for possession into the house of A. ... I have caused to enter." See also *idem*, "One Hundred New Selected Nuzi Texts," *AASOR* 16 (1936), p. 106; P. Koschaker, *Über einige griechische Rechtsurkunden aus den östlichen Randgebieten des Hellenismus* (Leipzig, 1931), p. 14, and "Fratriarchat in Keilschriftrechten," *ZA* 41 (1933), p. 33, n. 3. Further corresponding legal terminology is found in the use of *uštērib* and *ušēṣî* for "causing to enter" and "to leave" the period of service. One document, *JEN V* 299, states that the paying of the debt by the *ditennu* before the alloted time constitutes an infringement of the agreement. He must then supply a substitute to work in his stead (lines 12-13). See comments to vs. 5 for a formal declaration of a *ditennu*.

3) Nos. 38 and 58 both mention a woman "with her offspring," *qa-du še-er-ri-šu*; No. 39 involves *A. it-ti$_4$ ni-iš bi*-[*ti-šu*] "A. with the people of [his] house;" No. 63 deals with two men who enter *it-ti mārē*[^{meš}*-ni*] *it-ti aššāti*^{meš}*-ni ù it-ti* [*mārāti*]$^{ti\text{-}meš}$*-ni* "with [our] sons, with our wives, and with our [daughters]."

4) No. 65:5-7 *ù T. aš-ša-ta* ^{Id}*Š. u-ša-ḫa*-[*as*-]*su* "T. shall provide Š. with a wife." The same provision is also found in No. 64.

5) No. 64:15-23. The wife and children must remain for they are considered part of the master's property. A girl once provided by the master as a wife for a slave may have to remain in such a capacity for her entire life. *JEN* V 437 tells of

האשה וילדיה, "the wife and her children," is the semantic analogue to the Nuzi Akk. *aššatu qadu šerrišu* "the woman together with her offspring"—a phrase often found in these documents.[1])

5. "But if the slave declares, 'I love [אהבתי] my master, and my wife and children: I do not wish to go free'."

This is a formal declaration whereby the individual voluntarily chooses to remain a slave for life. A similar change of status from temporary to permanent bondage is accompanied by a formal voluntary declaration on the part of a *ditennu* in a document from Nuzi: *ù ra-ma-ni-ma ra-ma-ni i-na še-er-še-er-ri-ti i-it-ta-an-ni* "So of my free will I have cast myself in chains (i.e., bondage)." [2])

6. "His master shall take him before God [האלהים]. He shall be brought to the door or the doorpost , and his master shall pierce his ear [ורצע את אזנו] with an awl: and he shall then remain his slave for life [ועבדו לעלם]." [3])

---

a certain Tulpišenni who gave his daughter Warḫazizza to Teḫibtilla as a daughter-in-law: "And T. will give (her) to any one of his slaves as a wife. In case her first husband dies, he shall give (her) to a second. In case her second husband dies, he shall give (her) to a third. In case her third husband dies, he shall give her to a fourth. As long as W. lives, she shall not leave T's house." For other examples, see Speiser, "One Hundred Nuzi Texts," *AASOR* 16 (1936), texts 23, 30, 42.

The children of such a marriage also remain perpetual slaves of the owner. See Koschaker, *NKRA*, p. 83: *mi-nu-um-me še-er-ra-šu ša uš-tu lìb-bi ša F. ša ú-uṣ-ṣú-ú a-na A. lu-ú amātu*[meš-tu] *ù lu-ú ardū*[meš-du] "Whatever children F. bears shall remain the male and female slaves of A." In "Fratriarchat," *ZA* 41 (1933), p. 18, Koschaker states that the clauses which stipulate the girl's remaining in the household along with her children are characteristic of the documents that deal with the marriage of slaves. Cf. also A. Saarisalo, "New Kirkuk Documents Relating to Slaves," *StOr* V/3 (1934), pp. 24 ff.

1) Nos. 38.2, 58:3, and 64:17 (*ù šerrišu*). For the meaning of *šerru* "children born of slaves and offspring of a second wife, to be distinguished from *māru*, i.e., child born of free parents," see Saarisalo, *op. cit.*, p. 76, n. 3, and Koschaker, *loc. cit.*, n. 2. A peculiarity of the fringe Akkadian of Nuzi is the prevailing employment of a masculine suffix (here *šu*) with a feminine antecedent (here *aššatu*).

2) Speiser, "One Hundred Nuzi Texts," *AASOR* 16 (1936), No. 29. The first word of the declaration in Exodus, אהבתי "I love," has legal overtones. The juridical aspect of its antonym, שנא, is evident in Dt. 21:15-17. For a similar function of the latter's interdialectal equivalent, Akk. *zêru*, see *CAD*, Vol. 21, pp. 97-98. The interdialectal equivalent of אהב, Akk. *râmu*, appears together with *zêru* in a document from Alalakh concerning division of property. See D. J. Wiseman, *The Alalakh Tablets* (London, 1953), p. 35, No. 7:20-23 *[I]A. bītam ša i-ra-am-mu li-is-sú-úq-ma li-il-qí bītam ša i-zi-ir-ru [f]B. li-il-qí*. The quasi-juridical status of both these terms is further confirmed by the use in this tablet of the technical legal phrase *lisūqma lilqî* "to have a preferential choice" (lit. "let him choose and take") found in LH 60:25-26 and 170:58-59. See also Koschaker, *NKRA*, pp. 36-52, and Driver and Miles, *The Babylonian Laws*, Vol. II (Oxford, 1960), pp. 183-184.

3) Cf. Ug. *ʿbdk an wdʿlmk*, C. H. Gordon, *Ugaritic Textbook* (Rome, 1965), 67:II:12, 20.

The change of status from a temporary to a permanent slave is marked by a formal ceremony which takes place in the presence of האלהים. This term has been interpreted to mean judges,[1]) court,[2]) or temple door.[3]) It originally referred, however, to the symbols of private house gods, with the ceremony taking place by the door or the doorpost of the master's house. Since a permanent slave becomes part of the total property acquisitions of his owner, his inclusion within the family estate would most probably be brought under the aegis of the house gods for witness and protection. The slave would thereby become permanently attached to that household legally and cultically.[4])

האלהים would then fulfill a role here similar to one of the quasi-juridical functions of the *ilāni* at Nuzi,[5]) where the house gods serve

---

[1]) J. Z. Lauterbach, *Mekilta de-Rabbi Ishmael*, Vol. III (Philadelphia, 1949), p. 14, and others.

[2]) Abarbanel and Cassuto, amongst others.

[3]) O. Loretz, "Ex. 21, 6; 22, 8 und angebliche Nuzi-Parallelen," *Biblica* 41 (1960), pp. 167-175.

[4]) Driver, *The Book of Exodus*, p. 211, commenting on the word "the door," states that this is the door "not, as has been supposed, of the sanctuary, but, if the ceremony is to bear any relation to the thing which it intended to signify, of his master's house. The ear, as the organ of hearing, is naturally that of obedience as well; and its attachment (Dt. 15:17) to the door of the house would signify the perpetual attachment of the slave to that particular household." In light of the juxtaposition of bringing the slave "to האלהים" and bringing him "to the door or doorpost," Driver thinks that it is perfectly possible that האלהים here refers "to the household gods, or Penates, of the master's house, kept and worshipped near the door: the ceremony would then have the effect of bringing the above into a relation of dependence on the gods of his master's family, and of admitting him to the full religious privileges of the family." Cf. B. Baentsch, *Exodus-Leviticus-Numeri* (in Nowack's *Handkommentar zum Alten Testament* [Göttingen, 1903]), p. 190; and Noth, *op. cit.*, p. 178," . . . means a domestic deity who had his place at the door. Thus permanent slavery is given a cultic seal, and the permanent slave is also drawn into the cultic community of the house." According to Z.W. Falk, "Exodus XXI:6," *VT* 9 (1959), pp. 86-88, the ceremony had to take place in the presence of God since he was so concerned with the slave's manumission. It is of further interest to note that the later Deuteronomic version of this law, Dt. 15:12-18, omits the word האלהים, and transforms the entire ceremony into a secular act. See M. Weinfeld, *Deuteronomy and the Deuteronomic School* (Oxford, 1970), Part 3.

This private home ceremony is typologically similar to various Mesopotamian public ceremonies. For a discussion of "Publizitätsformen," see Koschaker, *op. cit.*, pp. 78-79, where he refers specifically to changes in status of property and slaves in cuneiform documents.

[5]) A. E. Draffkorn, "*Ilāni/Elohim*," *JBL* 76 (1957), pp. 216-224. Ex. 21:5 deals with one of the *ilāni*/אלהים functions in domestic law. For their employment in communal law, see comments to Ex. 22:7-10. Cf. C. Gordon, "אלהים in its Reputed Meaning of *Rulers, Judges*," *JBL* 54 (1935), pp. 134-144, who already called attention to both sections.

as the protectors of the family estate.[1]) Since symbols of deities are known to be found near the doors of chapels,[2]) it is very possible that that they were also stationed by the doors of private homes.[3])

Perforation of the ear, Heb. ורצע את אזנו, is also found in MAL A 40:84-86, 101-103; 44:45 (Akk. *uznišu upallišu*). The latter involve a humiliatory punishment rather than a symbolic slave mark.[4])

---

[1]) Greenberg, "Another Look at Rachel's Theft of the Teraphim," *JBL* 81 (1962), pp. 239-248, does not accept Draffkorn's opinion, *op. cit.*, that the *ilāni* were symbols of inheritance. However, he does mention the possible protective role of the hearth gods (p. 247).

[2]) W. F. Leemans, "*Kidinnu*: Un symbole de droit divin babylonien," *Symbolae ad jus et historiam antiquitatis pertinentes Julio Christiano van Oven dedicatae* (Leiden, 1946), p. 43. A sale that was transacted in the presence of divine symbols was a permanent one and was also considered an act of publicity (pp. 44-45). The contract was placed under divine protection; he who violated the stipulations would be guilty of "perjury" (p. 47). For a discussion of a divine symbol found by a chapel door, see D.J. Wiseman, "The Goddess Lama at Ur," *Iraq* 22 (1960), pp. 166-171.

[3]) E. Ebeling, "*Talīm*," *AfO* 5 (1928-29), pp. 218-219, describes a terracotta figurine of a protective male being that has inscribed on its right arm: *ir-ba rābiṣ šúl-mi* "Enter guardian of well-being," and on its left arm: UD.DU[= È] = (*ṣī*) *rābiṣ* ḫul (= *limuttim*) "Depart, guardian of evil." He identifies this figurine as a *talīm*. As his evidence Ebeling cites *KAR* III, 298:43 ff.: *ṣalmē*[meš] *ta-lim ṭiṭi ša* [iṣ] ... *na-šu-u i-na idi-šu-nu ir-*[*ba rā*]*biṣ šúl-mi ṣi-i rābi*[*ṣ limuttim tašaṭar* ....] "Clay figurines of *talīm* that are ... elevated of wood; on their arms [you should inscribe:] 'En[ter, guard]ian of well-being; depart guardia[n of evil'....]" The *talīm* apparently supervised the traffic through the door of the house. See Speiser's discussion of this text and terracotta in "*ṬWṬPT*," *JQR* 48 (1957-1958), pp. 211-212.

In one Old Babylonian document (P. Koschaker and A. Ungnad, *Hammurabi's Gesetz*, Vol. VI [Leipzig, 1923], No. 1752), a formal oath is taken by the owner of the house before symbols or emblems of deities placed by the judges alongside the house (*i-na pu-ut bi-ti-šu*, or read *i-na pu-ut bi-ti šu-a-ti*) in order to determine the correct deposition of property. These images or altars of the gods are not, however, the house gods, and this is not a private ceremony. The end of the document describes the "cleansing" (i.e., freeing from further claims or encumbrances) of the house before the gods. The same formula, *pūtam ullulum*, is also used in conjunction with the release of slaves—a ceremony that usually takes place near divine images. (Cf. Driver and Miles, *Babylonian Laws*, Vol. I, pp. 225-230.) This is one more indication of the similarity in treatment of property and slaves in cuneiform law; cf. p. 50, n. 4. Thus both in Mesopotamia and Israel changes in the status of slaves are formally marked by a ceremony in the presence of divine symbols. For a ceremony of the manumission of a slave at the gate of a temple (Akk. *bāb ilim ubbibšu*), see J. Lewy, *Die Kültepetexte der Sammlung Hahn*, 31:5. (Dr. M. Weinfeld drew my attention to this text.)

[4]) E. Ring, *Israels Rechtsleben im Lichte der neuentdeckten assyrischen und hethitischen Gesetzesurkunden* (Stockholm, 1926), p. 75, n. 2, objects to the formal identification of these two acts that is made by E. Jacob, "Die altassyrischen Gesetze und ihr Verhältnis zu den Gesetzen des Pentateuch," *ZVRW* 41 (1925), p. 358. According to the view expressed in the *Mechilta* to Ex. 21:6 (*Mekilta de-*

Laws dealing with slaves are found at the very end of LH, laws 278-282. In Exodus, however, they occupy prime importance by being placed first. This marked emphasis, it has been suggested, is due to the Israelites' recent freedom from bondage and their concern for the well-being and protection of other slaves.[1]) Since slaves are also created in the divine image, they, too, must be treated like human beings and not like chattels. This, in turn, explains the decided emphasis in biblical legislation on the various limitations of the owner's authority over his slave (cf. comments to Ex. 21:20-21, 26-27).

7-11. This pericope has been interpreted as the biblical counterpart to a type of marriage contract known from Nuzi—the *ṭuppi mārtūti ù kallūti/kallātūti* "document of daughtership and daughter-in-lawship,"[2]) a legal institution which has been studied by Koschaker [3]) and Mendelsohn.[4]) The usual stipulations of such a contract allow the purchaser, upon adopting a girl, to marry her himself or give her in marriage to one of his sons or slaves.[5]) The girl remains under the

---

Rabbi Ishmael, Vol. III, trans. J. Z. Lauterbach [Philadelphia, 1949]), p. 16, and in *B.T. Qiddushin* 22a, the perforation of the ear was a punishment for the ear. This symbolic act is connected with the idea that the ear is the organ of obedience. Cf. the views of Driver and Baentsch on p. 50, n. 4, and LH 282.

[1]) Cf. both Abarbanel and Cassuto in their respective commentaries to Exodus. This, moreover, is the explicit reason given in Dt. 15:15.

[2]) I. Mendelsohn, "The Conditional Sale into Slavery of Free Born Daughters in Nuzi and the Law of Ex. 21:7-11," *JAOS* 55 (1935), pp. 190-195, and *Slavery in the Ancient Near East* (New York, 1949), pp. 12 ff. Cf. also E. Neufeld's study of these documents in *Ancient Hebrew Marriage Laws* (London, 1944), pp. 68-76. For a complete study of cuneiform marriage law, see A. van Praag, *Droit matrimonial assyro-babylonien* = *Archaelogisch-Historische Bijdragen, Allard Pierson Stichting* 12 (Amsterdam, 1945), esp. pp. 80-84.

[3]) *NKRA*, pp. 82-91 (on p. 84 he first designated this kind of marriage as *adoptiones in matrimonium servile*), and "Fratriarchat," *ZA* 41 (1933), pp. 13-28 (where on pp. 18 ff., esp. pp. 21-22, he changed the formal designation to *adoptiones in matrimonium*). According to Koschaker, "Fratriarchat," pp. 20-22, just as *mārtūtu* is significant of the jurisdiction involved, so *kallātūtu* reflects the purpose of the relationship. For another interpretation, cf. H. Levy, "Gleanings From a New Volume of Nuzi Texts," *Or* 10 (1941), p. 216, n. 2. See also the discussion of these documents in C. Gordon, "The Status of Women Reflected in the Nuzi Tablets," *ZA* 43 (1936), pp. 146-169, esp. pp. 150-153; Driver and Miles, *The Assyrian Laws* (Oxford, 1935), pp. 164-165; and A. Saarisalo, "New Kirkuk Documents Relating to Slaves," *StOr* V/3 (1934), pp. 74-76.

[4]) See above, n. 2.

[5]) Some documents add further conditions: he may sell her outside to a "man in the gate," or even turn her into a prostitute. For all references, see Mendelsohn, *loc. cit.*

jurisdiction of her adopter or designated husband/s for life, [1]) unless the agreement is broken and a settlement made.[2])

The law in Exodus resembles the Nuzi documents in that it, too, pertains to the sale of a young girl by her father to a purchaser who must ensure her with a marital status. The biblical law, however, differs from the cuneiform in many aspects: (1) the girl is no longer considered a type of property that can be passed on from one husband to the next; [3]) (2) the original stipulation of the marriage must be fulfilled; if the purchaser refuses to marry her, he is guilty of a breach of contract and must let her be redeemed (vs. 8); (3) she must never be sold outside that one nuclear family (vs. 8); (4) if she is designated for her master's son,[4]) she is then treated like any other free maiden (vs. 9); (5) if the master should later take another wife, he must not fail to provide her (his first wife) with three basic necessities (vs. 10); (6) if he does not fulfill this responsibility, she is freed without having to make any payment (vs. 11).

7. "When a man sells his daughter as a slave [אמה], she shall not be freed as male slaves are."

Even though this law pertains to a girl who is sold by her father in order to get married and does not pertain to a case of female slavery, such a girl, nevertheless, is designated an אמה.[5]) Unlike male slaves, however, she does not obtain her freedom automatically, i.e., she is not manumitted on the seventh year, but she is provided with the protection of marriage for life.

8. "If she proves to be displeasing [6]) to her master, who has designated her for himself [לו יעדה], he must let her be redeemed; he shall not have the right [לא ימשל] to sell her to outsiders [עם נכרי], since he broke faith with her [בבגדו בה]."

---

[1]) Speiser, "One Hundred Nuzi Texts," *AASOR* 16 (1936), No. 23:12-13: *šum-ma* 10 *awēlūti*^{meš} *mu-uz-za-šú im-tù-ut ù* 11 *awēla a-na aš-šu-ti i-na-an-din* "If ten of her husbands should die, she may be given as wife to the eleventh." Cf. Nos. 30, 33, 42.

[2]) *Ibid.*, Nos. 23, 30.

[3]) Koschaker, "Fratriarchat," *ZA* 41 (1933), p. 26, remarks that all traces of a personal relationship toward the woman are absent from these Nuzi marriage documents.

[4]) There is no mention, however, of her being sold to a slave.

[5]) For the difference between the juridical status of this term and שפחה, see Jepsen, "*Amah* und *Schiphchah*," *VT* 8 (1958), pp. 293-297, 425. Jepsen further indicates that these terms can no longer be used to identify source documents.

[6]) Heb. רעה בעיני; cf. Gen. 28:8. The interpretation of this verse is based on the reading of the *qere* (יעדה) לו.

יעד is probably the technical term designating this type of marriage.[1]) (There appears to be, moreover, a close semantic relationship between this verb and Akk. *uddû* [D-stem of *idû*] "to designate, appoint, assign" in the marriage law of MAL A 43:21-22: *māru ša aššata ú-di-ú-ni-šu-ni* "a son to whom they have assigned a wife.") [2]) Two other biblical legal terms relating to marriage are the verbs ארש, referring to a free woman (Ex. 22:15; Dt. 22:23, 25, 27-28), and חרף,[3]) which refers to an actual slave (Lev. 19:20).

The stipulation "if she proves to be displeasing . . . he must let her be redeemed" is not found in any of the Nuzi marriage documents. Only in the law of Exodus is the purchaser guilty of a breach of contract when he does not fulfill his obligation to marry her.

לא ימשל in this context means "not to have the right." [4]) The legal function of משל here is similar to that of its interdialectal semantic equivalent שלט in the Aramaic papyri, e.g., אנת שליט למלקח "you have the right to take (pledges)." [5])

עם נכרי includes anyone who is not a member of that nuclear family.[6]) A similar stipulation is found in *HSS* V 73, lines 27-28: *ana awēli nakri la inandin* "she may not be sold to any outsider."

בגד. בבגדו בה in legal terminology is the interdialectal functional equivalent of Akk. *nabalkutu* "to break an agreement," e.g., *mannummê ša ibalkatu* "whoever breaks the agreement." [7])

---

[1]) For three different interpretations of the verb יעד as reflected in the versions —"betrothal" (Septuagint, Vulgate), "marriage" (Peshitta), "designation/promise" (Onkelos, Pseudo-Jonathan)—see B. Cohen, *Jewish and Roman Law*, Vol. I (New York, 1966), p. 329, n. 288. A complete discussion of the Rabbinic exegesis of this law is found on pp. 328-335.

[2]) Cf. also l. 28. Further examples may be found in *CAD*, Vol. 7, p. 32. The cognate Hebrew verb ידע also has a similar meaning of "selection" in several Biblical passages, e.g., Jer. 1:5; Amos 3:2.

[3]) Is this verb related to the *ḫuruppatu* tokens of engagement in MAL 42:17;43:20?

[4]) Cf. Saadya Gaon's translation in M. Zucker, *Rav Saadya Gaon's Translation of the Torah*, Heb. (New York, 1959), p. 336.

[5]) A. Cowley, *Aramaic Papyri of the Fifth Century B.C.* (Oxford, 1923), No. 10:16-17. For the neo-Babylonian model of the Aramaic לא ישלט, Akk. *la išallat*, see Muffs, *Studies in Aramaic Legal Papyri from Elephantine* (= *Studia et Documenta ad Iura Orientis Antiqui Pertinentia* 8 [Leiden, 1969]), pp. 178, 178*. Cf. also J. J. Rabinowitz, *Jewish Law* (New York, 1956), p. 129.

[6]) Cf. Cassuto, *Exodus*, p. 187. For the meaning of עם, see Speiser, " 'People' and 'Nation' of Israel," *JBL* 79 (1960), pp. 157-163. For another interpretation, cf. A. Cody, "When is the Chosen People Called a *Gôy*," *VT* 14 (1964), pp. 1-6. For נכרי "outside the family," cf. Gen. 31:15; Ps. 69:9; and Ecc. 6:2. Cf. also Jud. 19:12. Cf. Weinfeld, "נכרי," (Heb.), *Encyclopaedia Biblica*, Vol. 5 (Jerusalem, 1968), pp. 866-867.

[7]) Koschaker, *NKRA*, p. 11, n. 4; Speiser, *AASOR* 10 (1930), p. 8; and

9. "And if he designated her for his son, he shall deal with her as is the practice with free maidens [כמשפט הבנות יעשה לה]."

כמשפט הבנות יעשה לה is a technical phrase meaning "to treat as a free(-born) woman." Its earliest possible analogue in cuneiform legal texts is found in a Sumerian di.til.la document from Ur III: dumu. uru.gim in.dí[m]-*m[a].[1]) This phrase, translated by Falkenstein, "sie zu einem Sohne der Stadt gemacht hat," grants full rights of a citizen to the individual.[2]) It is then found in a Nuzi contract together with an explicative clause: *ša ki-i mārat [A]r-ra-áb-hi i-p[u]-ša-aš-ši a-na amti*[ti] *la ú-ta-ar-ši* "She shall treat her as a daughter of Arrapha; she shall not return her to (the status of) a slave girl."[3]) (Speiser has already called attention to the fact that this is "an officially recognized and legally protected designation.")[4]) It reappears once again in an Assyrian document pertaining to a girl who is adopted of her own free will.[5]) The adopting father agrees that "he will not ill-treat (her) nor prostitute (her);"[6]) *ki-i mārti-šu-ma Aš-šu-ra-ia-e ú-pa-us-si* "he must treat her as his own daughter, an Assyrian."[7])

W. von Soden, *AHw*, Vol. 8, p. 695. For the legal overtones of בגד "to break a relation/agreement with someone," cf. Jud. 9:23; Mal. 2:10-11, 14-15; and the manifold references in the Bible where the verb is employed to symbolize Israel's breaking its covenant agreement with God, e.g., Hos. 6:7. Cf. P. A. H. de Boer, "Some Remarks on Exodus XXI:7-11," *Orientalia Neerlandica* (Leiden, 1948), p. 165, and A. Ehrlich, *Randglossen zur hebräischen Bibel*, Vol. 4 (Leipzig, 1928-29), p. 265.

1) A. Falkenstein, *Die neusumerischen Gerichtsurkunden* (= *Abhandlungen der Bayerischen Akademie der Wissenschaften, phil.-hist. Klasse*, N.F. 40 [Munich, 1956]), Text 178:15, p. 122.

2) *Ibid.*, p. 123. Cf. also Koschaker, *Über einige griechische Rechtsurkunden aus den östlichen Randgebieten des Hellenismus. Abhandlungen der Sächsischen Akademie der Wissenschaften, phil.-hist. Klasse*, Vol. 42, Nr. 1 (Leipzig, 1931), p. 71, n. 3; E. Szlechter, "L'affranchissement en droit suméro-akkadien," *AHDO-RIDA* 1 (1952), p. 184; and Driver and Miles, *Babylonian Laws*, Vol. I, p. 225.

3) Speiser, "One Hundred New Selected Nuzi Texts," *AASOR* 16 (1936), No. 42:21-22.

4) *Idem*, "Nuzi Marginalia," *Or* 25 (1956), p .14. Cf. Koschaker, "Fratriarchat," *ZA* 41 (1933), p. 16.

5) M. David and E. Ebeling, "Assyrische Rechtsurkunden," *ZVRW* 44 (1929), No. 5. Cf. Kraeling, *Aramaic Papyri*, 7:32, 34, 38, 39, 40.

6) Akk. *la u-la-ma-an-[ši]*, *la u-ma-az-zi-[ši]*. The translation is that of Driver and Miles, *Assyrian Laws*, p. 283 (cf. philological notes on p. 494). For other translations of the second verb, cf. David and Ebeling, *loc. cit.*, "to sleep with;" von Soden, *Grundriss der akkadischen Grammatik* (Rome, 1952), p. 33, "to make pregnant," and *AHw*, Vol. 7, p. 637, *mazā'u* "to violate."

7) Akk. *kī(ma) X epēšu* is the customary way of expressing "to treat a person;" cf. *CAD*, Vol. 4, pp. 196-197, and p. 232, 2′d (esp. the first example). The Hebrew equivalent of the idiom found here in vs. 9 is also present in Ex. 21:31.

10-11. "If he marries another [אחרת], he must not diminish from this one her food [שארה], her clothing [כסותה], or her conjugal rights (?) [ענתה]. If he fails her in these three ways, she shall go free, without payment."

The interdialectal semantic equivalent of the Heb. אחרת "another wife" is found in both LI 28 dam.egir.ra and in MAL A 46:99 *urkittu*.[1]

According to the provisions of this verse, the husband must continue to support his rejected wife with three basic commodities: שארה, כסותה, ועֹנתה. Another specific maintenance clause appears in LI 28, a law which at first appeared to pertain to a situation similar to the one described in Exodus.[2] However, with the publication of a new Sumerian text of this law,[3] it was discovered that the provision was not for a rejected wife per se, but rather for one who had been stricken with a type of disease: "If a man's first wife has *lost her sight* or has become paralytic, she shall not leave the house; (if) her husband takes a second wife, the latter wife shall support the first wife." (Variant: "He shall support the latter wife (and) the first wife.") A similar set of circumstances is described in LH 148, where a man who marries a second wife after his first wife becomes sick with a certain disease (Akk. *la'ābu*) is not permitted to divorce her, but must continue his support for the rest of her life (*a-di ba-al-ṭa-at it-ta-na-aš-ši-ši*).[4] Hence, all three collections of laws—LI, LH, and Exodus—obligate the husband to continue to provide for the maintenance of his first wife who has been subsequently bypassed in favor of another. In LI and LH the reason is because of illness; in Exodus it is left unstated.

The basic items required for the minimal support of a woman are listed in LI 27, the law directly preceding the one discussed above:

Ehrlich, *Randglossen*, Vol. I, p. 349, already noted the specific nuance of the Heb. בנות "free maidens" in this context. Cf. also Rabinowitz, *Jewish Law*, p. 57, n. 78, and the remarks of A. ibn Ezra and S. D. Luzatto in their respective commentaries, *ad loc.*

[1]) For the meaning of Akk. *urkittu* "a second/subsequent wife" taken while the first one is yet alive, see Driver and Miles, *Assyrian Laws*, pp. 232-233, and van Praag, *Droit matrimonial assyro-babylonien*, p. 93.

[2]) Cf. the translations of both F. R. Steele, "Lipit-Ishtar Law Code," *AJA* 52 (1948), pp. 425-450, and S. N. Kramer, "Lipit-Ishtar Lawcode," *ANET*, p. 160.

[3]) M. Civil, "New Sumerian Law Fragments," *Studies in Honor of Benno Landsberger on His Seventy Fifth Birthday, April 21, 1965* (Chicago, 1965), pp. 2-3.

[4]) For an example of the praxis of this law, see Falkenstein, *Gerichtsurkunden*, Text 6, and pp. 9 ff.

"If a man's wife has not borne him children (but) a harlot (from) the public square has borne him children, he shall provide grain, oil, and clothing for the harlot." [1]) The provision here is for three commodities, the same number as found in the law of Exodus. This triad of barley or food rations, Sum. še.ba, Akk. *eprum*; oil, Sum. ì.ba/ì.giš, Akk. *piššatum*; and clothing, Sum. túg.ba/síg.ba, Akk. *lubuš/ltum*, which constitutes the basic maintenance allotment in LI 27, is quite common throughout Mesopotamian legal texts. In fact, as the following sampling of documents stemming from different periods shows, this threefold provision became somewhat stereotypic.

1. For the upkeep of a wife of a freeman by a slave (Ur III):

   "As long she lives, Lubaba (the slave) is obliged to give her 6 še gur.lugala 10 ma.na síg.gi 6 sìla ì.giš "6 *kors* of royal barley, 10 *minas* of *gi* wool, and 6 *silas* of olive oil." [2])

2. For the upkeep of a wet-nurse:

(a) *ana ittišu* 3, III: 47-50:

(47) um.me.gá.lá.a.ni.šè
a-na mu-še-niq-ti-šu

(48) mu.III.kam še.ba.i̯a.ba
*III šanāte*meš *ep-ra piš-šá-tam*

(49) síg.ba túg.ba.bi
lu-bu-uš-ta

(50) in.na.ni.íb.kala(g)
ú-dan-nin

"He maintained (lit. "strengthened") his wet nurse three years with food, oil, and clothing." [3])

(b) LE 32:

šum-ma awīlum mār-šu a-na šu-nu-qí-im a-na tar-bi-tim id-di-in-ma še.ba ì.ba síg.ba mu.3-kam *la id-di-in* 10 *ma-na tar-bi-it māri-šu* i.lal.e-*ma mār-šu i-ta-a-ar-ru* "If a man gives his son away for having him nursed (and) for upbringing, but does not furnish rations of food, oil, (and) clothing for three years,

---

[1]) The translation is taken from Kramer, *loc. cit.*

[2]) Falkenstein, *op. cit.*, Text 8:4-10, p. 10.

[3]) B. Landsberger, *Die Serie ana ittišu* (*Materialien zum sumerischen Lexicon*, Vol. I [Rome, 1937]), p. 45. Cf., however, *CAD*, D, p. 86.

then he shall pay 10 *minas* for the upbringing of his son and shall take back his son." [1]

3. For the upkeep of a priestess:

LH 178 is concerned with the devolution of the property of priestesses and pertains to a woman who is not permitted to dispose of a *šeriktum* "grant" given her by her father during his life time. Upon her father's death, it is taken by her brothers who administer it, and who, in turn, must supply her *ki-ma e-mu-uq zi-it-ti-ša* še.ba ì.ba *ù* síg.ba "food, oil, and clothing according to the value of her share." [2]

4. For the upkeep of a sister:

In an OB document from the time of Rim-Sin four brothers obligate themselves to provide a specific amount of barley, oil, and clothing annually for their sister. The brother who fails to provide this threefold maintenance quota forfeits his inheritance.[3]

5. For the upkeep of parents by real or adopted children:

OB documents from the first dynasty of Babylon,[4] from the time of Samsuiluna,[5] from Larsa,[6] and one from NB times, [7] make the provision of different amounts of barley, oil, and clothing obligatory upon the children.

6. For the upkeep of a deserted wife:

MAL 36 deals with the legal consequences if a husband has not left his wife *la-a* ìa.gis *la-a* síg *la-a lu-bu-ul-ta la-a ú-ku-ul-la-a* "neither oil, nor wool, nor clothing, nor food" (l. 86).[8]

7. For the upkeep of a slave:

---

[1]) See A. Goetze, *The Laws of Eshnunna* (New Haven, 1956), p. 92, for further references. Cf. also LE 9.

[2]) Driver and Miles, *Babylonian Laws*, Vol. I, pp. 374 ff. For the actual praxis of this law, see R. Harris, "The *nadītu* Laws of the Code of Hammurapi in Praxis," *Or* 30 (1961), pp. 163-169.

[3]) E. Chiera, *Old Babylonian Contracts* = *University Museum Publication of the Babylonian Section*, Vol. VIII/2 (Philadelphia, 1922), Text 116:8-9, 11, pp. 123-124.

[4]) A. Poebel, *Babylonian Legal and Business Documents from the Time of the First Dynasty of Babylon* = *Babylonian Expedition of the University of Pennsylvania, Series A: Cuneiform Texts*, Vol. VI/2 (Philadelphia, 1909), Text 28, pp. 29-31, and Text 48, pp. 35-38.

[5]) Chiera, *op. cit.*, Text 153:19-20, pp. 131-132.

[6]) C. F. Jean, "Nouveaux contrats de Larsa," *RA* 26 (1929), pp. 104-107.

[7]) F. E. Peiser, "Aus Rom," *OLZ* 7 (1904), p. 39.

[8]) For text and discussion see, Driver and Miles, *Assyrian Laws, ad loc.*

A neo-Babylonian document from the time of Nabonidus pertains to a slave who fled from one owner to another who provided him with *epri piššatum ù* túg*lubuštum* "food, oil, and clothing." [1]

In sum the basic necessities of life were epitomized in Mesopotamian legal texts by a formulaic triad of commodities.[2] This, then, has a direct bearing upon Ex. 21:10. There, too, a threefold obligation of support is placed upon the husband. The first two items, Heb. שארה "her, meat/food," [3] and כסותה "her clothing," are the functional equivalents of the Sum. še.ba and síg.ba, Akk. *eprum* and *lubuštum*. (The Akkadian cognate to the first item in the biblical triad, *šīru*, is also found as part of a list of basic provisions in OB [4] and NA [5] documents.)

The third item, Heb. עֹנתה, however, is much more difficult to interpret. This *hapax legomenon* has been a crux throughout the centuries, and several different interpretations have been offered to explain it. The most commonly accepted meaning of the word found in commentaries and dictionaries is "her conjugal rights." [6] Another interpretation, "her dwelling," related to Heb. מעון, has also been adopted by a few commentators.[7] However, in the light of all the extra-biblical evidence adduced above, it is here suggested that Heb. עֹנתה is none other than the functional equivalent of the third item in the traditional cuneiform formula, i.e., Sum. ì.ba, Akk.

---

1) Peiser, *Keilinschriftliche Bibliothek*, Vol. IV (*Texte juristischen und geschäftlichen Inhalts* [Berlin, 1896]), No. 44:7, 11, pp. 244-247. For further references, see *CAD*, Vol. 7, pp. 167-168.

2) Cf. I. J. Gelb, "The Ancient Mesopotamian Ration System," *JNES* 24 (1965), pp. 230-243, who documents the distribution of these commodities in the old Mesopotamian ration system.

3) Cf. Mic. 3:2, 3, and Ps. 78:20.

4) M. Schorr, *Urkunden des altbabylonischen Zivil- und Prozessrechts* (Leipzig, 1913), Nos. 19:35, 65:15, 125:12, 223:7. For the formulaic triad of commodities, see in addition Nos. 19:33-34, 78:7, 242:6.

5) B. Parker, "Economic Tablets from the Temple of Mamu at Balawat," *Iraq* 25 (1963), pp. 86-100. The word appears in several documents involving debts with security as one of the provisions that must be paid for by the creditor. (I owe this reference to my colleague, Prof. Y. Muffs.)

6) See *Mechilta, ad loc.* (in J. Z. Lauterbach's edition, *Mekilta de-Rabbi Ishmael* [Philadelphia, 1949], pp. 27-29) and *T. B. Kethubboth* 47b-48a (where several of the Rabbis still contend that the word should be interpreted differently, cf. Cohen, *Jewish and Roman Law*, Vol. 1, p. 330, n. 292), the commentaries of Saadiah, Rashi, ibn Ezra, Ramban, Abarbanel, Ehrlich, Dillmann, Holzinger, Baentsch, McNeil, Driver, Heinisch, Beer, Keil-Delitzsch, Noth, and the dictionaries of Brown-Driver-Briggs and Koehler-Baumgartner. The word עֹנתה is understood to mean "her time" and is then interpreted euphemistically.

7) Ibn Ezra (but immediately rejected), Rashbam, and Cassuto. See p. 60, n. 1.

piššatum. Whatever its ultimate etymological derivation, Heb. ענתה appears to be an otherwise unknown equivalent for "oil, ointments."[1])

The importance of oils for the protection of the skin against the hot sun is well known throughout the ancient Near East.[2]) Thus in the light of the over-all importance of oil and ointments in hygienic,[3]) ritualistic,[4]) and legal practices,[5]) it is no wonder that this important commodity would become part and parcel of any basic maintenance allotment. Conjugal rights, on the other hand, are nowhere mentioned in the documents from the ancient Near East as an integral requirement for marital support. It is hardly likely, moreover, that a husband would be obligated to fulfill such a demand on behalf of a rejected wife.[6])

The specific order of the three items in Exodus: food, clothing, and oil, is also found in several OB [7]) and Elamite documents.[8]) In the latter the interdialectal semantic equivalent for oil is *kupurtum*. In one contract provision is made for 14 gin k[u.babbar *ana*] *ip-ri*[*im*] *ù*

[1]) The writer was pleased to note that after having proposed this interpretation there appeared an article by E. Oren, "Concerning שארה, כסותה, ועונתה, Ex. XXI: 10," (Heb.), *Tarbiz* 33 (1964), p. 317, in which a similar identification of the word was made by citing LI alone, without any further indication of the plethora of Mesopotamian documentation at hand. However, on the basis of *lectio difficilor*, it seems preferable not to emend the text as Oren is led to do (Heb. עֲנֻגָּה "ointments(?)") comparing *Toseftah Terumoth* 9:14. N. H. Tur-Sinai, "כסותה, ועונתה, שארה," (Heb.), *The Language and the Book*, Vol. 2 (Jerusalem, 1950), pp. 215-218, and *Peshuto Shel Miqra*, (Heb.), Vol. I (Jerusalem, 1962), pp. 114-115, after thoroughly discussing the problem, is led to emend the text to read עֻגֹתֶהָ "her cakes." See now S. M. Paul, "Exod. 21:10 A Threefold Maintenance Clause," *JNES* 28 (1969), pp. 48-53. See in addition, J. Schacht, *An Introduction to Islamic Law* (Oxford, 1964), p. 167, where in Islamic law, maintenance of a wife by a husband consists of food, clothing, and lodging. (Prof. J. J. Finkelstein—written communication.)

[2]) R. Forbes, *Studies in Ancient Technology*, Vol. III (Leiden, 1965), pp. 2-3.

[3]) *Ibid.* [4]) *Ibid.*, pp. 3 ff.

[5]) E. Kutsch, *Salbung als Rechtsakt im alten Testament und im alten Orient* (Berlin, 1963). On p. 1 he discusses the general importance of oil in the ancient Near East. For the use of oil in a marriage ceremony, see MAL 42-43, and for the mention of oil as one of the requirements stipulated in Egyptian marriage contracts, see E. Lüddeckens, *Ägyptische Eheverträge* (Wiesbaden, 1960), pp. 261-262.

[6]) Hence this is not comparable to the clause in the Aramaic documents, E. G. Kraeling, *The Brooklyn Museum Aramaic Papyri* (New Haven, 1953), 7, p. 206, lines 38-40, where, according to the interpretation of H. L. Ginsberg, "The Brooklyn Museum Aramaic Documents," *JAOS* 74 (1954), p. 159, denial of conjugal rights by either spouse is considered an act of repudiation. The biblical passage pertains not to an act of repudiation but to the question of support.

[7]) Chiera, *op. cit.*, Text 153:19-20; Poebel, *op. cit.*, Text 48:31 and Text 28.

[8]) V. Scheil, *Mémoires de la Mission Archéologique de Perse*. Vol. 24. *Mission en Susiane. Actes Juridiques Susiens* (Paris, 1933), 332;17-18, 333:13-15. Cf. p. 10, n. 18.

lu-bu-ši-im ù ku-pu-ur-ti-im "14 shekels of silver for food, clothing, and ointment." [1])

The same sequence of commodities, moreover, is found in a biblical passage where its specific legal aspect may still be noted. In Hos. 2:7 adulterous Israel claims to follow her lovers who supply her with her fundamental needs: "my *bread* and water, my wool and flax [i.e., *clothing*], my *oil* and drink." Since she does not realize that it was God who had provided her all the time with this basic support (vs. 10), he shall proceed to deprive her of her regular maintenance allotment (vs. 11).[2])

Finally, Ecclesiastes (Ecc. 9:7-9) in the delightful passage where he advises man to enjoy his life to the utmost, highlights, among other things, these very three items in the same identical order: "Up, eat your *bread* with joy, and drink your wine with a glad heart.... At all times let your *clothes* be sparkling clean, and *oil* on your head not be lacking. Enjoy life with the woman you love....[3])

12. "He who fatally strikes [מכה · · · ומת][4]) a man shall be put to death."

This absolute ban on composition for homicide is without parallel in all Near Eastern law.[5]) Since homicide is considered to be contrary to the divine order (cf. Gen. 9:6), it cannot be atoned for by a pecuniary or property settlement; the murderer must be put to death. The religious precept of the sanctity of a human life is here embodied within a legal formula.

In cuneiform laws, however, such a religious motivation is absent,[6]) e.g., HL 1-5, where the penalty for homicide is the pledging of one's estate as security along with the surrender of a specified number of persons to the family of the slain (HL 1-4) or a monetary settlement

---

[1]) *Ibid.*, 333:13-15. Text 332:17-18 has še . ba [t]úg . níg . lám *ù qu-pu-úr-ta-am*.

[2]) Cf. also Ezk. 16:18-19. For the use of oil in other non-ritualistic passages, see, e.g., II Sam. 12:20; Isa. 61:3; Ps. 23:5, 45:8; Ruth 3:3; II Chron. 28:15.

[3]) In Egyptian literature, cf. J. A. Wilson, "The Instruction of the Vizier Ptah-Hotep," *ANET*, p. 413; "A Song of the Harper," *op. cit.*, p. 467, l. 10; and in Mesopotamian literature, cf. Speiser, "The Epic of Gilgamesh," *op. cit.*, p. 90, lines 6-14.

[4]) An example of hendiadys. This verse as well as vss. 15-17 are participially formulated. For the various types of cuneiform and biblical legal formulations, see Appendix II.

[5]) See Greenberg, "Some Postulates of Biblical Criminal Law," *Yehezkel Kaufmann Jubilee Volume* (Jerusalem, 1960), pp. 5-28.

[6]) LH, moreover, omits the general case of homicide altogether. For an actual trial for homicide, see T. Jacobsen, "An Ancient Mesopotamian Trial for Homicide," *Analecta Biblica* 12 (1959), pp. 130-150.

(HL 5). Furthermore, in both MAL A 10 and B 2 where capital punishment is contemplated, its execution is left entirely up to the discretion of the next of kin: [1] "If he chooses, he may put them/him to death; or if he chooses, he may be willing to settle [2] and take his share." [3] When homicide is viewed merely as an economic crime against the family or clan, the loss may be subsequently repaired by means of composition.

LH, HL, and Exodus all employ similar juridical terminology in describing a case of homicide as "striking to death":

(1) LH 207:14-15 *šum-ma i-na ma-ḫa-ṣí-šu im-tu-ut* [4])
(2) HL 3-4 *ták-ku . . . u̯a-al-aḫ-zi . . . a-ki*
(3) Ex. 21:12 מכה . . . ומת

13-14. If he did not do it by design,[5]) but it came about by an act of God [והאלהים אנה לידו], I will assign you a place to which he can flee. When a man schemes against another and kills him [6]) treacherously, you shall take him from my very altar to be put to death."

These verses distinguish between accidental or unintentional homicide and premeditated or intentional murder. Specific examples of the former are listed in Num. 35:22-23, where the expressions בפתע בלא איבה "of a sudden without enmity," i.e., without malice aforethought; בלא צדיה "unintentionally;" בלא ראות "without seeing," i.e., inadvertently; "though he was not an enemy (אויב) of his and did not seek him harm;" define accidental or unintentional (Heb. שגגה vss. 11,15) homicide. Dt. 19:4-5 prefaces a case of accidental homicide with the expression בבלי דעת "unwittingly," and "without having been his enemy (אויב) in the past." (Cf. also vs. 6 כי לא שנא הוא לו מתמול "since he had never been the other's enemy.") In cases of accidental homicide the culprit, who is nevertheless called a murderer (Heb. רוצח), is not put to death but may flee to an asylum—here the

---

[1]) This is T. Meek's translation of Akk. *bēl napšāte* in *ANET*.

[2]) Akk. *magāru* translated in Driver and Miles, *The Assyrian Laws* (Oxford, 1935), p. 497, "to accept composition."

[3]) Since both laws are so similarly worded, MAL B 2 may be used to restore several of the gaps in the mutilated text of MAL A 10. For another example of the discretion of the individual in the execution of capital punishment, cf. the Edict of Telepinus in O. R. Gurney, *The Hittites* (Baltimore, 1962), p. 98. Contrast these cuneiform laws, on the other hand, with Num. 35:31 which prohibits the taking of ransom for the murderer's life. Cf. also HL 197, 198 (adultery).

[4]) Cf. LH 116:40-42.

[5]) Heb. צדה; cf. Num. 35:20, 22; I Sam. 24:11.

[6]) Heb. להרגו "to kill him;" cf. the commentaries of Saadya and ibn Ezra, *ad loc.*

altar—which grants him the protection of the deity.[1]) Such an institution, which ensures the safety of one guilty of manslaughter, is without parallel in the entire ancient Near East.[2]) This sacred site, however, is not afforded to one guilty of premediated or intentional murder, for in such a case he is to be taken down "from my very altar to be put to death" (vs. 14).[3])

Homicide is defined as murder if the assailant schemed against his victim by lying in wait (Ex. 21:14), if a murderous instrument was used (Num. 35:16-18), or if "he pushed him in hate or hurled something at him on purpose and death resulted, or if he struck him with his hand in enmity and death resulted..." (Num. 35:20-21); cf. Dt. 19:11. In such cases the "avenger of blood"—though not specifically mentioned in Exodus—is responsible for the execution of the murderer.[4]) In accidental or unintentional homicide, on the other hand, such retaliatory action is considered wrong, but the blood avenger is "not guilty of a capital crime." [5])

Cases of unintentional homicide are also found in both LH 207-208 and HL 3-4. In the former, lack of intention is expressed by the phrase *i-na i-du-ú la am-ḫa-ṣú* "I did not strike him knowingly" (206:10-11);[6]) this offense is subject only to a monetary settlement. The latter em-

---

[1]) For the cities of refuge, see Num. 35:9-15, 22-28; Dt. 4:41-43; 19:1-10; Jos. 20.

[2]) Greenberg, "The Biblical Conception of Asylum," *JBL* 78 (1959), pp. 125-132; "Avenger of Blood," *IDB*, Vol. I (1962), p. 321; "City of Refuge," *IDB*, Vol. I (1962), pp. 638-639. Cf. B. Dinur, "The Religious Character of the Cities of Refuge and the Ceremony of Admission into Them," (Heb.), *Eretz-Israel*, Vol. III (Jerusalem, 1954), pp. 135-146; Y. Kaufmann, *Sefer Yehošuaᶜ*, Heb. (Jerusalem, 1959), pp. 259-270. See, however, J. J. Finkelstein's discussion of *bīt napṭarim* which has certain aspects of an asylum—"Some New *Misharum* Material and its Implications," *Studies in Honor of Benno Landsberger* (Chicago, 1965), pp. 238-239. His conclusions are now accepted by B. Landsberger, "Jungfräulichkeit," *Symbolae David*, Vol. 2 (Leiden, 1968), p. 99.

[3]) Cf. I Ki. 1:50 ff.; 2:28 ff.

[4]) Though it is questionable whether blood vengeance is found at all in the Mesopotamian corpora, cf. M. David, "The Codex Hammurabi and its Relation to the Provisions of the Law in Exodus," *OTS* 7 (1950), p. 160—otherwise, Driver and Miles, *Assyrian Laws*, p. 33, even if the latter were correct, the remark of E. Merz, *Die Blutrache bei den Israeliten* (Leipzig, 1916), p. 62, is still important to bear in mind: "Schon im alten Israel galten Bluttaten an Volksgenossen nicht mehr als reine Privatdelikte, sondern auch als religiöse Schuld." In Israel, moreover (a society that lacked a strong central authority), the defense of life is one of the main duties of kinship, cf. Greenberg, "Avenger of Blood," *IDB*, Vol. I, p. 321. Consequently the "avenger of blood" plays an important role in that society; cf. Merz, *loc. cit.*

[5]) Dt. 19:6.

[6]) Cf. LH 227:52-53 *i-na i-du-ú la ú-gal-li-bu* "I did not cut (it) off knowingly."

ploys the phrase *ki-eš-šar-ši-iš ua-aš-ta-i* "only his hand is at fault," i.e., he acted without premeditation (3:6-7, 4:8).[1]) Here the law prescribes the number of persons to be surrendered to the family of the slain as composition. This number, incidentally, is exactly one half the number surrendered in cases of murder (cf. HL 1-2). The technical phrase expressing lack of intention in HL has been compared to the wording of Exodus, והאלהים אנה לידו—ידו "his hand," but not "his head," is at fault, i.e., accidental rather than premeditated homicide.[2]) The emphasis, however, in this expression should be placed not on ידו but rather on האלהים, which here means "an act of God, fate, chance." Cuneiform analogues to such "acts of providence" are found in LH 249:38-39 *i-lum im-ḫa-sú-ma im-tu-ut* and 266:77 *li-pí-it ilim.*[3])

These two verses contain the only first-person references to the deity in the legal portion of the Book of the Covenant: ושמתי (vs. 13) "I will assign," and מזבחי "my altar" (vs. 14); and the only examples of direct address (with the exception of Ex. 21:2, 23): לך "(I will assign) you" (vs. 13), and תקחנו "you shall take him" (vs. 14). This feature remains unique to the biblical corpora.[4])

15. "He who strikes his father [מכה אביו] or his mother shall be put to death."

Though LH 195 pertains to a similar offense: "If a son strikes his father" (Akk. *a-ba-šu im-ta-ḫa-aṣ* = Heb. מכה אביו), the punishment differs: "They shall cut off his hand," i.e., only the peccant member is punished.

Only in biblical legislation does the parents' authority receive a divine sanction (cf. Ex. 20:12), and this helps to explain the severity of the punishment in Exodus. The Israelite society, moreover, is family centered having its basic nucleus in blood kinship, while the core of the Mesopotamian society is economic and political. Thus, an offense against the familial authority in Israel is treated much more gravely than in Mesopotamia.[5])

It is also of interest to note that in the biblical corpora the father

---

[1]) J. Friedrich, *Die hethitischen Gesetze* (Leiden, 1959), p. 17.

[2]) *Ibid.*, p. 90. Similarly, A. F. Pukko, *Die altassyrischen und hethitischen Gesetze und das Alte Testament* (= *StOr* 1 [1925]), p. 129.

[3]) Cf. Driver and Miles, *Babylonian Laws*, Vol. II, pp. 274-275. For other examples, cf. *ARM*, Vol. II, 24:9 *ilum uḫalliq*; Vol. III, 61:10 *ilum ikkal.*

[4]) Cf. Alt, "Die Ursprünge des Israelitischen Rechts," *Kleine Schriften*, Vol. 1, pp. 306-307.

[5]) J. Pedersen, *Israel*, Vols. I-II (London, 1954), pp. 353-354, cites this verse in his discussion on the important role of kinship in biblical law.

and mother are often mentioned together, e.g., Ex. 20:12; 21:15, 17; Lev. 19:3, 20:9; Dt. 21:18-19, 27:16, implying the basic equality of both parents.[1]) This verse is the first of three cases where capital punishment is prescribed for offenses other than murder.

16. "He who kidnaps [גנב] a man—whether he has sold him or is still holding him [ונמצא בידו]—shall be put to death" [מות יומת].

LH 14 also deems kidnapping a capital offense and employs a similar mode of expression: Akk. *iš-ta-ri-iq id-da-ak* = Heb. ... גנב מות יומת. Whereas LH, however, limits its provisions to the kidnapping of a minor of the *awīlum* class (Akk. *mār a-wi-lim ṣe-eḫ-ra-am*), the injunction in Exodus is all-inclusive.[2]) The law of kidnapping in LH, moreover, is the direct continuation of the laws pertaining to theft and lost property in general, cf. LH 6-13. Thus this crime is classified as just one other offense against property, and it is characteristic of LH, as well as other cuneiform collections, to punish such property offenses by death, cf. LH 6-11, MAL A 3a and HL 126. In Exodus, on the other hand, the crime of kidnapping is not related to property offenses; the two are classes apart. And whereas no crime against *property* is penalized by capital punishment, the repeated emphasis on the sanctity of an individual, coupled with the Israelite abhorrence of the wrongful deprivation of one's liberty, made every theft of a *human being*, automatically converting a free man into a slave, punishable by death.[3])

If the interpretation given in some commentaries to Ex. 20:15, לא תגנב "you shall not kidnap," is correct,[4]) this would further help to explain the severity of the penalty in Ex. 21:16: the sanctity of an individual's freedom is protected by a divine commandment (cf. Ex. 21:15, 17, and Ex. 20:12).

---

[1]) For LE 26, 27, 28; LH 192, 193; HL 28, 29, see Yaron, *Eshnunna*, pp. 96-98.

[2]) Cf. Alt, "Das Verbot des Diebstahls im Dekalog," *Kleine Schriften*, Vol. I, p. 340, n. 1. Dt. 24:7, however, restricts this law to the kidnapping of a fellow Israelite. This later limitation is then attributed in both the Septuagint and Targum translations to the law in Exodus.

[3]) Ring, *Israels Rechtsleben*, p. 140, correctly emphasizes this point. The severity of the punishment in LH, however, may also be related to the crime of kidnapping; cf. LH 15 ff. For another explanation of the difference between LH and Exodus, see Cazelles, *Études*, p. 149. Unlike the law pertaining to the theft of animals, Ex. 21:37 and 22:3, there is no difference in the penalty here whether the kidnapper has sold him or whether he is still found in his possession.

[4]) This interpretation which is found in the *Mechilta* both here and in Ex. 21:16 was independently arrived at by Alt, *op. cit.*, pp. 333-340. Cf. M. H. Gottstein, "Du sollst nicht stehlen," *ThZ* 9 (1953), pp. 394-395.

A partial analogue to the Heb. ונמצא בידו, "or is found holding him,"[1]) is found in HL 19, which adds to a similar case of manstealing the condition "but if his master discovers him." Curiously enough, the restitution legislated in HL 19 is far greater than the corresponding penalty for a case of homicide (i.e., formerly twelve persons, now six, as contrasted to HL 1, which provides four persons in case of murder and two for manslaughter).

A document from the time of Hammurabi deals with a case of kidnapping that eventually led to murder.[2]) In stating that the manstealer was caught "red-handed" with the kidnapped party, the tablet employs an analogue to the Heb. ונמצא בידו, Akk. *i-na qá-ti-šu iṣ-ba-at*: (1) *aš-šum* [I]*Ri-ba-am-ì-lí Š*[*u*]-*b*[*a-ri-i*]*m* (2) *ša* [I]*I-din-ia-tum ú-sí-pu-šu-ma* (3) *iš-ri-qú-šu* (4) [I]*A-bu-um-ra-bi rē'ûm* (5) *i-na qá-ti-šu iṣ-ba-at* "Concerning the shepherd A. who seized in the possession of I., the Subarean, R., whom I. had abducted [3]) and kidnapped." LH employs the same expression in 9:4-5 for the seizing of lost property in one's possession.[4])

17. "He who contemns [מקלל] his father or mother shall be put to death."

Once again (cf. above, vs. 15) the biblical emphasis on the honor due to one's parents makes any offense against them—verbal or physical—punishable by death.[5]) Capital punishment for "disrespect" (קלל) [6]) towards parents is unparalleled in any other collection of Near Eastern law.[7])

---

[1]) For Heb. נמצא "be caught," cf. S. Iwry, "הנמצא—A Striking Variant Reading in 1QIs[a]," *Textus* 5 (1966), p. 37. Cf. also Ex. 22:1, 3.

[2]) A. Riftin, *Ancient Babylonian Juridical and Administrative Documents in Collections in the USSR*, Russian (Moscow, 1937), No. 46. See also Landsberger, "Gerichtsprotokoll über einen Mordprozess," *ZA* 43 (1936), pp. 315-316.

[3]) Landsberger, *op. cit.*, p. 315, n. 4.

[4]) See Koschaker's discussion in *Rechtsvergleichende Studien zur Gesetzgebung Ḫammurapis* (Leipzig, 1917), pp. 46-54. Cf. also LH 19:1-2; 253:80-81. A similar phrase, *ina qāti kašādu*, is found in a tablet (*VAB* VI 245:7 ff.) pertaining to stolen produce.

[5]) Cf. also Lev. 20:9 and Dt. 27:16. For an actual case of such "disrespect" and insubordination to parental authority, cf. Dt. 21:18 ff., and its cuneiform analogue in *AASOR* 10 (1930), Nr.4. In the Septuagint vss. 16 and 17 are reversed, thus juxtaposing the two offenses against parents.

[6]) A complete study of the various shades of the verb *qll* is available in the monograph by Brichto, *The Problem of "Curse" in the Hebrew Bible* (Philadelphia, 1963). His comments to this verse are found on pp. 132-135. Cf. Ehrlich, *Randglossen*, Vol. I, p. 349; Cassuto, *Exodus*, p. 188; and already Philo, *On the Special Laws*, *The Loeb Classical Library*, Vol. 7 (Cambridge, 1950), Book II, 248, p. 461.

[7]) LH 192 deals only with the repudiation of a father by an adopted son, and capital punishment is not prescribed.

A document dealing with the case of a son who respects or disrespects his mother has been brought to light from Ugarit.[1]) This is the only extra-biblical document known to the writer in which the respective verbs "to respect" and "to disrespect" are used in conjunction with one's behavior toward a parent. The pertinent lines follow: *ù a-nu-um-ma* 2 *mārū*^meš^*-ia* *^I^Ia-at-li-nu rabû ù ^I^Ia-an-ḫa-mu ṣeḫru ma-an-nu-um-me-e i-na libbi-šu-nu ša iz-zi-iz i-na di-ni it-ti ^f^Bi-da-wa ù ša ú-qa-al-il-il ^f^Bi-da-wa umma-šu-nu* 5 *me-at šiqil kaspa ú-ma-al-li a-na šarri ù naḫlapta-šu i-šak-kán-ma a-na sikkuri ù i-pát-ṭar a-na sūqi ù ma-an-nu-um-me-e i-na libbi-šu-nu ša ú-kab-bi-i[t] ^f^Bi-da-wa [um-]ma-šu a-na šu-wa-ti ta-na-an-din.* The father states, "Now of my two sons, Iatlinu is the elder and Ianḫamu is the younger. Whichever of them enters into legal proceedings with B. and shows disrespect towards B., his mother, shall pay 500 shekels of silver to the king, place his garment on the (door) bolt [i.e., a sign of total severance],[2]) and depart outside; but whichever of them shows respect to B., his mother, to him shall she deed it [i.e., the inheritance]."

18-19. "When men quarrel and one strikes the other [יריבֻן · · · והכה] with stone or fist, and he does not die but has to take to his bed [ונפל למשכב]—if he gets up and walks [והתהלך] outdoors upon his staff, the assailant shall go unpunished [ונקה], except that he must pay for his idleness [שבתו יתן] and his cure [ורפא ירפא]."

This section introduces the laws pertaining to bodily assaults. The first case deals with a man who, while engaged in an argument,[3]) strikes his opponent in a sudden heat of passion with a stone or with his fist. If the injured party recovers sufficiently to be able to walk around outdoors with the aid of his staff, the assailant must merely make indemnification for any loss of income and for all medical expenses. This injury, however, is not subject to the laws of talion (cf. Ex. 21:23 ff.). As will be seen below, talionic punishment applies

---

[1]) F. Thureau-Dangin, "Trois contrats de Ras Shamra," *Syria* 18 (1937), pp. 245-255.

[2]) This symbolic act is most likely related to one recorded in Nuzi documents pertaining to the expulsion of a faithless wife, where the woman is first stripped of her clothing and then driven out of the house. See C. Kuhl, "Neue Dokumente zum Verständnis von Hos. 2:4-15," *ZAW* 52 (1934), pp. 102-109, and C. Gordon, "Hos. 2:4-5 in the Light of New Semitic Inscriptions," *ZAW* 54 (1936), pp. 277-280. Additional examples of this custom are found in the latest volume of Nuzi texts, *HSS* XIX 1:14, 10:38-39, *et al.* Cf. Yaron, *JJP* 15 (1965), pp. 179 ff.

[3]) Heb. ריב refers to a verbal altercation and not to a physical attack; cf. Gen. 26:20-22; Neh. 13:11, 17; and all other cases cited in biblical dictionaries.

only to injuries resulting from an originally premeditated intentional assault. Since the injury here was due to an act which in and of itself was not unlawful—the two men were involved in a quarrel and not in a fight—and since there was no original intent on causing bodily harm,[1]) the law of talion does not apply, and the punishment is thereby much less stringent. The original intention of the guilty party is here, as well as elsewhere, of decisive importance in determining the punishment.

LH 206 pertains to a somewhat similar offense, one who is injured by a blow received from a second party in an affray (but not in a quarrel). If the man swears, "I did not strike him deliberately" (Akk. *i-na i-du-ú la am-ḫa-ṣú*), i.e., with malice aforethought, he merely has to pay the cost of the physician. It should be noted that this offense immediately follows those offenses covered by the laws of talion, LH 196-205, and yet is not subject to that punishment. Here, too, the reason must be that since the injury was unintentional,[2]) as the oath clearly indicates, a monetary rather than a talionic punishment is prescribed.

HL 10, though making no mention of the intention of the act, is similar to LH 206 in that the assailant must pay the doctor's fee. It adds, moreover, several details of its own: "If anyone batters a man so that he falls ill, he shall take care of him. He shall give a man in his stead who can look after his house until he recovers. When he recovers, he shall give him six shekels [latter version: ten shekels] of silver, and he shall also pay the physician's fee." The law in Exodus is comparable to HL in the following points:

(1) HL, "he falls ill"—Heb. ונפל למשכב "he takes to bed."
(2) The recovery of the injured party is stated: HL, "when he recovers"—Heb. אם יקום והתהלך בחוץ על משענתו "if he then gets up and walks outdoors upon his staff." [2])
(3) Payment is made in both laws upon recovery. Exodus then adds that the guilty party is thereby absolved: When the injured party can walk about outdoors, "the assailant shall go unpunished,[3])

[1]) Cf. the remarks of Philo, *On the Special Laws*, III, 104-107, pp. 540-543; and Alt, "Die Ursprünge," *Kleine Schriften*, Vol. 1, p. 287.

[2]) Cf. the comment of Driver and Miles, *Babylonian Laws*, Vol. I, p. 412.

[3]) Note the iterative force of Heb. התהלך "walks around". Cf. Speiser, "The Durative *Hithpa'el*: A *tan*-Form," *JAOS* 75 (1955), pp. 118-121.

[4]) Heb. ונקה (נקי) is the interdialectal semantic, functional, and juridical equivalent of Akk. *zakû*; cf. *CAD*, Vol. 21, pp. 23 ff.

except that he must pay...." (This is also implied in HL.)

(4) Both laws stipulate that upon recovery two payments are made. In HL they consist of a pecuniary settlement and the doctor's fee; in Exodus, רק שבתו יתן ורפא ירפא "he must pay for his idleness and his cure."

(5) One of the two payments is exactly the same, i.e., the medical/doctor's fee. (This condition is also found in the corresponding section of LH.) [1]

(6) Neither in HL nor in Exodus is an oath taken.

20-21. "When a man strikes his slave, male or female,[2] with a rod,[3] and he dies there and then,[4] he must be avenged. But if he survives a day or two, he is not to be avenged, since he is the other's property."

This law is without precedent in all other ancient Near Eastern collections, where the case of a slave being killed by his master is never mentioned. The biblical law introduces a new evaluation of the intrinsic worth of a slave, i.e., he is considered a human being in his own right. There is a concern here for the interest and protection of the slave as a person; hence, he is not treated merely as chattel of value solely to his master.[5]

Though the master is permitted to beat his slave in order to dis-

---

[1]) Heb. רפא ירפא is a denominative verb meaning to provide and pay for all necessary medical work. It is the semantic counterpart of LH a.zu (= *asâm*) *i-ip-pa-al*, and HL [LÚ]a.zu-*ia ku-uš-ša-an a-pa-a-aš-pát* [(*pa-a-i*)]. Since so many similarities exist between HL and Exodus in this section, it is possible that the payment of שבתו in the biblical law may be a partial analogue to one of the two remaining stipulations found in HL. In that case it would most likely refer to the general monetary settlement mentioned in the last clause of HL (and not to the provision of a replacement to look after the house, as suggested by F. C. Fensham, "Ex. XXI:18-19 in the Light of Hittite Law 10," *VT* 10 [1960], pp. 333-335). The fine in HL is probably a token compensation for the injuries suffered and for one's enforced idleness. For a discussion of Heb. שבת, see S. Talmon, "The New Letter from the Seventh Century B.C. in Historical Perspective," *BASOR* 176 (1964), p. 32.

[2]) The two are similarly equated in vss. 26, 27, 32.

[3]) The rod (Heb. שבט) is the usual instrument of discipline; cf. ibn Ezra and Nahmanides, *ad loc.* Cf. also Prov. 10:13; 13:24.

[4]) Heb. תחת ידו is taken as the antithesis of יום או יומים "a day or two" in the next verse. See Ehrlich, *Miqrah KiFshuto* (Heb.), Vol. 1 (Berlin, 1898), *ad loc.*; and Nahmanides, *ad loc.*

[5]) Cf. Driver and Miles, *Babylonian Laws*, Vol. I, p. 408; David, "Codex Hammurabi," *OTS* 7 (1950), p. 162; Cruveilhier, *Introduction*, p. 80; Ring, *Israels Rechtsleben*, p. 64. For another law legislated in the interest of the slave, see vss. 26-27.

cipline him,[1] should he die immediately from his master's blows his life is to be avenged,[2] for the blows then are assumed to have been struck with homicidal rather than with disciplinary intention.[3] In such a case, the law of homicide (vs. 12) applies equally to a slave, and the master is put to death.

The slave, however, is not yet considered to be the peer of a freeman. While freemen may not strike one another with impunity—whether the blow be struck intentionally or unintentionally—the master still maintains the prerogative to beat his slave for disciplinary purposes. Consequently, if the slave survives the beating for "a day or two," it is assumed that the intention of his owner was disciplinary and not homicidal;[4] hence "he is not to be avenged, since he is the other's property."[5] Once again the punishment (or, in this case, lack of punishment) meted out in a case of homicide is determined by the original intent of the party involved.

22-23. "When men fight [ינצו], and one of them pushes a pregnant woman and a miscarriage results, but no (other) misfortune [אסון] ensues, he [i.e., the one responsible] shall be fined as the woman's husband may exact from him, the payment to be based on reckoning [ונתן בפללים]. But if (other) misfortune [אסון] ensues, you shall give life for life."

---

1) See above, p. 69, n. 3.

2) Greenberg, "Crimes and Punishments," *IDB*, Vol. I, p. 738, suggests that if a foreign slave is intended, the law then demands that he "be avenged" by Israelite justice. Otherwise the phrase may be merely a license to the next of kin to avenge his death.

3) See the remarks of S. D. Luzatto, *Commentary to the Pentateuch*, Heb. (Tel-Aviv, 1965), p. 344; Driver, *Exodus*, p. 218; and Noth, *Exodus*, p. 181. Cf. also Philo, *On the Special Laws*, III, 140-141, pp. 562-565.

4) According to D. Daube, "Direct and Indirect Causation in Biblical Law," *VT* 11 (1961), p.248, "The law cannot exact retribution where the evidence leaves a degree of doubt; . . . unless the law intended to make beating illegal, the master's liability must be confined to the most flagrant clearest murder." Ehrlich, *Randglossen*, Vol. I, p. 350, and Cassuto, *Exodus*, p. 190, also suggest that the difference lies in the indirect nature of the slave's death.

In practice, however, slaves were not always unprotected by law. Cf. *HSS* IX 10 which deals with an actual case at Nuzi where a slave beaten with a rod (Akk. *i-na* [iṣ]*ḫaṭṭi ma-ḫi-iṣ* = Heb. יכה · · · בשבט, Ex. 21:20) applies to the judges for an official inspection of his wounds.

5) According to Luzatto, *op. cit.*, p. 345, the phrase "since he is the other's property" is the motivation for the master's right to discipline his slave (Cf. also the remarks of ibn Ezra and Nahmanides, *ad loc.*) Others assume that this phrase implies that the master has been sufficiently penalized by the loss of his own possession, and thus he is not subject to any further punishment; cf. Noth, *loc. cit.*

Laws dealing with the case of a miscarriage are found in most Mesopotamian legal collections:[1]

(1) SL 1-2[2]
(2) UM 55-21-71, iii, 2′-13′[3]
(3) LH 209-214
(4) MAL A 21, 50-52
(5) HL 17-18

All of these laws, including that of Exodus, regulate a pecuniary settlement for the loss of the fetus.[4] Though composition for homicide is a regular feature of cuneiform corpora,[5] the acceptance of a sum of money for the loss of a fetus in Exodus shows that according to biblical law, at least, a fetus is not considered to be a human being.[6] Hence, this case does not fall within the law of homicide[7]—else a monetary settlement would be prohibited.[8]

Though the exact amount of payment[9] for the fetus is not specifically stipulated in Exodus as it is in all the cuneiform laws, a recent study of the root *pll* has shown that the basic meaning of this stem is "to estimate, assess, calculate,"[10] and it has been suggested that the Heb.

---

[1]) The fact that so many of the legal corpora specifically refer to such a case, which apparently was not too common, may be due to the literary dependence of one corpus upon another.

[2]) Only in this collection is there a distinction made between an unintentional involuntary push (Sum. zag.ús) and an intentional blow (Sum. sìg). The penalty for the latter (20 shekels of silver) is twice as much as the former.

[3]) Provisionally taken as part of LI by Civil, "New Sumerian Law Fragments," *Studies in Honor of Benno Landsberger on His Seventy-Fifth Birthday, April 21, 1965*," (Chicago, 1965), pp. 4-6.

[4]) Whereas a monetary settlement for the loss of a fetus is the standard penalty in all the laws, MAL adds a talionic punishment in MAL A 50a: "[If a man] struck a(nother) man's [wife] and caused her to have [a miscarriage], they shall treat [the wife of the man] who caused the (other) man's wife [to have a miscarriage] as he treated her." Cf. also MAL A 52.

[5]) Cf. HL 1-5 and the following annotations to the laws of talion.

[6]) Talmudic law also considers the fetus to be non-viable; cf. *Mishnah Ohiloth* 7:6 and *T. B. Sanhedrin* 72b (and the comments of Rashi).

[7]) *Mechilta, ad loc.*, p. 63: "One is not guilty of death unless he kills a viable child."

[8]) For in biblical law, life and property are incommensurable; cf. above p. 39.

[9]) The interdialectal semantic analogue to the Hebrew expression for exacting a monetary penalty (ענש יענש כאשר) ישית עליו (בעל האשה) is found in a document from Ugarit, *PRU* IV 17:128, lines 9-10: (*ù šarru mu-ul-la-a*) *a-na muḫ-ḫi* (*PN* 3-*šu*) *il-ta-kán*—Heb. ישית עליו = Akk. *ana muḫḫi iltakan.*

[10]) Speiser, "The Stem *PLL* in Hebrew," *JBL* 82 (1963), p. 301-306, esp. 303.

ונתן בפללים be translated, "the payment to be based on reckoning," with the "reckoning" possibly being based on the estimated age of the embryo.[1] This then would be comparable to the first version of HL 17: "If anyone causes a free woman to miscarry—if (it is) the tenth month, he shall give ten shekels of silver; if (it is) the fifth month, he shall give five shekels of silver and pledge his estate as security." [2] Cf. HL 18.

Should the pregnant woman die,[3] the law of talion, "a life for a life," is put into effect. [4] Biblical law, however, neither sanctions vicarious talionic punishment, e.g., LH 210: "If that woman [a member of the *awēlum* class] has died, they shall put his daughter to death," nor accepts a monetary settlement for the loss of life, e.g., LH 212 and 214 for members of the *muškēnum* and *wardum* classes. MAL A 50, moreover, while prescribing capital punishment for the assailant in the event that the woman dies,[5] levies an additional monetary fine for the loss of the fetus: *ù šumma sinništu ši-it mi-ta-at awēlam i-du-uk-ku ki-mu-ú ša-a libbi-ša nap-ša-a-te ú-ma-al-la* "But if that woman dies, they shall put the man to death; he shall be fined for the (loss of the) fetus" (lit., "in place of her fetus, he shall pay a fine for [the loss of] life").[6] In the Bible, on the other hand, there is no additional penalty

1) The Septuagint translation of these verses makes a distinction between a fetus that is not yet fully formed (Gr. ἐξεικονισμένον) and one that is. If the latter is aborted, the guilty party is put to death. Philo, *On the Special Laws*, III, 108-9, p. 545, follows the Greek interpretation of this section. For further comments, see Speiser, *loc. cit.*, and Driver and Miles, *Babylonian Laws*, Vol. I, p. 416. Cf. however, J. J. Rabinowitz, "The Susa Tablets, the Bible and the Aramaic Papyri," *VT* 11 (1961), p. 68.

2) The same fines of ten and five shekels of silver are also levied in LH 209 for the fetus of a daughter of an *awēlum* and in LH 211 for the fetus of a daughter of a *muškēnum*.

3) For Heb. **אסון**, cf. Gen. 42:38, and the statement in the *Mechilta, ad loc.*, p. 66: "**אסון** here means only death."

4) It is a moot question as to whether talion was ever applied in practice as a judicial penalty. See Greenberg, "Crimes and Punishments," *IDB*, Vol. I, p. 742, and *T. B. Baba Qamma* 83b-84a.

5) This is similar to UM 55-21-71, iii, 7′-8′ (Civil, "New Sumerian Law Fragments," *Studies in Honor of Benno Landsberger*, p. 5): "If she [daughter of a free man] died, that man shall be [put to death]"—Sum. tukun. b[i b]a. úš nita. bi ì. [gaz]. e.

6) The last clause, Akk. *napšāte umalla*, has been mistranslated by Driver and Miles, *Assyrian Laws*, "he pays (on the principle of) a life (for a life)." It may mean "he shall compensate with a life" (Meek, *ANET*), i.e., he has to replace the dead embryo with a living person (cf. *PRU* IV 17.251, p. 237, lines 14-15: 10 *napšāte*^meš *ú-ma-al-lu-nim* "they shall compensate with 10 lives")—a highly unlikely procedure in such a case since the penalty for homicide in MAL A 10 and MAL B 2 is either

for the loss of the fetus if the woman also dies.[1]) Hence, the strict application of talion in the biblical corpus is to be understood in the light of other prescriptions current in Mesopotamian corpora: vicarious punishment,[2]) composition,[3]) and multiple punishment.[4])

23-25. "But if (other) misfortune ensues, you shall give life for life, eye for eye, tooth for tooth, burn for burn, wound for wound, bruise for bruise." [5])

---

capital punishment or composition. The translation proposed above in the text is based on the technical meaning of *mullû* well known from both Nuzi and Ugaritic Akkadian "to pay a fine" (for the loss of life). This exact idiom appears in another document from Ugarit, *PRU* IV 17.230, p. 153, l. 14: *napišta* 3-*šu ú-ma-al-lu-ú* "they shall pay threefold for this life," i.e., the life of the murdered man (cf. l. 9: *amīla* 3-*šu ú-ma-al-la*). This rendering is further substantiated by the juxtaposition in MAL A 50 of *napšāte umalla* in l. 73 with *idukku* "they shall put (him) to death" in l. 71—for the translation, see above in text—and similarly lines 75-79 with lines 80-81: "If that woman's husband has no son, if someone struck her so that she had a miscarriage, they shall put the striker to death (*idukku*); if her fetus is a girl, he shall pay a fine for (the loss of) life" (*napšātēma umalla*). Cf. also MAL A 50:69 and 52:91. Cassuto, *Exodus*, pp. 192-193 (without explaining the Akkadian idiom) also notes in passing that the murderer must pay for the value of the lost fetus.

Heb. מלא ל also has the meaning "to pay in full" in I Sam. 18:27, and in the letter published by J. Naveh, "A Hebrew Letter from the Seventh Century B.C.," *IEJ* 10 [1960] p. 134, l. 12: *wmlʾ lśr*.

[1]) Cf. the *Mechilta*'s comment *ad loc.* (p. 63, 66): "One who incurs the penalty of death is exempt from making monetary compensation."

[2]) Note also the application of vicarious talion in LH 116, 210, 230. For a similar repudiation of vicarious punishment, see comments to vs. 31, p. 83.

[3]) See above pp. 61-62, and cf. *Mechilta*, p. 67: "It is with life that he must pay for life. He cannot pay for life with money."

[4]) Cf. also MAL A 21: "If a man struck a(nother) man's daughter and has caused her to have a miscarriage, when they prosecute him, he shall pay two talents thirty minas of lead; they shall flog him fifty (times) with staves (and) he shall do the work of the king for one full month." Cf. the general remarks of Loewenstamm, "Biblical Law," (Heb.), *Encyclopaedia Biblica*, Vol. 5 (Jerusalem, 1968), p. 632.

[5]) Many modern commentators unnecessarily transpose these verses to follow vss. 18-19, e.g., Ehrlich, *Randglossen*, Vol. I, pp. 349-350, and Cazelles, *Études*, p. 56. Noth, *Exodus*, p. 182, in turn, does not realize the positional importance of this section. The entire sequence which now follows immediately upon the punishment of "a life for a life" is related to the case of a pregnant woman's miscarriage only in so far as these are most likely the penalties meted out for any bodily injury caused by original intent to do harm. The grouping became fossilized but was originally formulated in contrast to monetary composition for unintentional injuries (e.g., vs. 19).

It is of interest to note that in HL the laws of composition (HL does not contain the laws of talion) immediately precede the case of a miscarriage (HL 7-16 followed by 17). Thus in both Exodus and HL there is an associative juxtaposition of the two sets of laws. See the annotations to Ex. 22:4-5 for a similar legal juxtaposition,

In the section above, vss. 18-19, a monetary rather than a talionic punishment was prescribed for bodily injuries incurred as a result of an unpremediated assault climaxing a verbal dispute [1])—an act which in and of itself is not unlawful.[2]) Here, however, the guilty parties were engaged from the outset in a fight,[3]) i.e., an unlawful act with intent to inflict injury. Since there was an original intent to cause harm, this case differs from both the law of accidental homicide (vs. 12) and the law of bodily assaults (vss. 18-19); the punishment is much more stringent; and the assailant is held directly responsible for all ensuing consequences, including those which might befall an innocent bystander.

Talion, then, appears to be the penalty prescribed for all injuries caused by malice aforethought and with intent to inflict harm.[4]) This is further substantiated by its application in Dt. 19:19-21: "You shall do to him [the false witness] as he *schemed* to do to his fellow.... Nor must you show pity: life for life, eye for eye, tooth for tooth, hand for hand, foot for foot." [5]) An additional support for this interpretation may be found in LH 206, where in a case of unintentional injury (Akk. *i-na i-du-ú la am-ḫa-ṣú*) talion is not prescribed, while in the preceding laws for personal injury, LH 196-197, 200, the unqualified statements of talionic punishment imply that the injuries there were most likely inflicted with intent to harm.[6])

The laws of miscarriage in LH, LH 209-214, are also in close proximity to the laws of talion, LH 196-205, with only the cases of accidental bodily assaults intervening, LH 206-208.

[1]) Heb. יריבן (ריב "quarrel, disputation") always refers to a verbal act.

[2]) Cf. Philo, *On the Special Laws*, Book III, 104-107, pp. 541-543.

[3]) Heb. ינצו (root נצה) refers to an act of fighting. Cf. Ex. 2:13, 25:11; Lev. 24:10; II Sam. 14:6. In Is. 58:4 the two words ריב ומצה form an hendiadys.

Note that legal vocabulary is very exact and the use of these two different verbs may very well imply different shades of meaning.

[4]) This was already noted by both the *Mechilta*, pp. 62-63, 68-69, and Philo, *On the Special Laws*, Book III, 195-197, pp. 597-599.

In Islamic law, moreover, talion is applied only in cases of intentional homicide and bodily injury. See J. Weismann, "Talion und öffentliche Strafe im Mosaischen Rechte," *Festschrift für Adolf Wach*, Vol. I (Leipzig, 1913), p. 58, and O. Spies and E. Pritsch, "Klassisches Islamisches Recht," *Handbuch der Orientalistik*, 111/1, *Orientalisches Recht* (Leiden, 1964), pp. 234-235.

That homicide is considered to be intentional even if the object of the assault was not murderous but was with intent to inflict injury, is already noted by Weismann, *op. cit.*, pp. 57 and 74.

[5]) The regulation in Deuteronomy adds an entirely new dimension to the law of talion. Talion is prescribed here for attempted or contemplated (but not real!) injury. The talionic formulation is also found in Lev. 24:19-20.

[6]) Cf. the remarks of Driver and Miles, *Babylonian Laws*, Vol I, pp. 412-413.

The principle of *lex talionis*, which is first formulated in LH, has been called primitive [1]) and barbaric.[2]) It is strange then to note that in two of the legal corpora preceding LH, LU and LE (42 ff.), monetary settlements rather than talionic penalties are prescribed.[3]) Furthermore, even though LH does introduce talionic physical punishment for offenses committed by one member of the *awēlum* class against another, it still permits pecuniary compensation for similar offenses of an *awēlum* against a *muškēnum*; (cf. LH 196-197 and 198; 200 and 201; 210 and 212). New light has recently been shed on this problem by Finkelstein:

> "In the first place the idea of physical punishment for physical injuries was an *innovation* in Hammurapi's laws, for we know that in earlier law collections pecuniary compensation was the rule for all cases and classes.... It is not the idea of physical punishment which is 'eine altertümliche rein moralische Satisfaktion barbarischer Art' (Kraus, *Edikt*, pp. 149 ff.). It is rather the all but universal primitive practice of treating physical assaults, including homicide, as private civil invasions remediable by pecuniary satisfaction, which far from perceiving any moral—and therefore criminal issue in such acts, is the truly 'barbaric' situation. In short, what the talionic rules in LH actually herald is the enlargement of the scope of criminal law beyond the spheres of god and king (i.e., blasphemy and sedition) which had long before constituted the sole realm of criminal action, to embrace for the first time—albeit in a crudely formulated fashion, ... a class of delicts that had previously been treated purely as civil torts. Far from indicating a legal handicap of the *awēlum* by contrast with the *muškēnum*, these laws, therefore, actually mark the formal elevation of physical invasions against the *awēlūtum* to the status of crimes (i.e., actions considered to be detrimental to the welfare and moral order of the society-at-large, and punishable by the public authority without necessary consideration of any deprivation or injury sustained by individuals as a consequence of such acts), while identical invasion against the *muškēnūtum*, like those against slaves, remained within the realm of private or civil damages." [4])

This distinction between intention and lack of intention also seems to play a role in the two laws pertaining to bodily injuries inflicted upon slaves, vss. 20-21 and vss. 26-27. The laws are not grouped together in the legal corpus, as one would expect, but are appendixed to the corresponding block of legislation which pertains to injuries to freemen incurred through an intentional or unintentional bodily assault. See the respective annotations to these two laws.

[1]) Cazelles, *Études*, p. 152.

[2]) F. R. Kraus, *Ein Edikt des Königs Ammi-Ṣaduqa von Babylon* (Leiden, 1958), pp. 149 ff.

[3]) HL (7 ff.), though later than LH, also prescribes monetary settlements.

[4]) J. J. Finkelstein, "Ammiṣaduqa's Edict and the Babylonian 'Law Codes',"

Thus the principle of *lex talionis*, far from being a primitive residuum,[1]) is actually an important advance in the history of jurisprudence.[2]) It not only granted the *awēlum* class added protection—for any physical offense against the *awēlūtum* would now be much more severely prosecuted and could not be composed by a mere financial settlement—but, in addition, it became an expression of equality—for talion was restricted only to members of the highest class; [3]) all others, members of an inferior social standing, had to be content with composition.[4]) Early biblical jurisprudence is also guided by the principle of talion, but rather than the state prosecuting the offense,[5]) it still (in Exodus, at least) is within the realm of the injured party or family to execute punishment.[6]) Hence, in the Bible talion comes to curb unlimited retribution, personal vendetta, and excessive retaliation.[7]) Moreover, since a class system is lacking in the early Israelite society, *lex talionis* is applied to all members of the community except slaves: all then—with this one exception—are treated as equals. Talion is equitable: the rich receive the same punishment as the poor—a punishment which is limited to the exact measure of the injury and is restricted to the culprit himself. Talion, furthermore, serves as a deterrent: the rich, who could otherwise afford to pay for the injuries inflicted, would now "pay" with the same limb as the injured one of the other party.

JCS 15 (1961), p. 98. Cf. also A. S. Diamond, "An Eye for an Eye," *Iraq* 19 (1957), pp. 154, and R. Haase, "Körperliche Strafen im altorientalischen Recht," *RIDA*, 3e serie, 10 (1963), pp. 55-61, 74-75. Haase also lists examples of what he calls "echte und uneigentliche" talion in cuneiform law (p. 73). On pp. 61-63 he assembles a complete list of penalties found in the various legal collections.

1) Biblical talion is also regarded by many as exhibiting primitive archaic features; cf. T. J. Meek, *Hebrew Origins* (New York, 1960), pp. 62, 71, 74. See, however, S. E. Loewenstamm, Review of A. Goetze, *The Laws of Eshnunna*, in *IEJ* 7 (1957), p. 194, and Yaron, *Eshnunna*, pp. 174 f.

2) The common view that talion is "a fundamental principle of early law and was only gradually replaced by a system of fixed composition" (Driver and Miles, *Babylonian Laws*, Vol. I, p. 408) is no longer tenable. See Diamond, *op. cit.*

3) Cf. Cruveilhier, *Introduction*, p. 57, and W. Seagle, *Men of Law from Hammurabi to Holmes* (New York, 1947), p. 27.

4) Talion embodies that which a monetary settlement necessarily lacks: no substitution or composition is acceptable—only equal punishment for those of equal rank. It becomes, strange to say, a mark of class distinction.

5) Note the use of a plural verb in the LH formulations.

6) Note the use of the singular נתת in the biblical formulation; Weismann, *op. cit.*, pp. 4, 25, 33.

7) Contrast the boast of Lamech in Gen. 4:23.

Several blatant differences still remain, however, between the principle as enunciated in LH and in the Bible. Though LH endorses *lex talionis* in cases of bodily injury, it, unlike the Bible, accepts composition in cases of homicide, e.g., LH 207.[1]) The biblical corpora, moreover, neither sanction vicarious talion (e.g., LH 116, 210, 230; cf. also MAL A 50, 55), nor do they penalize a peccant member on the basis of this principle (e.g., LH 192-195, 218, 226, 253).[2]) Furthermore, LH itself does not execute the penalty of talion mechanically for all physical invasions against the *awēlum* (e.g., 202 and 203—smiting of the cheek); [3]) this inconsistency is not to be found in the biblical collections of law.

Albright sums up the uniqueness of the biblical concept of talion in the following words:

> "This principle may seem and is often said to be extraordinarily primitive. But it is actually not in the least primitive. Whereas the beginnings of *lex talionis* are found before Israel, the principle was now extended by analogy until it dominated all punishment of injuries or homicides. In ordinary Ancient Oriental jurisprudence, men who belonged to the higher social categories or who were wealthy simply paid fines, otherwise escaping punishment.... So the *lex talionis* (is) ...the principle of equal justice for all!" [4])

---

[1]) Cf. Cazelles, *op. cit.*, p. 151. Note in particular Num. 35:31 which explicitly prohibits the acceptance of ransom from a murderer.

Even though biblical legislation does not prescribe the principle of talion in a case of accidental homicide, composition is never mentioned as a possible substitution. The formula of "a life for a life" is still operative—though somewhat indirectly—since the death of the high priest atones for the homicide. For this interpretation, see Greenberg, "The Biblical Conception of Asylum," *JBL* 78 (1959), pp. 125-132.

[2]) The only exception is Dt. 25:11-12. In a non-legal context, cf. Prov. 30:17.

[3]) For the insult of smiting another's cheek, cf. Driver and Miles, *op. cit.*, p. 412, n. 5, and R. Yaron, *The Laws of Eshnunna* (Jerusalem, 1969), pp. 190-191.

[4]) W. F. Albright, *History, Archaeology, and Christian Humanism* (New York, 1964), p. 74. Similar statements are found on pp. 98-99. For the distinction between talion as embodying the principle of retribution, and composition the principle of reparation, cf. Noth, *Exodus*, p. 182; Pedersen, *Israel*, Vol. I-II, pp. 329 A; and Weismann, *op. cit.*, p. 40.

Alt, "Zur Talionsformel," *ZAW* 11 (1934), pp. 303-305=*Kleine Schriften*, Vol. I, pp. 341-344, and Noth, *loc. cit.*, both seek the origin of the laws of talion in the cult—a view which in the light of the above discussion, and in particular the innovation of LH, is no longer tenable. For a suggested Amorite background, see Loewenstamm, *op. cit.*, p. 194 (citing B. Mazar), and W. G. Lambert, "A New Look at the Babylonian Background of Genesis," *JTS* 16 (1965), p. 289.

The penalty of talion is also found in the *Twelve Tables*, VIII: 2.

26-27. "When a man strikes the eye of his slave, male or female,[1]) and destroys it, he shall let him go free [2]) on account of his eye. If he knocks out the tooth of his slave, male or female, he shall let him go free on account of his tooth."

Since a slave is not considered the peer of a freeman, the laws of talion do not apply when he suffers an injury at the hand of his master. However, in an unparalleled example of concern for the interest of a slave, the law here provides for his release if the master should destroy his eye or knock out his tooth. The master himself must manumit the slave. The slave who formerly was not the equal of his master is now emancipated and achieves the status of a freedman.

It is of interest to note that the various bodily assaults upon the person of a slave are not listed together. This law—which does not mention an instrument of discipline as does vs. 20, where the beating of a slave is legally permitted for disciplinary reasons, and where the owner in such a case is acquitted (if the slave does not die immediately)—most likely follows the section of talion in order to indicate that these blows were delivered maliciously and willfully [3]) with intent to cause bodily harm and thus were not part of any lawful disciplinary chastisement. The owner then is held accountable and is punished by the release of his slave. The law once again takes into account the intention of the offender: a master may correct his slave, but he may not treat him as mere chattel to be maimed at his own caprice. The slave is a person in his own right and must be treated with proper restraint.

Cuneiform corpora, on the other hand, never mention bodily damages caused by the master to his own slave.[4]) Since an economic consideration (i.e., monetary compensation) is the overriding factor in these laws, the release of the slave is never contemplated. The owner would merely have to bear the loss that his blow caused the slave.

28-32. This section pertaining to the laws of the goring ox has its counterpart in both LE 54-55 and LH 250-252. Since several unique aspects of the law in Exodus, i.e., the stoning of the ox, the taboo sta-

---

[1]) Note the equation of the male and female slave. Cf. vss. 20, 27, 32.

[2]) For Heb. לחפשי, see above, p. 47, and n. 2 on that page.

[3]) Cf. Philo, *On the Special Laws*, III, 195-197, pp. 597-599 (for an eye); 201, p. 601 (for a tooth); and *Mechilta, ad loc.*, pp. 72-73.

[4]) Cases of injuries inflicted upon another's slave, however, are mentioned, e.g., LH 199, and HL 8, 12, 14, 16, and pecuniary settlements are made. HL 8, similar to Exodus, lists the blinding of a slave and the knocking out of his teeth. See Goetze, *The Laws of Eshnunna*, pp. 121-122, for a list of the injured parts of the body mentioned in the collections of LE, LH, HL, and Exodus.

tus of its flesh, and the execution of its owner, are not found in the corresponding cuneiform corpora, these laws have been called "much more primitive than the Babylonian." [1]) The key to the correct understanding and interpretation of these provisions, however, is not relative progress but rather relative emphasis. A completely different *Weltanschauung* motivates the biblical version, where an inherent religious evaluation—totally missing in the Mesopotamian parallels—predominates throughout the law.

28. "When an ox gores a man or a woman [2]) to death, the ox shall be stoned and its flesh shall not be eaten, but the owner of the ox is not to be punished." [1])

A parallel to this specific case is found only in LH 250,[4]) but in contrast to the biblical law, no punishment is prescribed for the ox: "If an ox, when it was walking along the street, gores a man to death, that case is not subject to claim," since the owner was not responsible. In Exodus, however, legal consequences follow, for the ox is stoned, and its flesh must not be eaten. The stoning of the ox [5]) and its taboo status are related, in turn, to the religious presupposition of blood-guilt: [6]) "For your lifeblood, too, I will require a reckoning: of every beast will I require it.... For in the image of God was man created" (Gen. 9:5-6). A beast that kills a human being destroys the image of God and thus is held accountable for being objectively guilty of a criminal action, even when the owner is not legally accountable or responsible.[7])

---

[1]) Driver and Miles, *Babylonian Laws*, Vol. I, p. 444. For a recent study of these laws, see Yaron, "The Goring Ox in Near Eastern Laws," *ILR* 1 (1966), pp. 396-406, and *The Laws of Eshnunna*, pp. 192-200.

[2]) Cf. Ex. 21:15, 17, 28, 29, 31, and p. 78, n. 1.

[3]) For Heb. נקי, see p. 68, n. 4.

[4]) In both laws the ox is not a gorer (contrast vs. 29 and LH 251), and the owner remains unpunished.

[5]) For the stoning of the ox, which represents communal participation in the extirpation of the homicidal beast, cf. Noth, *Exodus*, p. 182. Since execution by stoning is often found as the punishment for the violation of the religious order or for the offense of insurrection and sedition but is never prescribed for cases of homicide, J. J. Finkelstein, in an unpublished study on the laws of the goring ox, has suggested that the penalty of stoning here is for an "insurrection against the divinely ordained hierarchy of terrestrial authority." The ox's goring a human being to death is an "insurrection against the established order" since "man was ordained to rule over earthly life." It is thus equated with other insurrections against the religious order such as the cursing of YHWH, the rebellion against one's parents, idolatry, etc.

[6]) Cf. above, p. 61.

[7]) Greenberg, "Postulates," *Kaufmann Vol.*, p. 15: "A beast that kills a man

29-30. "If, however, that ox has long been a gorer [נגח], and its owner, though warned [הועד בבעליו], has failed to guard it [לא ישמרנו] and it kills a man or woman [1]) [והמית איש או אשה]—the ox shall be stoned and its owner, too, shall be put to death. If ransom is laid upon him, he must pay whatever is laid upon him to redeem his life."

The case of an owner who was warned that his ox was known to gore but did not take the necessary precautions to safeguard his ox, which subsequently gores a man to death, is the subject of LH 251 and LE 54. Both the biblical and cuneiform laws have several points in common: [2]) (1) a habitual gorer, (2) an official warning, (3) a lack of precaution in spite of the warning, (4) the fatal accident, (5) the punishment:

(1) The habitual gorer, is called *nakkāpum* in LH [3]) and נגח in Exodus. (Cf. the use of the verb נגף in vs. 35.)

(2) *ba-ab-tum a-na be-lí-šu u-še-di-ma* (LE)
ba-ab-ta-šu ú-še-di-šum-ma (LH) [4])
הועד בבעליו (Exodus) [5])

(3) *alap-šu la ú-*<*še*>*-ši-ir-ma* (LE)
qar-ni-šu la ú-šar-[r]i-im alap-šu la ú-sa-an-ni-iq-ma (LH)
לא ישמרנו (Exodus) [6])

---

destroys the image of God and must give a reckoning for it . . . . The religious evaluation inherent in this law is further evidenced by the prohibition of eating the flesh of the stoned ox. The beast is laden with guilt and is therefore an object of horror. . . ." He further points out in his article, "The Biblical Conception of Asylum," *JBL* 78 (1959), p. 128, that this is "the most striking legal expression of the objectivity of blood guilt—i.e., its occurrence even without criminal intent . . . . Here, where there can be no intent since the killer is a brute, the law nonetheless regards the animal as blood guilty and requires that it be stoned." See also *IDB*, Vol. I, p. 739. Cf. Driver, *Exodus*, pp. 220-221; Cassuto, *Exodus*, pp. 194-195; and Loewenstamm, *IEJ* 7 (1957), p. 196.

1) See above, p. 79, n. 2.

2) Cf. Goetze, *op. cit.*, p. 136.

3) For LE, Goetze, *loc. cit.*, posits a voiced labial and transcribes *nakkābum*.

4) There is no parallel to the Akk. *bābtum* "city ward/authorities" in the law of Exodus. This institution apparently did not yet exist at the time of the formulation of the biblical version of the law.

5) Goetze, *loc. cit.*, n. 9, on the basis of the cuneiform analogues suggests "that the original text [of Exodus] may have been not *hū'ad* . . . but *hōda'*" (= Akk. *ušēdi*); cf. Heb. נודע in vs. 36. However, if the biblical law is considered a strongly influenced adaptation of its cuneiform antecedents rather than a direct translation, Heb. הועד would be the perfect semantic, if not etymological, parallel to Akk. *ušēdi*.

6) An interesting suggestion is offered by Goetze, *op. cit.*, p. 137, n. 11, whereby

(4) *awīlam ik-ki-im-ma uš-ta-mi-it* (LE)
mār a-wi-lim i[k-k]i-ip-ma u[š-ta]-mi-it (LH)
המית איש או אשה (Exodus) [1]

Though there are many stylistic and linguistic similarities between the cuneiform and biblical laws, which would indicate that a common legal tradition found its way into three separate legal collections, they still differ in regard to motivation and legal consequences. The sole concern of the two cuneiform laws is an economic one, and thus they compensate the victim's family for its loss. These laws, moreover, deal "only with the liability of the owner of the ox. The ox is of no concern to the law since no liabilities attach to it." [2]) In Exodus, however, a religious presupposition predominates: bloodguilt rests upon the ox, and hence it is summarily executed.[3]) The biblical legislation, furthermore, repudiates the commutability of paying an indemnification to the family of the slain man [4]) by stating that the owner of the goring ox should also be put to death. However, since this is a case of criminal negligence in which the owner did not commit the crime

---

Heb. ישמרנו through metathesis would be made to agree with Akk. *ušarrim* of LH. However, the Hebrew verb employed here, שמר, is none other than the analogic equivalent to the Akk. *sunnuqu* found in LH. The Akk. verb does not mean "to tie up" (Meek, *ANET*, p. 176, and Driver and Miles, *Babylonian Laws*, Vol. II, pp. 89, 264), but rather "to take proper precautions, watch over." This meaning is amply demonstrated by its many occurrences in Mari. Its correct translation in LH would be, "he has not watched over him," "he has not made him (the ox) safe/secure." For comments on the verb *sanāqum/sunnuqum* "Überwachung," see W. von Soden, *ZA* 49 (1950), p. 182, who rightly objects to the previously cited translation of LH. (Cf. also R. Borger, *Babylonisch-Assyrische Lesestücke*, Vol. 1 [Rome, 1963], p. LXXVII.) M. Held, "A Faithful Lover in an Old Babylonian Dialogue," *JCS* 15 (1961), p. 17, following von Soden, cites further corroborative evidence and compares, in turn, the verse in Exodus here under discussion. Finkelstein, "Sex Offenses in Sumerian Laws," *JAOS* 86 (1966), p. 364, n. 30, reads *ú-‹še›-ši-ir* "(if he did not) keep (his ox) in line" for the difficult *pašir* of LE 54. Cf. von Soden, *BiOr* 13 (1956), p. 34. This then would be the equivalent of LH *usanniq*. Compare furthermore the use of Akk. *naṣāru* (which corresponds to the Heb. שמר) in LE 56, a law which pertains to the guarding of a wild dog and which immediately follows the section on the goring ox.

[1]) For point n. 5, the punishment, see the discussion in the text.

[2]) Greenberg, "Postulates," *Kaufmann Vol.*, p. 16. Cf. A. van Selms, "The Goring Ox in Babylonian and Biblical Law," *ArOr* 18[4] (1950) = *Symbolae Hrozný*, p. 327: "The fundamental idea which underlies the whole system is that of protection of property. . . . The main object is not to prevent crime, or to punish criminals, but to provide compensation for the loss the other party has suffered."

[3]) See the comments to vs. 28 on pp. 78-79.

[4]) For the practice of composition for homicide, see comments to vs. 12, pp. 61-62.

himself, he is permitted to redeem his life, if the slain person's family so permits, by paying a ransom.[1]) But the sum of money that is set,[2]) be it noted, is neither a composition nor an indemnification to the victim's family, but rather a ransom for his own life which is otherwise forfeit.[3]) And a ransom is acceptable only in this specific case of culpable negligence, for when a human being commits homicide, "You may not accept a ransom for the life of a murderer who is guilty of a capital crime; he must be put to death" (Num. 35:31).[4]) Composition is applicable only in a system which is motivated entirely by economic presuppositions: the family has suffered a loss, thus payment in kind must be made and is acceptable. In the Bible, however, homicide is an unpardonable offense, since it is considered to be, in addition to everything else, a flouting of the divine will; hence, no matter nor manner of composition is acceptable.

One further note concerning the relative position of these laws in their respective legal corpora.[5]) In LH the phenomenon of an ox goring a human to death is subcategorized under the same section with all other incidents involving the use of an ox in which property settlements must be made (LH 241 ff.). "Interest is not focused on the victim." In the Bible, however, this law is a direct continuation of the section concerning crimes committed by one man against his fellow man. "Man as a legal entity is a class apart. The incident is classified not according to the similarity of circumstances but according to whether the victim is a human being or not."

31. "So, too, if it gores a minor, male or female,[6]) [the owner] shall be dealt with according to the same rule." [7])

---

[1]) Since no civil authorities are mentioned here, the ransom was most likely set by the family. [2]) For Heb. יושת עליו, see p. 71, n. 9.

[3]) Cf. Merz, *Blutrache*, pp. 98-100. This is also clearly indicated by the addition of Heb. פדין נפשו "redemption for his life" which explicates Heb. כֹפר "ransom." Cf. also Ps. 49:8-9.

[4]) Contrast MAL A 10 and B 2 where capital punishment for homicide is left to the discretion of the next of kin. Cf. also the Edict of Telipinus, Gurney, *The Hittites* (Baltimore, 1962), p. 98.

[5]) The following, including the quotations, is taken from Finkelstein's unpublished paper on the goring ox. For another example of the importance of the position of a law in a legal corpus, see the comments to Ex. 21:16, p. 65.

[6]) So *Mechilta*, *ad loc.*, p. 88. A preferable translation would be "son or daughter." Cf. Ehrlich, *Randglossen*, Vol. I, p. 351, who contrasts the Heb. בן and בת of this verse with the following עבד and אמה "male and female slave." He also compares this to the use of בנות "free maidens" in Ex. 21:9. For the similar status of male and female, cf. p. 79, n. 2.

[7]) For the same Hebrew expression, see above, vs. 9, p. 55.

The biblical laws concerning the goring ox apply equally as well in a case where a son or a daughter of a freeman is gored to death. This is another example (cf. above, pp. 72-73) of the repudiation of the practice of vicarious talion (e.g., LH 116, 210, 230).[1])

32. "But if the ox gores a slave, male or female,[2]) he shall pay thirty shekels of silver to the master [כסף שלשים שקלים יתן לאדניו] and the ox shall be stoned."

The ambiguous status of the slave is here characterized by both the acceptance of composition[3]) on behalf of his death and the stoning of the ox. The latter is another reflex of the religious principle embodied in Gen. 9:5, for the slave is still considered a human being.

This law provides the only example in the legal corpus of Exodus where a specific sum of money is recorded.[4]) The inverted Hebrew word order used to express the amount of the monetary penalty, כסף שלשים שקלים יתן לאדניו, "silver, thirty shekels he shall pay to his master," is relatively rare but does appear in biblical texts [5]) and in Babylonian legal documents.[6])

33-34. "When a man opens a pit—or when he has dug a pit but

---

[1]) This fact was first noted by D. H. Müller, *Die Gesetze Ḥammurabis und ihr Verhältnis zur mosaischen Gesetzgebung sowie zu den XII Tafeln* (Wien, 1903), pp. 166 ff. Cf. also A. Jepsen, *Untersuchungen zum Bundesbuch* (Stuttgart, 1927), p. 64; Cassuto, *Exodus*, pp. 194-195; and Greenberg, "Postulates," p. 23. Cf., however, Loewenstamm, "מדה כנגד מדה," *Encyclopaedia Biblica*, Vol. 4 (Jerusalem, 1962), p. 844.

[2]) See above, p. 78, n. 1, and p. 79, n. 2.

[3]) This is in contrast to Ex. 21:20, where the master himself committed homicide and composition is not acceptable. In criminal negligence, however, the law compensates the master for his economic loss.

[4]) Cf. moreover Ex. 22:16 with Dt. 22:29. In cuneiform corpora the exact amount of the penalty is almost always stated; cf. LH 252 for the specific case.

For the comparative prices placed on slaves several centuries prior to the laws of Exodus, see Mendelsohn, "On Slavery in Alalakh," *IEJ* 5 (1955), pp. 65-72, where a slave at Nuzi is also valued at thirty shekels. Though this sum equals ½ maneh—the price paid in LH 252 for the goring to death of a freeman's son—no exact correspondence can be drawn because of the fluctuation of the weights in different geographical areas and in different centuries. Cf. also the remarks of Cazelles, *Études*, p. 59.

[5]) Cf. II Sam. 24:24; Neh. 5:15.

[6]) For an example coming from a neo-Babylonian document, see H. Petschow, *Neobabylonisches Pfandrecht* (Berlin, 1956), p. 159, lines 11-13: *kaspa-a*$_4$ 2 *manû* 1/3 (!) *šiqlu in-ni-ṭer-ru*; *kaspa-a*$_4$ 2 *manû* 1/3 (!) *šiqlu* [*ina*] *qaqqadi-šu ana* ^{Id}*Nabû* (!)-*šum-ukîn i-nam-din*-ʾ "The silver, 2 minas 1/3 shekel shall be paid back; he shall pay the silver, 2 minas 1/3 shekel, to N. in full."

has not covered it—and an ox or an ass falls into it, the one responsible for the pit must make restitution; he shall pay the price to the owner [ישלם כסף ישיב לבעליו], but shall keep the dead animal."

Damage caused to another's property through culpable negligence must be compensated in full. Although this specific case is not found in the cuneiform corpora, it may be conjectured that the clause, "but [the guilty party] shall keep the dead animal," has been added to offset an existing custom whereby the injured party received both the dead animal and compensation. The law in Exodus would then come to legislate on behalf of both the injured party who receives full compensation, and the guilty party who still receives the dead ox.

An interesting semantic parallel to vs. 34—(בעל הבור) ישלם, כסף ישיב לבעליו "(The one responsible for the pit) must make restitution; he shall restore [i.e., pay] the price to the owner"—is found in LH 125:79 ff.: *ú-ša-lam-ma a-na be-el makkūrim i-ri-a-ab* "He shall make restitution, and he will restore in full to the owner of the property." In both cases the verb *šlm* (Heb. פיעל, corresponding to the Akk. D-stem) is used absolutely without a direct object and is followed by an explicative clause employing the verb "to restore/replace" (Heb. ישיב: Akk. *iriab*).

35-36. "When a man's ox injures [1]) his neighbor's ox and it dies, they shall sell the live ox [2]) and divide its price; they shall also divide the dead animal. If, however, the ox has long been known as a gorer, and its owner has failed to guard it, he must restore ox for ox, but shall keep the dead animal."

LE 53 is an exact parallel to vs. 35: *šum-ma alpum alpam ik-ki-im-ma uš-ta-mi-it ši-im alpim ba-al-ṭì ù šīr* [3]) *alpim mi-tim be-el alpim ki-la-la-an i-zu-uz-zu* "If an ox gores another ox to death, both owners shall divide the price of the live ox and the flesh of the dead ox." When there is no culpable negligence involved, LE and Exodus provide for

---

[1]) Heb. יגף. It is somewhat unlikely that the same collection of laws would employ different legal terminology to describe a parallel case. Thus the juxtaposition of יגח "gores" (vss. 28, 31, 32, and נגח "gorer" vs. 29) and הועד "warned" (vs. 29) with יגף (vs. 35) and נודע (vs. 36—where the root נגח is also found) is a possible indication that these sections were originally incorporated from different sources.

[2]) For another example of negligence coupled with the selling of an ox, cf. Goetze, "On § 163, 164/5 and 176 of the Hittite Code," *JCS* 20 (1966), p. 132.

[3]) For the corrected reading of Sum. uzu (= Akk. *šīru* "flesh") for Sum. daḫ (= Akk. *taḫḫum* "price," Goetze, *Laws of Eshnunna*, pp. 73 and 132), see *CAD*, Vol. 1, p. 366, Vol. 2, p. 67, and Landsberger, "Jungfräulichkeit," *Symbolae David*, Vol. 2, p. 102.

the equal division of both the assets and liabilities between the two owners. In the case of a habitual goring ox (vs. 36), on the other hand, the owner, who was guilty of culpable negligence, must restore a live ox to the injured party; the dead ox, however, remains in his possession.[1])

21:37 and 22:2b-3. "When a man steals an ox or a sheep, and slaughters it or sells it, he shall pay five oxen for the ox, and four sheep for the sheep.[2]) He must make restitution; if he lacks the means, he shall be sold for his theft. But if what he stole—whether ox or ass or sheep—is found alive in his possession, he shall pay double."

The penalties incurred in crimes of theft are much greater than those found in cases of culpable negligence where the party involved was not directly guilty and profited nothing by the damage, and thus is obligated to pay only the exact equivalent of the loss. Here, however, since the guilty party is the man himself, and not his animal, and since he derived a direct benefit from his theft—he sold the animal or slaughtered it—he must make multiple restitution in kind. Similar penalties of multiple restitution for the theft of domestic animals are found in LH 8 and HL 57 ff. Several of the laws in the Hittite collection, analogous to Ex. 21:37, exact a higher penalty for the theft of cattle than for sheep, e.g., HL 57, 63 and 67, 69. But whereas the reparations in HL often reach as high as thirtyfold,[3]) the maximum in Exodus is fivefold.[4])

If the stolen animal is found alive in his possession (22:3), the thief has only to pay double.[5]) The same penalty is found in HL 70: "If anyone steals an ox,[6]) or a horse, or a mule, or an ass and its owner

---

[1]) See above, remarks, to vs. 34, p. 84. Cf. Yaron, *Eshnunna*, p. 193. For an actual court case allegedly involving two oxen, cf. *JEN*, Vol. 4, 341:4-19.

[2]) Cf. II Sam. 12:6. A greater multiple restitution (sevenfold) is found only in a non-legal section, Prov. 6:31.

[3]) HL 57-59, which are later changed to penalties of fifteenfold. Cf. LH 8 for another example of a thirtyfold penalty.

[4]) Cf. above, n. 2. For the various attempts to explain the difference between the four and fivefold restitution, consult the commentaries to Exodus. The earliest explanations are already found in the *Mechilta, ad loc.*, p. 99.

[5]) A double penalty is also exacted from a burglar (Ex. 22:6). For a similar penalty, cf. Ex. 22:8, and LH 120, 124, 126.

[6]) The word for an "ox," Sum. g u d, is accidentally omitted from Goetze's translation in *ANET*. Cf. Friedrich, *Die hethitischen Gesetze*, *ad loc.*

For an analogue to these verses in early Greek law, see Mühl, *Untersuchungen zur altorientalischen und althellenischen Gesetzgebung*, pp. 24-25.

traces it out,[1]) he shall receive the respective (animal). In addition (the thief) shall give it a second time, and he shall pledge his estate as security." [2])

Whether Ex. 22:2b—"He must make restitution; if he lacks the means, he shall be sold for his theft"—is to be interpreted as the continuation of 21:37,[3]) interpolated after 22:3,[4]) or meant to conclude 22:2a,[5]) the verse should be understood in the light of LH 8, which exacts capital punishment for a thief who is unable to make sufficient restitution.[6]) Whereas Mesopotamian corpora frequently demand the death penalty for offenses against property, e.g., breaking and entering, looting, trespassing, theft—cf. LE 12-13; LH 6-11, 21, 22, 25; MAL A 3—in the biblical corpora no offense against property is punishable by death. Life and property remain incommensurable. This, in turn, reflects "a basic difference in judgments of value, rather than stages in a single line of evolution." [7])

22:1-2a. "If the thief is seized [8]) while tunneling, and he is beaten to death, there is no bloodguilt [9]) in his case. If the sun has risen on him, there is bloodguilt in that case."

Within the section pertaining to the theft of livestock which are normally kept outside the house, a law on larceny is interpolated, which pertains to attempted theft of property from within the house.[10])

---

[1]) The Hit. verb, *ga-ni-eš-zi* (third-person singular of Hit. *kaneš*), is the semantic equivalent to the Heb. מצא employed in Ex. 22:3.

[2]) Though biblical commentators (medieval, Driver, Cassuto, and others) interpret the double fine in Exodus to consist of the stolen animal plus one other, Friedrich, *op. cit.*, p. 41, n. 3, unlike Goetze, (whose translation has been followed in the text above), assumes that in HL the thief has to return twofold in addition to the original stolen animal.

[3]) Y. ibn Ganah, *Sefer Hariqmah*, (Heb.), Vol. I (Jerusalem, 1964), p. 364, ll. 9 ff.; ibn Ezra, *ad loc.*; Ehrlich, *op. cit.*, *ad loc.* This is the interpretation adopted in the new JPS translation of the Torah. It is also accepted by Tur Sinai, *Pᵉshuto shel Miqrah* (Heb.), Vol. I (Jerusalem, 1962), p. 117.

[4]) Cf. the alternate possibilities suggested by Noth, *Exodus*, p. 183.

[5]) Rashi, *ad loc.*; Cassuto, *Exodus*, p. 197; and Greenberg, "Postulates," p. 18, n. 26.

[6]) Since the amount of the penalty is so exorbitant (thirtyfold to the church or state, tenfold to a private individual), it must have been practically impossible to make proper restitution.

Akk. *ša na-da-nim la i-šu* "(if) he does not have sufficient to make restitution" (LH 8) corresponds to the Heb. אם אין לו "if he lacks the means" (Ex. 22:2b).

[7]) Greenberg, *op. cit.*, p. 17. Cf. above, p. 39.

[8]) Cf. above, p. 66, n. 1.

[9]) Heb. דמים; cf. Num. 35:27, where the singular דם is employed.

[10]) For the juxtaposition of laws pertaining to the theft of property from within and without the precincts of a house (i.e., temple or palace), cf. LH 6 and 8, and the comments of Driver and Miles, *Babylonian Laws*, Vol. I, pp. 81, 84. See also

When there is any presumption of danger to the life of the house-owner, he is permitted to protect himself even at the expense of the life of the housebreaker. Thus, if the offense takes place at night, when there is a chance that the housebreaker might have resorted to homicide, and the housebreaker is slain, this is considered a case of self-defense [1]) on the part of the owner of the house and falls within the category of justifiable homicide. Such is not the case, however, if the offense takes place during the day, when the owner of the house may not protect his property at the expense of the life of the housebreaker, who, it is assumed, came only to rob and not to commit homicide; hence, if the housebreaker is slain, the houseowner incurs bloodguilt.[2])

LE 13 also makes a distinction between unlawful entry by day and by night: "A man who is caught in the house of a *muškēnum*, inside the building at high noon [*i-na mu-uṣ-la-lim*] shall pay ten shekels of silver. He who is caught inside the building at night [*i-na mu-ši-im*] shall die; he shall not live." A similar distinction is made in LE 12, where one who is caught in the field of a *muškēnum* at night is also put to death.[3]) LE and Exodus still differ, nevertheless, in regard to one basic principle. Whereas cuneiform law prescribes capital punishment for such a crime against property (cf. also LH 21, where the crime of breaking into a house is punished by the hanging of the thief in front of the breach which he has made), Exodus merely permits the slaying of the housebreaker; it does not designate this as the prescribed punishment.[4]) Once again it is to be noted that no crime against property per se—even the presumption of theft—warrants capital punishment.[5])

4-5. "When a man lets his livestock [בעירה] loose to graze [יבער] in another's land, and so allows a field or a vineyard to be grazed bare [בער],[6]) he must make restitution according to the top yield from that

---

LE 12 *ina eqel muškēnim* "in the field of a *muškēnum*," and LE 13 *ina bītim ša muškēnim* "in the house of a *muškēnum*." Cf., furthermore, HL 93-95 and 96-97. HL 93 also deals with unlawful entry. See also Appendix I, p. 110, n. 1.

[1]) Cf. Cassuto, *Exodus*, *ad loc.*

[2]) Cf. Abarbanel, *ad loc.*

[3]) Cf. Greenberg, *IDB*, Vol. I, p. 739. For analogues to Hellenistic law and the Twelve Tables, see Mühl, *Untersuchungen*, p. 27, and Yaron, *Laws of Eshnunna*, p. 182. For LE 13, see now Landsberger, *op. cit.*, p. 72.

[4]) Greenberg, "Postulates," *Kaufmann Jubilee Volume*, p. 18. See Jer. 2:34 for an allusion to this law.

[5]) Cf. above, p. 39.

[6]) Heb. יבער and בער are both denominative verbs from בעיר "livestock."

field or vineyard. When a fire is started and spreads to thorns, so that stacked, standing,[1]) or growing grain [lit. "field"] [2]) is consumed, he who started the fire must make restitution."

This section pertains to the damage of fields caused by either the grazing of animals or by fire. Both laws stipulate that the one responsible for the damage must make adequate restitution. The fine, however, is much greater in the first case (restitution from the "top yield"), since the man allowed his animals to graze on fields other than his own. In the second case, where the damage was caused by accident [3]) and not by intent, he must merely make the losses good, but need not pay from the top yield of the field or vineyard.

A similar juxtaposition of (1) a man who lets his livestock graze in another's field (vs. 4), and (2) a fire that consumes the grain of a neighboring field (vs. 5), is also found—though in reverse order— in HL 105-6 and 107.[4]) Both the biblical and Hittite compilations, moreover, place these laws in the section pertaining to robbery.[5])

The LXX and Samaritan versions both seem to have preserved an

---

יבער "to graze bare" is explicated by the following two clauses: "He set loose (Heb. שלח in the פיעל) his livestock (בעירה) and so allows a field or vineyard to be grazed bare (בער)."

A semantic analogue to these clauses is found in LH 58:71-74 pertaining to a shepherd who has let his sheep graze in another field: Akk. *rē'ûm ṣēnam a-na eqlim id-di-ma* [= Heb. שלח את בעירה], Akk. *eqlam ṣēnam uš-ta-ki-il* [= Heb. בער בשדה (אחר)] "(If) the shepherd drove the sheep into a field and has allowed the sheep to graze in the field." Cf. also LH 57:52-53.

1) Cf. Jud. 15:5.

2) Heb. שדה. A preferable interpretation is that of ibn Ganah, *Sefer Hariqmah*, p. 288, lines 5 ff., and Saadya, *ad loc.*, "or everything else in the field."

3) Cf. Driver, *Exodus*, p. 225, and Abarbanel, *ad loc.*

4) See p. 73, n. 5. The juxtaposition of these two laws in HL lends some support to the correctness of the Masoretic text. Cf. Pedersen, *Israel*, Vol. I, p. 535, note to p. 405. (Note also that both vss. 4 and 5 start with כי indicating separate laws.) The text has been called into question, however, since the time of Hoffman, "Versuche zu Amos," *ZAW* 3 (1883), p. 122, who emended it to read הַבְּעֵרָה "the fire" for בְּעִירֹה and וּבָעֲרָה שָׂדֶה "and burnt a field" for וּבִעֵר בִּשְׂדֵה. Additional support for this reading is now found in the Aramaic Targum of Neofiti, where the text reads ארום ייקד גבר חקל או כרם וישלח יקידתא ויוקד בחקלא דחורן. See G. Schelbert, "Exodus XXII 4 im palästinischen Targum," *VT* 8 (1958), pp. 253-263. The text then would differentiate between the willful (vs. 4) and unintentional (vs. 5) setting on fire of another's field. For earlier views, cf. J. Teicher, "A Sixth Century Fragment of the Palestinian Targum?," *VT* 1 (1951), pp. 125-129, and J. J. Weinberg, *Meḥqarīm beTalmud*, (Heb.), Vol. I (Berlin, 1937-38). See now, A. Toeg, *Tarbiẓ* 39 (1970), pp. 223-231.

5) Cazelles, *Études*, p. 162. Both Ex. 22:4 and HL 105, 107 also mention a "vineyard."

ancient tradition in their variant readings, which, in turn, may help shed light on the ambiguous phrase of vs. 4: מיטב שדהו ומיטב כרמו ישלם "He must make restitution according to the top yield from that field or vineyard." According to their reading, if only small sections are damaged, compensation is based upon the normal yield of those sections ("according to its produce"); but if the whole is ruined, the choicest sections shall serve as the standard.[1]) Hence, compensation has to be made according to the choicest sections of the field of the damagee. The Masoretic version may then be interpreted accordingly: "He [i.e., the one who allows his neighbor's field to be grazed bare] must make restitution according to the top yield from that field or vineyard [i.e., the field or vineyard of the damagee]." [2])

6-8. "When a man gives money or goods to another for safe-keeping [כי יתן איש אל רעהו כסף או כלים לשמר], and they are stolen from the man's house—if the thief is caught, he shall pay double; if the thief is not caught, the owner of the house [בעל הבית] shall depose before God [האלהים] [3]) that he has not laid hands on [4]) his neighbor's property.[5]) In all charges [6]) of misappropriation [7])—pertaining to an

[1]) For a discussion of whether this variant reading reflects an authentic tradition (cf. Cazelles, *op. cit.*, p. 64, n. 4) or is merely an interpolation, see E. J. Bickerman, "Two Legal Interpretations of the Septuagint," *RIDA*, 3e série 3 (1956), pp. 81-104, who also presents the Rabbinic controversy concerning the precise interpretation of the Masoretic text. For a dissenting view, cf. J. J. Rabinowitz, "Ex. XXII:4 and the Septuagint Version Thereof," *VT* 9 (1959), pp. 40-46. For a note on the penalties involved here, see D. Weiss (Halivni), "Notes on the Mishna and Baraita," (Heb.), *Tarbiz* 27 (1957), p. 21, n. 25.

[2]) Even without the benefit of the Samaritan and Septuagintal tradition, many commentators—Rabbinic, medieval, and modern—have interpreted the verse to mean that payment must be made according to the best crops of the damagee's field. In Mesopotamian law damage to crops was assessed by the yield obtained from adjacent fields, e.g., LH 42:3, 43:8, 55:37, 62:43, and NB 2:31, 34, 3:40.

Daube, "Direct and Indirect Causation in Biblical Law," *VT* 11 (1961), p.258, points out the difference between these verses and Ex. 21:28-34. There the "chief basis for liability is ownership of object causing damage; here the responsibility is primarily for doing something, for setting the agent to work, rather than because an object belonging to him does something or because he has not prevented [it].... Here indirect but active causation is the basis of liability."

[3]) See Cazelles, *Études*, p. 67, and Cassuto, *Exodus*, p. 199, for various ways of interpreting this difficult clause. Cf. also the comments of Saadyah and ibn Ezra, *ad loc.*

[4]) For Heb. שלח יד ב־, cf. Es. 9:15. Cf. P. Humbert, "Étendre la main," *VT* 12 (1962), pp. 383-395.

[5]) For Heb. מלאכה, cf. Gen. 33:14 and I Sam. 15:9 (referring to animals); and II Ch. 17:13.

[6]) Heb. דבר "word, charge, case, dispute" (for the last, cf. Ex. 18:16, 22) is the semantic and functional analogue to Akk. *awātu* and *dabābu.*

[7]) Heb. פשע "breach of faith."

ox, an ass, a sheep, a garment, or any other loss [על כל אבדה], whereof one party alleges, 'This is it'—the case of both parties shall come before God [האלהים]: he whom God [האלהים] declares guilty [1]) shall pay double to the other."

This section commences with the laws of the deposit of mobilia which are subsequently stolen. When the thief is apprehended (vs. 6), he must pay a twofold penalty. Although a similar twofold penalty is inflicted upon a dishonest bailee in LH 120, 124, and 126, in a case of theft (LH 125), if one is to judge from the other laws pertaining to stolen and lost property (LH 6-11) [2]) where capital punishment is meted out to the culprit, the thief when apprehended would most likely be given the death sentence. The biblical corpus, however, as noted several times above, never punishes any crime against property with death.[3])

If the thief is not apprehended (vs. 7), the bailee must depose before האלהים that he has not misappropriated the articles given him for safekeeping. This deposition before some supernatural authority [4]) has analogues in cuneiform law, where an oath before the gods (Akk. *ilāni*) was resorted to in cases where the judges did not have sufficient evidence or information to render a decision on their own. When human authorities cannot reach a final verdict, whether because of lack of evidence or because of contradictory statements on the part of the litigants, the case is referred to higher powers.[5]) Hence, both the deadlocked legal cases of Ex. 22:7, where concrete evidence of theft is lacking, and Ex. 22:8, which extends to all charges of suspected misappropriation and breach of trust where a dispute arises and there is no conclusive proof by which to decide, would fall into this same category, and thus a similar oath to the deity is resorted to in order to resolve the impasse.[6]) The one declared guilty—

---

[1]) Heb. יַרְשִׁיעֻן is a declarative הפעיל; cf. Dt. 25:1; I Ki. 8:32.

[2]) Cf. MAL A 3.

[3]) See above, p. 87.

[4]) Cf. Ex. 22:8, 10.

[5]) This has often been interpreted as an ordeal; cf. Driver and Miles, *Babylonian Laws*, Vol. I, pp. 466-469, in general, and H. Liebesny, "Evidence in Nuzi Legal Procedure," *JAOS* 61 (1941), pp. 130-142; Speiser, "Nuzi Marginalia," *Or* 25 (1956), pp. 15-23; Draffkorn, "*Ilāni/Elohim*," *JBL* 76 (1957), pp. 216-224, for a complete discussion of such an oath at Nuzi in particular. For another function of the *ilāni*, see the comments to Ex. 21:6, pp. 50-51.

For the role of ordeal in Israel, see R. Press, "Das Ordal im alten Israel," *ZAW* 51 (1933), pp. 121-140, 227-255.

[6]) Heb. האלהים in vss. 7-8 is the functional equivalent to Akk. *ilāni* (plural)

whether depositor or bailee—is punished like a thief [1]) for his illegal gain and must pay double (cf. Ex. 22:3, 6).

The loss of deposited mobilia is also the subject of LE 37: "If the man's [the depositary's] house is either broken into or collapses (and), together with the property of the depositor which he gave him [i.e., to the depositary], loss on the part of the owner of the house is incurred, the owner of the house shall swear for him an oath in the gate of the temple of Tishpak (saying): 'Together with your property, property of mine was lost; I have not engaged in conspiracy or fraud.' If he [i.e., the depositary] swears for him (such an oath), he [i.e., the depositor] shall have no claim against him [i.e., the depositary]." [2]) The depositary in a case of housebreaking is not responsible for the loss of deposited goods if he takes an oath that his own property was lost and that he has not engaged in any illegal action, thereby offsetting the possibility of an act of fraud on his part. In Ex. 22:7 the depositary likewise vindicates himself by taking an exculpatory oath: "If the thief is not caught, the owner of the house shall depose before האלהים that he has not laid hand on his neighbor's property." In both instances he thereby escapes liability for the loss of the deposit.

LH 125 also pertains to a case of housebreaking which results in the loss of deposited property along with the depositary's property. It further adds that since the owner of the house (i.e., the depositary) was so careless as to allow the deposited goods to get lost, he has to compensate the depositor in full and must search for the lost property. Here, unlike LE and Exodus, negligence (Akk. *egû*) on the part of the

---

in the communal law of Nuzi and is to be understood as a plural agent. This is further indicated by the plural pointing of the verb יַרְשִׁיעֻן in vs. 8 of the Masoretic text—a reading which is to be preferred to the singular pointing ירשיענו in the Samaritan version. This expression, which was later interpreted as referring to the highest human authority in the community, is most probably a reflex of pre-Israelite times. Cf. the discussion on this same word in a different context in Ex. 21:6, pp. 50-51.

The technical formulation in vs. 7, Heb. ונקרב בעל הבית אל האלהים, is not the functional equivalent to Akk. *ana ilāni* (*la*) *iqerrib* found at Nuzi (e.g., *JEN* 89:10-12; 216:14). Akk. *qarābu* in that idiom means "to have a claim or a right to, to be qualified for," and may be compared to the use of Heb. קרב in Ex. 12:48 and Lev. 21:17-18 (Speiser). In the present verse (Ex. 22:7), however, קרב is part of a technical legal expression for the taking of an oath (órdeal?) before האלהים. The *Mechilta*, p. 116, already interpreted this phrase as the taking of an oath.

[1]) Cf. Luzatto, *ad loc.*

[2]) This translation is taken from Goetze, *Laws of Eshnunna*, pp. 97-98; cf. his critical notes and discussion on pp. 98-105. See now Landsberger, "Jungfräulichkeit," *Symbolae David*, Vol. 2, p. 99, who reads *lu-uq-qú-ut* "was plundered," in l. 18.

depositary is specifically mentioned, and the depositor must be indemnified under all circumstances; the liability of the depositary is absolute. Hence there is no mention of any oath in this case.[1])

The legal formula for deposit is similar in the three laws:

(1) LE 36:14-15 *šum-ma awīlum bu-še-šu a-na na-ap-ṭà-ri a-na ma-ṣa-ar-tim id-di-in-ma* "If a man gives property of his to a *napṭarum* [2]) for safekeeping."

(2) LH 124:53-59 *šum-ma a-wi-lum a-na a-wi-lim kaspam ḫurāṣam ù mi-im-ma šum-šu ... a-na ma-ṣa-ru-tim id-di-in-ma* "If a man gives silver, gold, or anything the like to another man for safekeeping."

(3) Ex. 22:6 כי יתן איש אל רעהו כסף או כלים לשמר "If a man gives money or goods to another for safekeeping."

Heb. יתן לשמר is the semantic parallel to Akk. *ana maṣṣarūtim iddin*. Moreover, in all three laws the depositary is called "the owner of the house:" LE 37:20 and LH 125:75, *bēl bītim*, and Ex. 22:7, בעל הבית.[3])

9-12. "When a man gives to another an ass, an ox, a sheep or any other animal to guard, and it dies or is injured [4]) or is carried off, with no witness about, an oath before the Lord shall decide between the two of them that the one of them has not laid hands on the property of the other; the owner must acquiesce,[5]) and no restitution shall be

---

[1]) An oath is mentioned, however, in both LH 120 and 126: the former pertains to the lost property of the depositor, the latter to that of the bailee.

For a detailed study of LH 125 and its apparent internal inconsistency, see Koschaker, *Rechtsvergleichende Studien zur Gesetzgebung Ḫammurapis, Königs von Babylon* (Leipzig, 1917), pp. 29 ff.; Driver and Miles, *Babylonian Laws*, Vol. I, pp. 239-241; and Goetze, *op. cit.*, pp. 102-104.

[2]) See Finkelstein, "Some New *Misharum* Material and its Implications," *Studies in Honor of Benno Landsberger*, p. 238, and below, p. 63, n. 2.

[3]) The Hebrew phrase על כל אבדה "or any other loss," which appears at the end of the list of items mentioned in vs. 8, serves the same functional purpose as the common Akkadian catchall term *mimma šumšu* "anything the like" (lit. "whatever its name"), which sums up the list of items for deposit in LH. Interestingly enough the exact semantic analogue to the Hebrew appears at the end of LH 125—*mimmašu ḫalqam* "anything that is lost." (Cf. another summarizing phrase, וכל בהמה "or any other animal," in vs. 9 below.)

[4]) Heb. ומת או נשבר. Cf. the remarks to Ex. 22:13. For Heb. שבר as applied to animals, cf. Lev. 22:22; I Ki. 13:28; Ez. 34:4, 16; Zach. 11:16.

[5]) Heb. ולקח בעליו is difficult. The present translation follows Ehrlich, *Miqrah KiFshuto*, *ad loc.* (with reference to Ps. 6:10). An alternate suggestion is "the owner shall take (the animal)"—but this could not apply, of course, when the animal was carried off. (It must be added, however, that some commentators delete ונשבה as a dittography.) This interpretation, which is already found in the *Mechilta*, *ad loc.*, p. 124, is favored by Cazelles, *op. cit.*, p. 71.

made. But if [the animal] was stolen from him, he shall make restitution to its owner. If it was torn by beasts, he shall bring it as evidence; he need not replace what has been torn by beasts."

This section pertains to the laws of the safeguarding of animals. If there are no witnesses present and the animal dies or is injured or is carried off—all three acts are beyond the control of the bailee—an oath before the deity is sufficient to settle the case.[1]) The owner must accept this oath, and he then has no subsequent claims upon the bailee. The latter is also absolved from paying any penalty when he brings evidence that the animal was torn by beasts. The bailee must make restitution only when the animal is stolen, for it is then assumed that he was negligent in guarding the animal. In sum he is held responsible only in case of theft [2]) but is exempt in all instances of *force majeure*.[3])

In LH 267 a shepherd in charge of another's cattle is also held responsible for losses due to negligence, e.g., when an infection breaks out in the fold, but is exempt from acts beyond his control, e.g., "the stroke of a god," LH 266. In this latter case, furthermore, when the animal dies from "the stroke of a god" (266:77 *lipit ilim*),[4]) and in HL 75, "If he contends: 'It died by the hand of god' " (75:75 *ina qāti* dingir^{lim} *-u̯a-ra-aš* ba.ug$_6$), an oath before the deity is required,[5]) as it is in the law of Exodus, and no restitution is made to

---

[1]) Since there were no witnesses present (Heb. ראה, cf. Lev. 5:1), only the deity could make the final decision; cf. above, pp.90-91. Interestingly enough, vs.10 employs the name of YHWH in the oath rather than האלהים (vss. 7-8). This is most likely an example of the use of different source material in which the oath before YHWH would be a modernizing of a pre-Israelite formulation.

[2]) In the case of the theft of goods (Ex. 22:7), however, the bailee only has to take an exculpatory oath in order to be acquitted. In an attempt to explain the reason for the difference between these two laws, two answers have been offered. According to the *Mechilta*, p. 124, the section of Ex. 22:6-8 pertains to an unpaid bailee who does not receive any compensation for safeguarding the deposit and thus is exempt when anything is stolen. Ex. 22:9-12, however, is interpreted as falling within the category of a paid bailee who is held liable in case of theft since he is being compensated for his labors and thus has heightened responsibility. Another suggestion is found in the commentaries of Rashbam, Luzatto, Cassuto (and already in the Karaite work of Benjamin Nahwendi—Zucker, *Rav Saadya Gaon's Translation of the Torah*, pp. 164-165), all of whom distinguish between the first section which pertains to mobilia deposited within the house, and the second section which pertains to livestock kept in the fields. The latter, since they are constantly out in the open, demand much more care and hence the added responsibility. Cf. also Philo, *On the Special Laws*, IV, 35, p. 29.

[3]) Cf. *Mechilta*, *ad loc.*, p. 121.

[4]) Cf. LH 249:38 *i-lum im-ḫa-sú* "a god struck it."

[5]) The technical legal expression employed for the oath in LH 266 is *rēʾûm*

the owner of the animal. In all of these laws when death is the result of *force majeure*, the loss falls upon the owner.

The case of livestock being devoured by a wild beast is also prevalent in Mesopotamian law: SL 8, New Sumerian Law Fragments III 9′-11′,[1]) and LH 244, 266—by a lion, and HL 75—by a wolf. In the latter two, the one in charge can acquit himself by taking an exculpatory oath, while in Ex. 22:12 he is acquitted when he brings the torn animal as evidence to the owner.[2])

13-14a. "When a man borrows [an animal] [3]) from another and it dies of injuries [or "is injured or dies"—ונשבר או מת], its owner not being with it, he must make restitution. If its owner was with it, no restitution need be made."

If the owner is not present, the borrower bears the full onus for all injuries occurring to the animal whose services he has enjoyed free of charge.[4]) The presence of the owner, on the other hand, frees the borrower from all responsibility.

In Nuzi documents pertaining to animals there is found an Akkadian phrase, *ul-te-eb-ir-šu ù im-tu-ut*, which is a hendiadys for "injuries that lead to an animal's death" (lit., "he injured it so that it died"). [5]) On the basis of this phrase, the equivalent Hebrew expression, ונשבר או מת, which appears in vs. 13, has likewise been rendered in the new JPS *Torah* translation as a hendiadys.[6])

---

ma-ḫar! (written *ḫi*) *ilim ú-ub-ba-am-ma*. For the use of *ubbubu* in oaths, see *CAD*, Vol. 4, p. 7. Cf. also W. Albright, *Yahweh and the Gods of Canaan* (New York, 1968), pp. 103-104.

[1]) Civil, "New Sumerian Law Fragments," *Studies in Honor of Benno Landsberger*, p. 7, and his comments on p. 8.

[2]) Cf. Gen. 31:39; Am. 3:12 (M. Weinfeld). Since Heb. עֵד "evidence, witness" is usually employed with persons, the pointing of Heb. עד as עַד "to" instead of עֵד, which is already found in the Septuagint and is offered as one of several suggestions in the *Mechilta*, *ad loc.*, p. 125, has been accepted by some scholars, the latest being Fensham, "*ʿD* in Exod. XXII:12," *VT* 12 (1962), pp. 337-339. The suffix of the verb יבאהו would then refer to the owner and not to the torn animal. The translation would be: "Let him [the bailee] bring him [the owner] to the torn animal; he [the bailee] need not make any restitution." Cf. also the comments of Ehrlich, *Randglossen*, *ad loc.*, and the conflate reading of the Targum Yerushalmi to this verse.

[3]) The elliptical phrase has been spelled out in both the Peshitta and the Targum Yerushalmi.

[4]) Since he has full use of the animal without any payment, he also has full responsibility. Cf. the comments of Philo, *On the Special Laws*, IV, 37-38, p. 31.

[5]) Cf. *JEN* IV 335:9-10.

[6]) If this interpretation is correct, there is the further possibility that the Heb. או "or" resolved the Akk. *ù* "and" in the hendiadys erroneously. For both Heb. ו

14b. "But if it was hired [or "if he was a hirer"—שכיר], he is entitled to the hiring fee(?) [בא בשכרו]."

Both the laconic nature of the Hebrew text and its linguistic difficulties complicate the interpretation of this law. According to the Rabbinic interpretation of the verse, the law pertains to a hirer, and he bears the same responsibility as a paid bailee, i.e., he is exempt only in a case of *force majeure*.[1])

In cuneiform corpora, laws pertaining to rented oxen are found in New Sumerian Law Fragments I 2′-III 11′,[2]) LI 34-37, LH 242-249, and HL 78 (cf. also HL 76). According to LH 244 if a hired ox is killed by a lion [3]) in the open country, the loss is sustained by the owner (244:5 *a-na be-lí-šu-ma*). LH 249 likewise exempts the bailee, a hirer, from payment if he takes an oath that the ox died by a "stroke of god." Hence LH, at least, would be in perfect agreement with the Rabbinic interpretation of the law in Exodus, i.e., the hirer is absolved from all liability in cases of *force majeure*. HL 76, on the other hand, while not specifically dealing with one who rents an ox, does mention the death of the ox and holds the bailee liable: "If anyone pawns [4]) an ox, a horse, a mule, or an ass, and it dies at its place, he has to make amends for it, and he shall pay its hire." The owner must be compensated for the use of the animal by being paid its hiring cost.

Since both phrases of the verse are very ambiguous, the law has been the subject of several different interpretations. According to Cassuto, the one who has hired an animal is exempt from any further payment, since the owner has already received his daily compensation up until the animal's death; hence the loss would be the owner's (cf. LH 249).[5]) According to Ehrlich, on the other hand, if the animal was hired, the owner would receive the price of its hire for the entire period for which

"and" and או "or" are subsumed under Akk. *ù*, and ו, rather than או, is what is expected in examples of hendiadys (Speiser—oral communication). The bracketed translation, however, may still be correct. For another example of the juxtaposition of these two verbs, though in reverse order, see Ex. 22:9, where the expression is not interpreted as a hendiadys.

[1]) Cf. *Mechilta*, *ad loc.*, pp. 128-129.

[2]) Civil, *loc. cit.* On p. 8 he lists the various sources that mention damages to hired oxen and their respective penalties; the example(s) from HL, however, are omitted. Cf. also the discussion in Driver and Miles, *Babylonian Laws*, Vol. I, pp. 435-441.

[3]) Cf. Civil, *op. cit.*, Law III 9′: "If a lion has killed the ox (while it was under) the yoke of a wagon, he shall not . . . ." The rest is too broken to be read. For other examples, cf. his chart on p. 8.

[4]) The exact meaning of the Hittite verb *appatariịa* is uncertain.

[5]) Cassuto, *Exodus*, p. 200.

it was hired [1]) (cf. HL 76). This verse,[2]) nevertheless, should probably be understood in contrast to the preceding vss. 13-14a pertaining to a borrower, for here the law would go into effect regardless of whether or not the owner was present at the time of the animal's death.

15-16. "If a man seduces a virgin [בתולה] who has not been spoken for [אשר לא אֹרָשָׂה] and lies with her, he must make her his wife by the payment of a bride price. If her father refuses to give her to him [אם מאן ימאן אביה לתתה לו], he must still weigh out silver in accordance with the bride price for virgins [כמֹהר הבתולֹת]."

The law of the seduction of a virgin is related to the above section pertaining to offenses against property in that it, too, pertains to compensation which must be made to reimburse an economic loss, in this case one sustained by the father.[3]) The girl is described as one "who had not been betrothed" [4]) (Heb. אשר לא אֹרָשָׂה), which means that her father had not yet received the bride price for virgins,[5]) and now, after her deflowering, is completely deprived of ever receiving it. Thus, the seducer is obliged to take the girl as his wife by the payment of a bride price (Heb. מהר ימהרנה לו לאשה) or—if the father is unwilling to permit his daughter to marry him—to pay her father the "bride price for virgins" (Heb. מֹהר הבתולֹת), i.e., in either case he must compensate the father for his monetary loss.

A law dealing with the seduction of a virgin is also found in MAL A 56: "If the virgin has given herself to a man, the man shall (so) swear and they shall not touch his wife; the seducer shall give the (extra) third in silver [6]) as the value of a virgin (and) the father shall

---

[1]) Ehrlich, *Randglossen*, Vol. I, p. 354.

[2]) Cf. also the various other suggestions made by Driver, Cazelles, and Noth. The opinion of Driver that the owner is prepared to take a risk since the animal "came for its hire," and hence compensation is unnecessary (cf. Cassuto), is to be seriously considered.

[3]) Cf. Driver, *Exodus*, *ad loc.* For the same concept in MAL, see the discussion in Driver and Miles, *Assyrian Laws*, pp. 36 ff., esp. p. 40. For a similar conclusion based upon sex offenses in Mesopotamian law, see Finkelstein, "Sex Offenses in Sumerian Laws," *JAOS* 86 (1966), p. 367.

[4]) For this translation, see Weiss, "A Note on אשר לא ארשה," *JBL* 81 (1962), pp. 67-69. His interpretation of the law is the one followed in the annotations to the text. For a study of מהר, see Loewenstamm, "מהר," *Encyclopaedia Biblica*, Vol. IV (Jerusalem, 1962), pp. 702-706.

[5]) If the girl has had a previous financé who died or deserted her, her father would have already received the bride price for virgins and would not be entitled to a second reimbursement. See Weiss, *loc. cit.*, who also brings Rabbinic support for this interpretation from the *Mechilta*, p. 130.

[6]) Meek, *ANET*. Cf. the different translations found in Driver and Miles, *Assyrian Laws*, *ad loc.*, and *CAD*, Vol. 2, p. 173.

treat his daughter as he wishes." [1]) The law in Exodus resembles this cuneiform law in that both pertain to an unmarried girl (Akk. *batūltu* = Heb. בתולה) who has been seduced, and whose seducer must pay the "price for virgins" (Akk. *šīm batūlti* [2]) = Heb. מֹהר הבתולת). The father, apparently, is not bound to give his daughter in marriage to the seducer. MAL, however, has an additional clause which is not found in the biblical law: "The father shall treat his daughter as he wishes," i.e., he may punish her in any way he sees fit.[3])

MAL A 55, while pertaining to a case of rape rather than to one of seduction, has several analogous features to the law in Exodus. The virgin is described as one whose father "had not been asked for her [hand in marriage]" (Akk. *ba-tu-ul-ta ša . . . a-ba-a-ša la-a ú-tar-ri-šu-ni*). This description of her status is similar to the Heb. בתולה אשר לֹא ארשה "a virgin who had not been spoken for." Note that both clauses employ the passive perfect tense of a related verb (Akk. *erēšu*, Heb. ארשׂ) in the intensive conjugation (Akk. Gt, Heb. פיעל).[4]) The ravisher, furthermore, if he has no wife, in addition to paying the price for virgins (cf. Ex. 22:15), must also marry the girl. However, "if the father does not (so) wish [Akk. *šum-ma a-bu la ḫa-a-di*], he [the father] shall receive the (extra) third for the virgin in silver (and) give his daughter to whom he pleases." Cf. Ex. 22:16, where the culprit must still pay the bride price for virgins even "if her father refuses to give her to him" [Heb. אם מאן ימאן אביה לתתה לו].[5])

---

[1]) See p. 96, n. 6. For a discussion of this law and other laws pertaining to sexual offenses, see Driver and Miles, *op. cit.*, pp. 36-65, and esp. Finkelstein, *loc. cit.*

[2]) Driver and Miles, *op. cit.*, pp. 61-65.

[3]) This apparently does not preclude the death penalty. Cf. *ibid.*, p. 60.

[4]) Whereas the exact Hebrew cognate equivalent of Akk. *erēšu* is ארשׁ (Ps. 21:3, cf. Ug. *ʾrš*), Heb. ארשׂ has also been related to this verb; cf. *ibid.*, p. 493, note on l. 9, and Ginsberg, on II Aqht 6:26-27 (oral communication). Akk. *erēšu* is also used of asking for a girl in marriage in the tablets from el-Amarna; cf. J. A. Knudtzon *Die El-Amarna-Tafeln*, Vol. I (Leipzig, 1907), 27:17; 29:17, 19, 21. See, however, Finkelstein, *op. cit.*, p. 357, n. 4.

[5]) In Dt. 22:28-29 (the case of the rape of a young woman who has not been betrothed) a clause similar to that of MAL A 55 is added to protect the woman against future divorce: "If a man comes upon a virgin who has not been betrothed and he seizes her and lies with her, and they are discovered, the man who lay with her shall pay the girl's father fifty [shekels of] silver, and she shall be his wife. Because he has violated her, he can never have the right to divorce her." Cf. MAL A 55: 33-37: "If he has no wife, the ravisher shall give the (extra) third in silver to her father as the value of a virgin, (and) her ravisher shall marry her (and) not cast her off." This protection clause, however, is not added in the biblical or cuneiform laws when the girl has willingly consented to her seducer.

For similar laws, cf. Dt. 22:23-27 (where she is described as already being betrothed) and HL 197. Both emphasize the place of the crime: town or open country (Deuteronomy), mountains or house (Hittite), and acquit the wife if the assault took place in the open country or mountains, where she is presumed not to be guilty of any willing collaboration on her part. If, however, the offense took place in the town or in the house, she is held equally responsible and the two of them are put to death. An important point of distinction must yet be noted. HL 198 adds that the husband or the king may spare the lives of the two convicted of adultery. (Cf. also LH 129 and MAL A 15.) This is impossible in biblical law where such a crime is considered a flouting of the divine will and as such is without pardon. Cf. Greenberg, "Postulates," *Kaufmann Volume*, pp. 12-13. In Mesopotamian law, however, adultery "was *de facto* not a capital crime.... It was at bottom a civil invasion of a husband's domain." Finkelstein, *op. cit.*, p. 372. For a further detailed explication of the Mesopotamian laws pertaining to sex offenses, cf. Finkelstein's study cited above, and Landsberger, "Jungfräulichkeit: Ein Beitrag zum Thema 'Beilager und Eheschliessung'," *Symbolae Iuridicae et Historicae Martino David Dedicatae*, Vol. 2, pp. 41-105. For a study of these laws in Deuteronomy, see Weinfeld, *Deuteronomy and the Deuteronomic School*, Part 3.

CHAPTER SIX

SUMMARY

A society structured on law was one of Mesopotamia's most important contributions to the advancement of civilization. Mesopotamian, or better, cuneiform law was characterized by several complementary features: the cuneiform script and the legal document; the predominate use of casuistic legal formulations; and a fundamental concept whose premise that "law on earth must be in harmony with cosmic law and order" [1]) accounted for the cultural dynamism and expansion of Mesopotamian civilization throughout the entire ancient Near East. Indeed, all cultures of the Fertile Crescent were attracted by the magnetism of cuneiform law; all, that is to say, except Egypt, where the Pharaoh was considered a god, and, as such, the source rather than the servant of the law.[2])

Law, impersonally conceived and secular in character, was embodied in two Akkadian terms: *kittum* (pl. *kīnātu*) "truth, right," i.e., the sum of cosmic truths, and *mēšarum* "equity, justice," i.e., the process whereby law was made to function equitably. Whereas the authority of the king as legislator was limited to the institution and implementation of *mēšarum*, for which he was granted the divine gift of the perception of *kīnātu*, the ultimate source of these "cosmic truths" themselves was apparently neither a human nor a divine agent, but most likely belonged to a metadivine realm. Hence, Shamash, the patron of justice, is not to be considered the *fons et origo* of law, but rather its custodian and guardian, and the king its temporary trustee.

The king, moreover, as the agent and servant of the law was held directly accountable to the gods for its just enactment. He earned a reputation of being a *šar mēšarim*, "just king," by assembling a collection of laws which constituted a report to the gods of his exemplary achievements. The legislator, by thus providing his

[1]) E. A. Speiser, "Cuneiform Law and the History of Civilization," *PAPS* 107 (1963), p. 538.

[2]) J. A. Wilson, *The Culture of Ancient Egypt* (Chicago, 1956), pp. 49-50. Cf. V. Arangio Ruiz, "La codification dans l'Égypte ancienne," *JJP* 11-12 (1957-1958), pp. 25-46; J. Pirenne, "La loi et les décrets royaux en Égypte sous l'ancien empire," *RIDA*, 3e série, 4 (1957), pp. 2-31.

people with just and equitable laws, assured for himself and for his family the reward of the deity to whom he had dedicated his collection.

Several of these legal collections—in particular LH—are characterized by a clear dichotomy between a prologue-epilogue frame and a juridical corpus. This literary arrangement provides, in turn, pertinent data concerning the style, content, and sources of both heterogeneous sections. The non-juridical frame, composed in hymnic-epic language, embodies the religious setting of law and describes the military, economic, political, and social achievements of the king—all in a long panegyric dedicated to the gods. Thus, the prologue-epilogue sections, though following traceable literary precedents, are directly related to the age and the person of the legislator. The juridical corpus, on the other hand, which is drafted predominantly, yet not exclusively, in traditional casuistic style and which employs formulaic legal terminology, incorporates, along with the legislator's innovations and reforms, the norms of customary legal practice which have evolved throughout the centuries prior to the actual compilation.[1])

In sharp contrast to the Mesopotamian secular concept of law, biblical law has a divine authorship. It is a revelation of the will of God and not a "humanly authored safeguard of cosmic truth."[2]) The deity alone is the ultimate source and sanction of law. In the light of this several unique features of biblical law can be singled out:[3])

(1) Since law is an expression of the divine will, all crimes are considered sins, and certain offenses (e.g., adultery and homicide) are not capable of pardon by human agency.[4])

(2) The whole of one's life is directly related to the will of God, to whom each and everyone is directly and personally responsible.

(3) Law is proclaimed publicly to the entire society and constitutes, moreover, a body of teaching for this community. Hence, explanatory, ethical, religious, and historical motive clauses are appended to many of the prescriptions.

(4) The sacredness of a human life becomes a primary concern of the law, i.e., whoever destroys a human life—whether man or beast—must give a reckoning for it. There is an absolute ban on composition.

---

[1]) P. Koschaker, *Rechtsvergleichende Studien zur Gesetzgebung Hammurapis, Königs von Babylon* (Leipzig, 1917), pp. 1-6; V. Korošec, "Le code de Hammurabi et les droits antérieurs," *RIDA*, 3e série, 8 (1961), pp. 12-27.

[2]) M. Greenberg, "Some Postulates of Biblical Criminal Law," *Yehezkel Kaufmann Jubilee Volume*, (Jerusalem, 1960), p. 12.

[3]) See above, pp. 37 ff., for further amplification and documentation.

[4]) Greenberg, *loc. cit.*

(5) Brutal, multiple, and vicarious punishments are all but absent.

(6) The laws of talion, which restrict retaliation to the actual offender and limit it to the exact measure of the injury, thereby according equal justice, are an important advance in the history of jurisprudence. Though this principle is already found in LH, it is now extended to encompass all freeborn members of the community. Slaves, who are not considered the peers of freemen and thus are not included within the scope of these laws, are nevertheless provided with additional protection within the law.

Moreover, since all law ultimately stems from God, legal injunctions (casuistically formulated) and moral exhortations along with religious prescriptions (apodictically formulated—and present only in biblical legal corpora) are all interwoven within a single juridical corpus.

Nevertheless, the early Israelite society was attracted by the magnetism and dynamism of Mesopotamian culture and institutions. Thus it was also very much influenced by cuneiform law. Israel was greatly indebted to its predecessors for its profound respect for the law; for understanding law to be the backbone of a society; for viewing man not as the source, but rather as the servant of the law; for legal terminology; for the casuistic formulation of law; and last, but not least, for many legal prescriptions which ultimately had an influence on the corresponding biblical laws.

Since in both form and content Israel proved to be an apt (yet independent) disciple of its legal predecessors, the question was posed whether the earliest collection of biblical laws, the so-called Book of the Covenant in Exodus, had a literary arrangement in common with several of the Mesopotamian compilations. Was a prologue-epilogue frame attached to this legal collection? Though the Mesopotamian examples of prologue-corpus-epilogue were easily discernible, since the heterogeneous sections occur on the same monument, the problem was far more complicated for the legal collection of Exodus. There was, however, certain external evidence which seemed to favor such an assumption and made it entirely feasible. It was suggested that the legal corpus proper, Ex. 21:2—22:16, along with its moral and cultic appendix, Ex. 22:17—23:19, were all part of one larger composite section, Ex. 19—24, which in its *final redaction* constituted a literary frame of redemptive history that bound the destiny of Israel to the discipline of law. The superstructure of the narrative of the theophany together with the literary units of Ex. 19:3b-6 and the

Decalogue (="prologue") and the pericope of Ex. 23:20-33 (="epilogue") were seen to be the structural and functional analogues to the extra-biblical prologue-epilogue frames. An analysis of some of the key phrases in the "prologue" section (גוי קדוש and ממלכת כהנים), moreover, pointed to the fact that this early collection of laws was meant to provide a constitution for the forthcoming institution of statehood and was geared to a new political entity about to leave its seminomadic state and become a settled society in a land of its own.

The actual collection of laws in this compilation, then, in common with cuneiform compilations, was the end result of a long process of development which incorporated, together with traditional customary law as it had evolved throughout the centuries, the additions and modifications of early Israelite jurisprudence. Therefore, in order to gain a true appreciation of the contribution of biblical law, one must first isolate those elements which were originally influenced by earlier sources. With the discovery of LH, scholars were inclined to make hasty, but often inconclusive, comparisons between biblical and Mesopotamian legal collections. However, subsequent finds of additional legal collections—LU, LE, LI, HL, MAL—coupled with the many documents from Nuzi, Alalakh, and Ugarit, pertaining to the actual practice of law, now provide a greater and sounder basis for such a comparison.

A study of the legal collection of Exodus in the light of these finds reveals that early biblical law remained within the legal orbit of its cuneiform predecessors. This eclectic compilation appears to have been influenced by several extra-biblical substrata, many of which are still contextually and linguistically identifiable. Several possible examples of the biblical adaption of cuneiform antecedents are included in the following brief outline, which is meant to be illustrative rather than exhaustive: [1])

1. *Laws*

   a) *Nuzi*—Ex. 21:2-6 reflects the formulaic terminology and legal provisions of Nuzi *Ḫāpiru* documents. It also highlights one of the functions of the Heb. האלהים, which is analogous to the Akk. *ilāni*. In Ex. 22:7-8, moreover, האלהים are mentioned in connection with communal law where, as

[1]) These few selected examples must be read in conjunction with the annotations to their respective verses.

is well known from Nuzi, an oath ordeal in the presence of the *ilāni* was resorted to when, either for lack of evidence or because of conflicting evidence, the legal proceedings reached an impasse which could only be resolved by recourse to higher powers.

b) *Ugarit*—A legal document from Ugarit contains an analogue to the usage of *qullulu* "to disrespect" and *kubbudu* "to respect" in describing a son's behavior towards his mother. Cf. Ex. 21:17 (קלל) and 20:12 (כבד).

c) *LI*—LI 27-28 is analogous to Ex. 21:10 in that a husband upon taking a second wife is obligated to continue to support his first wife with three basic commodities.

d) *LE*—LE 53 is very similar to Ex. 21:35-36 in that the assets and liabilities accruing in a case where one ox gores another to death are divided equally between the two owners.

e) *LH*—LH is the earliest extra-biblical collection which employs the laws of talion; cf. Ex. 21:23-25.

f) *HL*—HL 10, which pertains to one who is injured by a blow received from a second party, is analogous to Ex. 21:18-19 in several aspects:
   (1) The striking and the recovery of the injured party are both mentioned.
   (2) Two payments are made upon recovery, whereupon the guilty party is absolved.
   (3) One of the two payments is exactly the same, i.e., the doctor's fee.
   (4) Neither in HL nor in Exodus (unlike LH) is an oath taken.

g) *MAL*—MAL A 56 has several features in common with Ex. 22:15-16 pertaining to the laws of seduction:
   (1) Both deal with an unbetrothed girl who has been seduced.
   (2) The seducer must pay a certain "price for virgins" to the girl's father.
   (3) The father reserves the right to make the final decision concerning his daughter.

2. *Legal Terminology and Phraseology*

a) Casuistic formulations predominate throughout the juridical corpus.

b) Similar modes of legal expressions are found in:
   (1) laws of homicide—cf. LH 207, HL 3-4, Ex. 21:12.
   (2) laws of the goring ox—cf. LE 54, LH 251, Ex. 21:29-30.
   (3) laws of deposit—cf. LE 36, LH 124, Ex. 22:6.
   (4) an animal that dies of injuries—cf. Nuzi, Ex. 22:13.

c) The stipulation in Ex. 21:10 of three items provided for a rejected wife is most likely based on the stereotypic triad of commodities found in cuneiform documents from the time of Ur III down to NB times.

3. *Legal Juxtaposition*

a) HL 105-107 and Ex. 22:4-5 both juxtapose the laws of illegal grazing in another's field with the laws of a fire that consumes the grain of a neighboring field.

b) A close juxtaposition between the laws of a miscarriage and the laws of talion are found in both LH 209 ff. and Ex. 21:22 ff.

As the above outline indicates, much of the juridical content and formulation of these laws is pre-Mosaic and hence, pre-Israelite. Thus, the legal collection of Exodus emerges as an integral component of a vast juridical canvas which extended throughout the ancient Near East. All indications point to an eclectic adaptation of native and fringe Mesopotamian legal traditions, which is a testimonial to the extent to which the earliest compilation of biblical laws was indebted to the rich heritage of its Mesopotamian forebears.

An important question remains to be posed: How did Israel come into contact with cuneiform law precisely at this juncture in its history, i.e., the period of its transition from a seminomadic to a settled community? Since there was an overall cuneiform legal background in the Near East at this time, the legal traditions could have reached Israel by several different paths. A very close relationship has already been established between cuneiform material and the patriarchal narratives.[1]) Could the same sources for the Genesis substrata account for some of the underlying legal traditions in the book of Exodus? Were these legal traditions part of the cultural heritage from the patriarchal sojourn in Haran and Palestine during the pre-conquest days? [2]) Or could the Israelites have come in contact with cuneiform

[1]) For the latest presentation of these cultural correspondences, see Speiser, *Genesis* (New York, 1964).

[2]) Cf. R. Kilian, *Literarkritische und Formgeschichtliche Untersuchungen des Heilig-*

sources in some cultural center? [1]) At present it would be rash to propose any one specific solution. Further discoveries may provide further clues to help solve this problem.

In the meantime all that one can safely assume is that there was a general awareness of cuneiform law throughout the entire ancient Near East, and that cuneiform legal traditions played an important role in the early stages of Israelite law. This extra-biblical legacy was integrated, in turn, into the unique religious pattern of law which originated in Israel. This combination of an extra-biblical legacy together with the distinctive Israelite contribution to jurisprudence constituted the latest fusion of second millennium legal collections.

---

keitsgesetzes (Bonn, 1963), pp. 2-3; J. J. Stamm and M. E. Andrew, *The Ten Commandments in Recent Research* (Naperville, 1967), p. 36; and W. F. Albright, *Yahwe and the Gods of Canaan* (New York, 1968), pp. 101, 105.

[1]) H. Cazelles, *Études sur le code d'alliance* (Paris, 1946), pp. 168-183, thinks that Moses, whom he considers to be the actual draftsman of the juridical corpus, was exposed to these various legal traditions while yet in Egypt. A more likely center, however, would be Canaan which probably served as a "melting pot" for cuneiform law. Recent finds at Ugarit and Alalakh have demonstrated that "Canaanite law" itself is largely fringe Mesopotamian law. This was already noted by A. Alt, "Eine neue Provinz des Keilschriftrechts," *WO* 1 (1947), pp. 78-92 = *Kleine Schriften zur Geschichte des Volkes Israel*, Vol. 3 (Munich, 1959), pp. 141-157, who earlier had posited Canaanite sources for the biblical casuistic legal material in *Die Ursprünge des israelitischen Rechts* (Leipzig, 1934) = *Kleine Schriften*, Vol. 1, pp. 278-332. See, however, below, pp. 116-118.

For an indication of the existence of cuneiform literary material in Canaan, note the discovery at Megiddo of a fragment of the Gilgamesh epic written in Akkadian and dating from the Amarna age. See A. Goetze and S. Levy, "Fragment of the Gilgamesh Epic from Megiddo," *'Atiqot* 2 (1959), pp. 121-128.

APPENDIX I

VERSE ARRANGEMENT OF THE LAWS OF THE BOOK OF THE COVENANT

The legal portion of the Book of the Covenant (Ex. 21:12—22:16) has a demonstrable systematic external and internal arrangement of its individual laws and sections which follows the well known method of the concatenation of ideas, key words and phrases, and similar motifs.[1]) An attempt will be made here to show some of the associative reasoning behind the structure and particular development of the various links which together constitute this juridical corpus. The general outline—following the introductory section of 21:2-11, which determines the conditions whereby the respective parties are free to leave their owners, and which is structurally parallel to the intro-

---

[1]) This is a well known feature in the post-biblical literature of the Mishnah and Gemara. Several scholars have independently suggested an associative, external, and ideational ordering of laws in cuneiform collections as well. Cf. M. San Nicolò, *Beiträge zur Rechtsgeschichte im Bereiche der keilschriftlichen Rechtsquellen* (Oslo, 1931), pp. 71-72; W. Eilers, "*Die Gesetzesstele Chammurabis*," *AO* 31, 3/4 (1932), p. 10; G. Boyer, "Introduction bibliographique à l'histoire du droit suméro-akkadien," *AHDO* 2 (1938), p. 72; G. Cardascia, "La codification en assyrie," *RIDA*, 3e série, 4 (1957), pp. 69-71; and J. J. Finkelstein, "Ancient Near Eastern Law," *Encyclopaedia Biblica*, (Heb.), Vol. 5 (Jerusalem, 1968), p. 592.

For the "systematic" arrangement of the laws in LE, see H. Petschow, "Zur 'Systematik' in den Gesetzen von Eschnunna," *Symbolae Iuridicae et Historicae Martino David Dedicatae*, Vol. 2 (Leiden, 1968), pp. 131-143; and R. Yaron, *The Laws of Eshnunna* (Jerusalem, 1969), pp. 52-55.

For the order of the laws in LH, see G. R. Driver and J. C. Miles, *The Babylonian Laws*, Vol. I (Oxford, 1960), pp. 41-53, and Petschow, "Zur Systematik und Gesetzestechnik im Codex Hammurabi," *ZA* 23 (1965), pp. 146-172.

For the Hittite collection (Tablet I), see V. Korošec, "Le problème de la codification dans le domaine du droit hittite," *RIDA*, 3e série, 4 (1957), pp.93-105 (and references to his former study). For Tablet II, see *idem*, "Das Eigentum an Haustieren nach dem hethitischen Gesetzbuch," *Symbolae Koschaker*, pp. 37-49; and R. Haase, "Zur Systematik der zweiten Tafel der hethitischen Gesetze," *RIDA*, 3e série, 7 (1960), pp. 51-54.

For MAL, see G. Cardascia, "La codification en assyrie," *RIDA*, 3e série, 4 (1957), pp. 53-71.

D. Daube, *Codes and Codas in the Pentateuch* (Edinburgh, 1941) = *Studies in Biblical Law* (Cambridge, 1947), pp. 74-101, states that new provisions were joined as an appendix to the compilation, and not worked properly into the collection. See, however, S. E. Loewenstamm, review of A. Goetze, *The Laws of Eshnunna*, in *IEJ* 7 (1957), p. 196, n. 10, and below, p. 110, n. 1.

duction to the Decalogue where the freeing of the Israelites from their Egyptian taskmasters is given prime importance—may be sketched as follows: [1])

I 21:12-27	laws pertaining to crimes committed by one man against another (and one instance of an act of God, vs. 13).
II 21:28-32	laws pertaining to crimes committed by a man's property (an ox) against another man.
III 21:33-36	laws pertaining to damages caused by one man's property (a pit or an ox) against another's property (an ox).
IV 21:37—22:16	laws pertaining to crimes committed by one man (directly or indirectly) against another's property and cases of *force majeure*.

In sum: I—man and an act of God against man, II—property against man, III—property against property, IV—man and *force majeure* against property. In I and II human beings are the victims, in III and IV, property.

I 21:12-27 Laws pertaining to crimes committed by one man against another (and an act of God). This section is ordered according to the following categories:

(a) 21-12:17—a list of five capital offenses (all participially formulated) [1]) highlighting the sanctity of life and body:

(1) vs. 12—general law of homicide (fatal "striking").
vs. 13—accidental homicide (act of God), contrasted to

---

[1]) For several other attempts at discovering some type of prearranged ordering in the laws of Exodus, cf. L. Waterman, "Pre-Israelite Laws in the Book of the Covenant," *AJSL* 38 (1921), pp. 36-54, a somewhat forced reconstruction of the entire corpus into pentads and decads; U. Cassuto, *A Commentary on the Book of Exodus*, Heb. (Jerusalem, 1951), p. 184, and excellent comments on each individual section of laws (here occasionally incorporated); B. Dinur, "The Religious Character of the Cities of Refuge and the Ceremony of Admission into Them," (Heb.), *Eretz-Israel* 3 (1954), p. 137, n. 35; and H. Cazelles, *Études sur le code d'alliance* (Paris, 1946), p. 156, a very brief sketch of the principles behind the ordering of the laws. See recently V. Wagner, *ZAW* 81 (1969), pp. 176-182. Several commentators have attempted to find a link between these laws and the order of the Decalogue, e.g., *Mechilta*, Philo, ibn Ezra, Abarbanel.

There is an interesting correlation between the order of the laws here and that of LH which should be studied further.

For the explication and elaboration of all these laws, reference must constantly be made to the annotations found in ch. V which are here presupposed.

[2]) See Appendix II, p. 118, n. 1.

vss. 12 and 14; no death penalty prescribed; takes refuge at sanctuary (i.e., altar).

vs. 14—premeditated intentional homicide: no refuge allowed.

vss. 15-17—the only three cases where capital punishment is prescibed for a non-fatal offense; these three are equated (penaltywise) with homicide:

vss. 15-16—specific physical actions:

(3) vs. 15—striking of parents.

(4) vs. 16—kidnapping.

(5) vs. 17—physical (?) and/or verbal action: disrespect toward parents. [1])

(b) 21:18-27—a list of five offenses pertaining to assault and battery:

(1) vss. 18-19—introduction of two reponsible parties: "when men quarrel" (previously the action described was entirely one sided); one freeman inflicts an injury on another by "striking;" (but unlike vss. 12 and 15, death does not occur, and there is no death penalty; and unlike vs. 22 the offense is not premeditated); an instrument is mentioned ("stone or fist"); original act (i.e., quarrel) not unlawful.

(2) vss. 20-21—the fatal striking of a slave with an instrument, a "rod;"(up until this verse all cases dealt with freemen); associated with above in lawful nature of original act (i.e., if struck with disciplinary and not homicidal intentions). [2])

(3) vs.22—introduction of a third party, a pregnant woman who, while two men are engaged in a fight (a premeditated act with intent to harm), receives a blow which results either in the destruction of her fetus (which is considered less than life and for which compensation can be made) or in her death, for which the death penalty is prescribed; this penalty talionically formulated is then

---

[1]) For the order of vss. 15-17, cf. the comments of S. D. Luzatto, *Commentary to the Pentateuch* (Tel Aviv, 1965), *ad loc.*, and Cazelles, *op. cit.*, p. 52. Cf. also the descending order of Ex. 20:13-16. In the Septuagint, vss. 16 and 17 are reversed, thus juxtaposing both offenses against parents. Otherwise compare p. 107, n. 1.

[2]) The intent of the culprit is of the utmost importance in many of these laws and determines the severity of the punishment.

followed by a series of talionic rules for other (intentional) unlawful assaults leading to injuries of less than life (in descending order of severity: limb [also listed in descending order of the body: eye, tooth, hand, leg], burn, wound, bruise).

(4-5) vss. 26-27—talion, a penalty, limited to freemen, does not apply to injuries inflicted upon a slave; the slave, however, is manumitted for intentional unlawful assaults upon his body.

II 21:28-32 Laws pertaining to crimes committed by a man's property (an ox) against another man:

vs. 28—ox is not a habitual gorer; (ox put to death).

vss. 29 ff.—ox is a habitual gorer and strikes:

vs. 29—a freeman or woman (ox and owner put to death).

vs. 31—a son or daughter of a freeman (ox and owner put to death; no vicarious talion).

vs. 32—a male or female slave (only ox put to death).

vs. 30—is connected with vs. 22 of section (I) by the key phrase ונתן ... יושת עליו = ישית עליו ונתן.

III 21:33-36 Laws pertaining to damages caused by one man's property (pit or ox) against another's property (ox):

This section is related to (II) in the following ways:

(a) both sections pertain to an ox—here the victim.

(b) both pertain to cases of culpable negligence and the owner's responsibility: ולא ישמרנו (ox - vs. 29) = ולא יכסנו (pit - vs. 33).

(c) key phrase בעל השור (vs. 28) and בעל הבור (vs. 34).

(d) same sequence of non-habitual followed by habitual goring ox—vss. 28-29 and vss. 35-36.

Vss. 33-34 are related to vss. 35-36:

(a) in both the ox is the injured party.

(b) vss. 34 and 36 employ the identical phrase: והמת יהיה לו.

Monetary penalties are introduced (e.g., שלם "to compensate" vss. 34, 36, 37; 22:2, 3, 4, 5, 6, 8, [10], 11, [12], 13, [14], and the payments in vss. 15 and 16). Here is the last mention of any fatal injury (מת)—vss. 34, 35, 36)—thus ending a motif which started in vs. 12 of (I).

IV 21:37—22:16—Laws pertaining to crimes committed by one man (directly or indirectly) against another's property and cases of *force majeure*:

vs. 37—continuation of laws pertaining to oxen—still victims, this time stolen; introduction of key term גנב "to steal" (vss. 37; 22:1, 2, 3, 6, 7, 11).

vss. 1-2a [1])—cases of attempted theft from within house; and introduction of key term מצא "to find" (vss. 1, 3, 5, 6, 7).

vss. 21:37—22:2-3—continuation of monetary penalties.[2])

vss. 4-5—continuation of property offenses (agricultural damages); monetary penalties; internal connection of key homonymic stem בער.

vs. 4—whereas in vs. 3 the man himself is directly responsible for the crime (of theft), here his agent (an ox), which is intentionnally sent by him (שִׁלַּח), is responsible (for illegal grazing which is also a deprivation of property). [3])

vs. 5—indirect case of responsibility: property loss caused by fire; fine is less than vs. 4 (where he must pay from "choicest" produce, i.e., the greater the responsibility, the greater the penalty).

vs. 6—continuation of laws of theft, here loss of mobilia deposited for safekeeping, but culprit, unlike above cases, is unknown; twofold penalty as in vs. 3.

vs. 7—first of three deadlocked legal cases where litigant resorts to oath (ordeal)—cf. vs. 8 (also האלהים) and vs. 10.

vs. 8—key phrase שור, חמור, שה found above in vs. 3 and below in vs. 9: חמור, שור, שה.

vss. 9-12—mishaps to animals deposited for safekeeping:

---

[1]) Ex. 22:1-2a constitutes what appears to be an obvious interpolation which interrupts the natural continuation of the law of Ex. 21:37 and 22:2b-3. It has not yet been sufficiently noted, however, that in the Bible, as well as in the Talmud (cf. D. Halivni (Weiss), *Sources and Traditions*, Heb. [Tel Aviv, 1968], p. 58, and n. 2 on that page, and p. 542, n. 1, for Talmudic and biblical examples), additional comments or associative ideas, i.e., "footnotes," are usually inserted directly within the section pertaining to the relevant subject matter and are not appended at the end as a sort of coda. The remark to be added is included within the text immediately after the sentence which first calls it to mind, and once inserted, the original theme under discussion is then concluded, thus forming a sort of framework about a somewhat obtrusive centerpiece. This device is often found in the narrative sections. See annotations to these verses, esp. p. 86 and n. 10. Cf. also Ex. 23:4-5 which interrupts Ex. 23:3 and 6.

[2]) Twofold penalty for theft; four and fivefold penalty for any additional benefit accruing from the offense, i.e., selling or slaughtering the animal.

[3]) For another possible connection between vss. 4 and 5, see p. 88, n. 4.

vs. 9—same legal terminology as in vs. 6: ... כי יתן איש אל רעהו . . . לשמר.

vs. 10—same legal terminology as in vs. 7: אם לא שלח ידו במלאכת רעהו.

vs. 11—penalty in case of theft even when thief is not found—contrast vss. 3 and 6.

vss. 13-14a—mishap to an animal that is lent; monetary penalty.

vss. 15-16—another "property" offense: case of seduction, where penalty compensates for the monetary loss to the father.[1])

---

1) Cf. Cassuto, *op. cit.*, *ad loc.*

APPENDIX II

CUNEIFORM AND BIBLICAL LEGAL FORMULATIONS

The classification of laws according to their *Gattung* and *Sitz im Leben* was an extension of Gunkel's method of research into the various literary genres of the Bible. The legal material was the last to be studied, but once inaugurated by the studies of Jirku [1]) and Jepsen,[2]) the typological approach gained momentum.[3]) Jirku, basing his investigation on the cuneiform legal collections already known in his day (SL, LH, MAL, HL), stated, "It is an undeniable fact, which comparative study of law teaches us, that legal collections are always composed in a uniform style." [4]) Hence, the composite nature of the legal formulations found in the biblical corpora must be secondary.[5]) For "if Moses had in fact bequeathed to his people a codified law, then he would certainly have composed and promulgated these laws in a single homogeneous style." [6]) On the assumption of such an "iron law," [7]) he proceeded to divide biblical law into ten independent collections based on ten different stylistic formulations present in the Pentateuch.

Now cuneiform legal corpora do show a great deal of homogeneity in formulation, i.e., they are predominantly cast, from the time of LU on, in a casuistic mold: Sum. tukumbi,[8]) Akk. *šumma*,[9]) Hit.

---

[1]) A. Jirku, *Das weltliche Recht im Alten Testament* (Gütersloh, 1927).

[2]) A. Jepsen, *Untersuchungen zum Bundesbuch* (Stuttgart, 1927). He divided the Book of the Covenant into four sources: (1) Hebrew משפטים, which have the closest contacts with ancient Near Eastern law (= Jirku's "if" formulation and Alt's "casuistic" law), (2) Israelite משפטים, which are laws established in Israel by God (= Jirku's "participial" formulation), (3) religious and moral prohibitions, (4) cultic stipulations.

[3]) In that same year S. Mowinckel, *Le Décalogue* (Paris, 1927), investigated the *Sitz im Leben* of the Decalogue. According to him (p. 129) the JE narratives of exodus and Sinai are a reproduction of a New Year festival, enthronement and covenant renewal festival. In this festival he finds the setting for the Decalogue.

[4]) Jirku, *op. cit.*, p. 32.

[5]) *Ibid.*, pp. 32-33.

[6]) *Ibid.*, p. 52.

[7]) *Ibid.*, p. 160.

[8]) A. Poebel, *Grundzüge der sumerischen Grammatik* (Rostock, 1923), p. 423.

[9]) E. A. Speiser, "A Note on the Derivation of *šumma*," *JCS* 1 (1947), pp.

takku.[1]) However, a closer examination of the laws already known in Jirku's day, supplemented by additional legal material available today, completely disproves the existence of such an "iron law" which he posited for all legal corpora.[2]) Indeed, even LH contains several exceptions to the traditional *šumma*-form: [3])

36) "In no case is the field, orchard, or house belonging to a soldier, a commissary, or a feudatory salable" (Akk. *ul inaddin*).

38) "In no case may a soldier, a commissary, or a feudatory deed any of his field, orchard, or house belonging to his fief to his wife or daughter, and in no case may he assign (them) for an obligation of his" (Akk. *ul išaṭṭar... ul inaddin*).

39) "He may deed to his wife or daughter any of the field, orchard, or house which he purchases and accordingly owns, and he may assign (them) for an obligation of his" (Akk. *išaṭṭar...inaddin*).

40) "A hierodule, a merchant, and a feudatory extraordinary may sell his field, orchard, and house, with the purchaser assuming the feudal obligations of the field, orchard, and house which he purchases" (Akk. *inaddin...illak*).

187) "The (adopted) son of a chamberlain, a palace servant, or the (adopted) son of a votary, may never be reclaimed" (Akk. *ul ibbaqqar*).

321-328; T. J. Meek, "The Asyndeton Clause in the Code of Hammurabi," *JNES* 5 (1946), pp. 64-72.

[1]) E. A. Hahn, "Some Hittite Words in *ta-*," *Language* 12 (1936), pp. 108-120, and "The Shift of a Hittite Conjunction from the Temporal to the Conditional Sphere," *Language* 20 (1944), pp. 91-107.

[2]) For a study of the various stylistic formulations employed in Mesopotamian law, see now H. Petschow, "Zu den Stilformen antiker Gesetze und Rechtssammlungen," *ZSS* 82 (1965), pp. 24-38.

[3]) The translations here are taken from *ANET*. Although there is considerable controversy over the exact meaning of many of the technical terms found in these passages, this appendix wishes to concentrate solely on the style of drafting—hence no further comments will be made concerning the difficult legal vocabulary. The difference in the drafting of these five laws was already noted by G. R. Driver and J. C. Miles, *The Babylonian Laws*, Vol. I (Oxford, 1960), p. 125. According to R. A. F. Mackenzie, "The Formal Aspect of Ancient Near Eastern Law," *The Seed of Wisdom: Essays in Honour of T. J. Meek*, ed. W. S. McCullough (Toronto, 1964), p. 42, these apodictic laws were most likely royal decrees of Hammurabi that were incorporated by the legal draftsmen, yet not recast in casuistic style. For another attempt to resolve these five exceptions to the casuistic formulation, see Petschow, *op. cit.*, pp. 33-34. The apodictic formulation of MAL A 40 has been called by P. Koschaker, *Quellenkritische Untersuchungen zu den "altassyrischen Gesetzen"* = *MVAG* 26 (1921), Vol. 3, p. 12, "a police regulation" (Polizeivorschrift).

Other exceptions to the traditional casuistic formulation of legal prescriptions are found in MAL A 40, 41, 47 (all containing a mixture of formulations), 57-59, B 6, F 2; HL 48, 50-52, 54-56, 167, 178, 181-186; (and the Neo-Babylonian Laws).

The coexistence of several different legal formulations in a single compilation is now very clearly demonstrated by LE.[1]) Yaron, in a recent study, divides these laws typologically into five separate categories.[2]) These categories together with characteristic examples for each formulation are listed below: [3])

1. *Prices and Wages*

   1) 1 *kùr še'um a-na* 1 *šiqil kaspim* "1 *kor* of barley is (priced) at 1 shekel of silver."

   4) *idi* ^{iṣ}*eleppim* 1 *kurrum*^{um} 2 *qa ù* [1 *sū*]*t* 1 *qa idi malāḫḫim ka-la! u*$_4$*-mi i-re-de-ši* "The hire of a boat is 2 *qa* per *kor* (of capacity), and 1 *sūt* (and) 1 *qa* is the hire of the boat man. He shall drive it the whole day."

(Tariffs are similarly formulated in HL 178-183, 185 A.)

2. *šumma awīlum*

   This casuistic formulation predominates here, as it does in all other compilations including Tablet VII of *ana ittišu.* (The only outstanding exception is the Neo-Babylonian laws which consistently employ the *awīlum ša*-formulation.)

   43) *šum-ma awīlum ú-ba-an awīlim it-ta-ki-ís* 2/3 *ma-na kaspam išaqqal* "If a man severs a(nother) man's finger he shall pay 2/3 of a mina of silver."

3. *The split protasis*

   17) *mār awīlim a-na bīt e-mi-im ter-ḫa-tam li-bi-il-ma šum-ma i-na ki-la-al-li-in iš-te-en a-na ši-im-tim it-ta-la-ak kaspum a-na be-lí-šu-ma i-ta-a-ar* "Should a member of the *awīlum* class bring bride-money to the house of (his) father-in-law—if one of the two deceases, the silver shall revert to its owner." (Cf. LE 9.) [4])

---

[1]) 20 of the 59 laws do not employ the standard *šumma*-formulation.

[2]) R. Yaron, "Forms in the Laws of Eshnunna," *RIDA*, 3e série, 9 (1962), pp. 137-153, and *The Laws of Eshnunna* (Jerusalem, 1969), pp. 59-71. Cf. Petschow, *op. cit.*, p. 36, n. 70.

[3]) The translations are those of Goetze, *ANET.*

[4]) Cf. Petschow, *op. cit.*, pp. 35-36. For a slightly different reading of this law, see B. Landsberger, "Jungfräulichkeit," *Symbolae Iuridicae et Historicae Martino David Dedicatae*, Vol. 2 (Leiden, 1968), p. 72, (LE 9).

4. *The apodictic command* [1])

16) *mār awīlim la zi-zu ù wardum ú-ul iq-qí-a-ap* "To a coparcener or a slave a loan requiring security shall not be furnished." (Cf. LE 15.)

5. *awīlum ša* [2])

13) *awīlum ša i-na bītim ša muškēnim i-na bītim i-na mu-uṣ-la-lim iṣ-ṣa-ab-ba-tu* 10 *šiqil kaspam išaqqal* "A man who is caught in the house (on the premises) of a *muškēnum*, inside the building, at high noon, shall pay 10 shekels of silver."

Yaron finds the *Sitz im Leben* of these formulations in:

1) the actual life of the market
2) the law courts
3) the same as 2 but further refined
4) the naked command of a ruler
5) the sphere of the proclamation

Hence, it becomes quite evident that the *šumma awīlum* casuistic formulation is only one—though the predominant one—of many ways in which cuneiform legal prescriptions are cast. Yaron correctly concludes that the general uniformity of LH is the work of its draftsman, who selected one common mode of formulation, *šumma awīlum*, and imposed it upon the entire collection. LE, on the other hand, was not subject to a similar process of levelling.[3]) However, his further inference—"There is no reason to assume that any one legislator would express his rules in very different ways" [4])—is subject to question and further investigation. The same legislator may very well employ different types of formulations since the stylistic formulation may be directly related to the content of the law.

---

[1]) Cf. also LH 36, 38, 39, 40, 187; MAL A 40 (several clauses), F 2; HL 48, 50-51 (second clause), 56. Cf. Petschow, *op. cit.*, pp. 31-32. Yaron, *loc. cit.*, also lists LE 51-52 in this category, but they are actually examples of the *awīlum ša*-formulation.

[2]) Cf. also LE 12, 19, 51, 52; MAL A 40:42-45, 58-60, 61-62; 41:6-10; 47:7-13; HL 50-52; and all of NB. It is never employed in LH. Another similar formulation with *ša* alone appears in LE 12 and 13 (second case); MAL A 40:63-65, 68-76, 89-93; and HL (*kuiš*) 185:15 and 186. Cf. Petschow, *op. cit.*, pp. 29-31.
The biblical analogues to these formulations are איש אשר and אשר (Ex. 21:13).

[3]) Yaron, *RIDA*, 3e série, 9 (1962), p. 137. This levelling process becomes quite apparent when even the tariff sections of LH are conditionally formulated.

[4]) *Ibid.*, p. 138. Cf. J. C. Miles and O. R. Gurney, "The Laws of Eshnunna," *ArOr* 17^2 (1949), p. 176, who come to similar conclusions in their attempt to prove that the Eshnunna collection is not a law code.

The predominance of the *šumma* impersonal conditional formulation of these legal collections categorizes them typologically with traditional medical and omen compilations. Landsberger was the first to call attention to their similarity,[1] and he was followed in turn by Kraus,[2] Cazelles,[3] Gadd,[4] and Finkelstein,[5] all of whom have made further comments upon their stylistic affinities.

Contextually, casuistic law consists of a protasis, which contains the statement of the case (i.e., what is),[6] and an apodosis, which sets forth the solution (i.e., what shall be). An analysis of this type of law has recently been published by Mackenzie.[7] He points out that casuistic law (1) is strictly pragmatic and "amoral," i.e., appeals to no religious or ethical axioms; (2) does not express a formal obligation or prohibition, but rather contains a warning of likely consequences if an act is committed; (3) is incumbent upon the judges, the agents of the legislator who carry out its enactments, rather than the individual; and (4) must, as a corollary of (3), indicate a solution, i.e., in penal law —the penalty. Since this type of law determines a remedy, he calls it "remedial law." It "is a crystallization of jurisprudence based on the exercise of already customary law" (p. 37). Its origin is to be sought among the Sumerians.

The biblical counterpart [8] of this traditional Near Eastern formulation of law forms its protasis with the particle כי,[9] which introduces the main statement of the case, followed by a verb in the imperfect. Secondary and subordinate clauses are introduced by אם or או

[1] B. Landsberger, "Die Eigenbegrifflichkeit der babylonischen Welt," *Islamica* 2 (1926), pp. 370-371.

[2] F. R. Kraus, "Ein Sittenkanon in Omenform," *ZA* 43 (1936), pp. 77-113, shows how this form was adapted in the late Assyrian period to convey ideas of moral correctitude and their consequences. On p. 81, he categorizes the various classifications and characteristics of this literary form. In a much later study devoted to law, "Ein zentrales Problem des altmesopotamischen Rechts: Was ist der Codex Ḫammu-rabi," *Genava* 8 (1960), p. 288, he calls the legal compilations "wissenschaftliche Literatur" and "Omenliteratur;" cf. also p. 293.

[3] H. Cazelles, *Études sur le code de l'alliance* (Paris, 1946), p. 110.

[4] C. J. Gadd, *Ideas of Divine Rule in the Ancient East* (London, 1948), p. 79.

[5] J. J. Finkelstein, "Ammiṣaduqa's Edict and the Babylonian 'Law Codes', " *JCS* 15 (1961), p. 104.

[6] According to E. Gerstenberger, "Covenant and Commandment," *JBL* 84 (1965), p. 43, n. 24, "Case law . . . looks back to a potentially committed crime. . . ."

[7] Mackenzie, "The Formal Aspect of Ancient Near Law," *Meek Vol.*, pp. 35-37.

[8] For the various styles of biblical legal formulations, see Cazelles, *op. cit.*, pp. 109-114.

[9] For the legal use of Akk. *kī* "if" in subordinate clauses, see NB 6:26; cf. W. von Soden, *Grundriss der akkadischen Grammatik* (Rome, 1952), p. 215.

(Ex. 21:31, 36) and are also followed by a verb in the imperfect.[1]) Alt, in his classic form-critical study of Israelite law,[2]) states that the "hervortretende israelitische Volksbewusstsein" never appears in casuistic law, which is similar in both formal structure and content to other Near Eastern law and regulates only the relations between man and man.[3]) The prototype of biblical casuistic law, according to Alt, originated in the lay courts of the Canaanite population of Palestine and was adopted by the Israelites after they entered the land of Canaan.[4]) Though his form analysis of biblical law is correct, this writer does not share his view concerning the historical development of the casuistic material.[5]) For as de Vaux has correctly commented, "It is mere guesswork to speculate about the formulation of Canaanite law as long as we possess none of the legislative texts which embodied it, and the juridical texts of Alalakh and Ras Shamra suggest that it hardly differed at all from other Oriental laws. The fact remains that the Mesopotamian codes are compiled in casuistic form, and part of the Israelite law closely resembles them in style."[6]) Casuisti-

---

[1]) Both Heb. כי and אם are subsumed under Akk. *šumma*. The usual structural outline of cuneiform casuistic formulations consists of a sequence of the simple preterit, *t*, and present-future tenses. (The *t*-form, representing a stage secondary to the situation mentioned in the preterit clause, is followed by a present-future tense that contains the result or punishment. For a survey and discussion of the different explanations of this *t*-form, see Driver and Miles, *Babylonian Laws*, Vol. II, pp. 350-361.) Interestingly enough, biblical casuistic legislation also follows a threefold sequential pattern of tenses (i.e., imperfect, perfect, imperfect). After כי, a verb in the imperfect tense is found which is the functional analogue to the preterit following *šumma*. (In LH the preterit is predominately used; only occasional exceptions are to be found in a permansive, LH 126, or a present, LH 132, 138. The same is true of LE; cf. the list of verb tenses with *šumma* in A. Goetze, *The Laws of Eshnunna* [New Haven, 1956], pp. 179-180.) Could the imperfect tense here be another reflex of the original East-Semitic preterit found in biblical Hebrew and thus be morphologically parallel to the Akk. preterit? (Some of the better known examples of the preterit in Hebrew are (1) its use after the so-called conversive *wav*; (2) its occurence after the particles אז and טרם; (3) in proper names, e.g., ישמעאל.) The perfect tense, here functionally similar to the Akk. *t*-form, indicates a subsequent stage, and is followed, in turn, by a true imperfect tense (cf. Akk. present-future) which prescribes the action that is to be taken.

[2]) A. Alt, *Die Ursprünge des israelitischen Rechts* (Leipzig, 1934) = *Kleine Schriften zur Geschichte des Volkes Israel*, Vol. I (Munich, 1959), pp. 278-332.

[3]) *Ibid.*, p. 291.

[4]) *Ibid.*, p. 295. Cf. M. Noth, *Exodus*, trans. J. S. Bowden (Philadelphia, 1962), p. 174.

[5]) Cf. F. C. Fensham, "The Possibility of the Presence of Casuistic Legal Material at the Making of the Covenant at Sinai," *PEQ* 93 (1961), pp. 143-146.

[6]) R. de Vaux, *Ancient Israel*, trans. J. McHugh (New York, 1961), p. 146.

cally formulated laws were part of Mesopotamia's legacy to Israel.[1])

The origin and uniqueness of apodictic law, on the other hand, is a much more difficult problem. According to Alt, it has a "spezifisch israelitische Anschauung" [2]) that is "volksgebunden israelitisch und gottgebunden jahwistisch," [3]) and its origin is to be found in a cultic

---

Interestingly enough, Alt himself was one of the first to show the spread of cuneiform law to the Fertile Crescent. See his study, "Eine neue Provinz des Keilschriftrechts," *WO* 1 (1947), pp. 78-92 = *Kleine Schriften*, Vol. III (Munich, 1959), pp. 141-157.

[1]) The participial formulation, though present in Egyptian and Babylonian curse literature (cf. Cazelles, *op. cit.*, pp. 110-112, and J. G. Williams, "Concerning One of the Apodictic Formulas," *VT* 14 [1964], pp. 484-489), is quite unique to biblical legislation. Whereas Alt classifies it within the apodictic category of law and relates it to the curses of Dt. 27 (*Kleine Schriften*, Vol. I, pp. 308 ff.), W. Kornfeld, *Studien zum Heiligkeitsgesetz* (Wien, 1952), following Mackenzie, "The Forms of Israelite Law" (unpublished dissertation [Rome, 1949]), classifies it within the sphere of casuistic legislation. Kornfeld states that "das apodiktische Recht eine Handlung verlangt bzw. verbietet, welche die angesprochene Person erst setzen bzw. unterlassen soll, während die Gesetze der Partizipialform, völlig analog jenen der übrigen kasuistischen Formulierungen, der gerichtlichen Obrigkeit vorschreiben, welche Strafe verhängt werden müsse, nachdem die Tat begangen wurde" (p. 49); cf. also pp. 50, 54. For a similar view, see Gerstenberger, *Wesen und Herkunft des "apodiktischen Rechts"* (Neukirchen, 1965), p. 24. Cf. H. Gese, "Beobachtungen zum Stil alttestamentlicher Rechtssätze," *ThLZ* 85 (1960), pp. 147-150, who calls the participial formulation a "verkürzende Nachahmung . . . der kasuistischen Rechtsformulierung;" R. Kilian, "Apodiktisches und kasuistisches Recht im Licht ägyptischer Analogien," *BZ* 7 (1963), pp. 185-202, does not consider it to be in the same category as apodictic law since apodictic law does not consider consequences. (Cf. also his remarks in *Literarkritische und Formgeschichtliche Untersuchungen des Heiligkeitsgesetzes* [Bonn, 1963], pp. 1-2.) See, however, the remarks of Williams, "Addenda to 'Concerning One of the Apodictic Formulas'," *VT* 15 (1965), pp. 113-115, where he concludes that it is still closer to absolute prohibitions and commandments than to casuistic law. (Cf. also his first article mentioned above, "Concerning One of the Apodictic Formulas," *VT* 14 [1964], 484-489.) Both Noth, *loc. cit.*, and G. Fohrer, "Das sogenannte apodiktisch formulierte Recht und der Dekalog," *KuD* 11 (1965), pp. 49-74, conclude that the participial formulation is a compromise between the apodictic and casuistic formulations. According to the former (p. 179), "The brevity and absolute nature of these sentences stands close to the apodictic formulations; the explicit and emphatic description of the legal consequences (the condemnation to death) is reminiscent of the casuistic formulation." As for the latter (p. 72), it is "kasuistisches Recht in apodiktischer Formulierung." But rather than call it law he defines it as "Lebens- und Verhaltensregel in apodiktischer Formulierung" (p. 73; cf. p. 67). For a different view, cf. H. G. Reventlow, "Kultisches Recht im Alten Testament," *ZTK* 60 (1963), p. 282 (where he attacks Gese's position, *loc. cit.*), and pp. 287 ff.

[2]) Alt, *op. cit.*, p. 309.

[3]) *Ibid.*, p. 323.

setting.[1]) Objections to some of Alt's conclusions were first registered by Mowinckel and Landsberger. Whereas the former stated that the employment of this type of law in the cult does not necessarily imply—or in any way prove—its cultic origin, but only its "kultische Verwendung," [2]) the latter questioned Alt's distinction between two different categories of law: "Die Meinung von Alt kann ich mich nicht anschliessen. Grade der lebendige Predigtstil motiviert den Wechsel in der Satzform." [3]) However, no further evidence for this "living sermonic style" was offered.

Meek, in turn, objected to the uniqueness of apodictic law in Israel when he drew attention to its presence in extra-biblical legal compilations.[4]) Since, however, the cuneiform examples which he cited are all formulated in the third-person rather than in the second-person,[5]) they cannot be taken as exact parallels to the direct address of biblical apodictic law.

Mendenhall was the first to turn his attention to this aspect of the problem when he compared the second-person singular apodictic legislation to Hittite treaties.[6]) He was followed in turn by Heine-

---

[1]) Alt included the participial formulations, the curse dodecalogue of Dt. 27:15-26, the sexual offenses of Lev. 18, and the Decalogue all within the same sphere of apodictic law. K. H. Rabast, *Das apodiktische Recht im Deuteronomium und im Heiligkeitsgesetz* (Berlin, 1949), extended Alt's thesis to the book of Deuteronomy and the Holiness Code of Leviticus.

For several reviews of the studies of apodictic law, see Reventlow, "Kultisches Recht im Alten Testament," *ZTK* 60 (1963), pp. 267-304; Fohrer, "Das sogenannte apodiktisch formulierte Recht und der Dekalog," *KuD* 11 (1965), pp. 49-74; and E. Nielsen, *Die zehn Gebote* (Copenhagen, 1965), pp. 49-64.

[2]) Mowinckel, "Zur Geschichte des Dekalogs," *ZAW* 55 (1937), p. 220, n. 1. Cf. this same note (starting on p. 219) for further criticism of Alt's thesis.

[3]) Landsberger, "Die babylonischen Termini für Gesetz und Recht," *Symbolae Koschaker* (Leiden, 1939), p. 223, n. 19. Koschaker in "Keilschriftrecht," *ZDMG* 89 (1935), p. 23, n. 4, accepts Alt's distinction.

[4]) Meek, *Hebrew Origins* (New York, 1960), p. 72, and *ANET*, p. 183, n. 24. (For a complete list, see above, p. 115, n. 1.) Cf., however, the objections of I. Rapaport, "The Origins of Hebrew Law," *PEQ* 73 (1941), pp. 158-167, and J. J. Stamm, "Dreissig Jahre Dekalogforschung," *ThR* 27 (1961), p. 216.

[5]) Mackenzie, "Formal Aspect," *Meek Vol.*, p. 41: "This is the impersonal so-called 'jussive' formulation: 'So-and-so shall do this' or 'such-and-such shall be done.' Although this corresponds grammatically to the apodosis of the casuistic formulation, . . . yet it definitely comes under the heading of apodictic law, being formally a command or prohibition for the future, not the solution of an existing case. For example, Deut. 17:6. . . . This formulation is specially prevalent in the ceremonial legislation of the Priestly Code." Cf. Gerstenberger, *Wesen und Herkunft des "apodiktischen Rechts,"* pp. 66-70.

[6]) G. E. Mendenhall, *Law and Covenant in Israel and the Ancient Near East* (Pittsburgh, 1955), reprinted from *BA* 17 (1954), pp. 49-76, 126-146; cf. also his

mann [1]) and Baltzer.[2]) Gerstenberger,[3]) however, was unable to accept the covenant treaty-form as the origin of this type of law. After first presenting some very telling objections to Alt's proposed cultic origin for apodictic law,[4]) he states that the treaty formulation does not proscribe calumny, misdemeanors, etc., in and of itself for all people, but is limited to the actions of a specific vassal toward a specific king; the corresponding Israelite laws, on the other hand, are "an sich und absolut gültig" and are valid for all men and for all time. Furthermore, the general form of prohibition cannot be derived from a specialized treaty-form, and the characteristic sanction clauses appended to treaty stipulations are all but absent here.[5]) Gerstenberger does find, however, a very close relationship between apodictic legislation and wisdom literature, which in both form and content closely resemble the commandments in the legal sections of the Bible.[6]) For the ultimate *Sitz im Leben* of these commandments he posits the "Sippenethos."[7]) He does admit,

---

article, "Covenant," *IDB*, Vol. I, pp. 714-723. For a collection of "thou shalt (not)" laws in treaties, see D. J. McCarthy, *Treaty and Covenant* (Rome, 1963) = *Analecta Biblica* 21, p. 249; most of the list pertains to political matters.

[1]) G. Heinemann, *Untersuchungen zum apodiktischen Recht* (Hamburg, 1958).

[2]) K. Baltzer, *Das Bundesformular*, 2. Auflage (Neukirchen, 1964).

[3]) *Loc. cit.*

[4]) *Ibid.*, pp. 64, 90-95, and "Covenant and Commandment," *JBL* 84 (1965), pp. 47-48.

[5]) *Idem*, *Wesen und Herkunft*, pp. 100-105. Cf. also *JBL* 84 (1965), pp. 46-51, and McCarthy, *op. cit.*, pp. 159-160.

[6]) *Ibid.*, pp. 117 ff., and *JBL* 84 (1965), pp. 49-50, where he also notes the contribution made by J. Fichtner, *Die altorientalische Weisheit in ihrer israelitisch-jüdischen Ausprägung* (= *BZAW* 62 [1933]), in pointing out the affinity between the two genres. Gerstenberger concludes that "we are led to recognize a fundamental phenomenon in the Ancient Near East: the expression of moral precepts in collections of commandments and prohibitions which aim at the preservation of basic social institutions" (p. 50). He then compares this genre of "instruction" to Egyptian literature. On this last point of comparison, cf. Cazelles, *Études*, pp. 112 ff., and "Loi israélite," *SDB*, Vol. V, pp. 515-516. This view is also favored by McCarthy, *op. cit.*, p. 160.

[7]) *Wesen und Herkunft*, pp. 110-117, and *JBL* 84 (1965), pp. 50-51. He cites Jer. 35:6-7 as an example of this "family ethos." See K. Elliger, "Das Gesetz Leviticus 18," *ZAW* 67 (1955), pp. 1-25 = *Kleine Schriften zum Alten Testament* (Munich, 1966), pp. 232-259, for a comparable opinion concerning the apodictic formulas in Lev. 18. Fohrer, "Das sogenannte apodiktisch formulierte Recht und der Dekalog," *KuD* 11 (1965), pp. 51, 74, assumes that this type of law stems "aus dem (halb)nomadischen Lebensbereich." Reventlow, "Kultisches Recht im Alten Testament," *ZTK* 60 (1963), p. 283, however, rejects Gerstenberger's assumed *Sitz im Leben* for the apodictic formulation and reverts back to a cultic explanation: "Das apodiktische Recht gottesdienstlich verkündigtes Recht

nevertheless, that no direct proof for such an origin is available.[1])

Though wisdom literature is characterized by a direct address, and does afford the closest analogue to the apodictic commandment, Cazelles thinks that it belongs to a completely different literary genre: "Dans le code de l'alliance et la Décalogue il est réellement impératif et comminatoire.... Au contraire dans les livres de Sagesse, c'est une exhortation; il s'agit du bien de l'individu auquel on s'adresse et que l'on veut protéger contre ses entraînements." [2]) One is addressed to the conscience and is obligatory, since it is the will of God; the other is addressed to prudence and the practical, pragmatic nature of man.[3])

Gevirtz has compared West Semitic inscriptional curses to this type of legislation. Apodictically formulated prohibitions are found in these inscriptions in the second-person (though rarely) and third-person singular.[4]) He concludes that "it is this prohibitive-preventive function which invests the curse with a legal air." [5]) He does not claim, however, that the origin of this formulation is to be found in the curse-motif.

Before an attempt is made to reach some sort of conclusion, a brief

---

darstellt, das auf dem israelitischen Bundesfest mündlich zum Vortrag gekommen ist. . . ." Cf. also W. Beyerlin, "Die Paränese im Bundesbuch und ihre Herkunft," *Gottes Wort und Gottes Land*: *Festschrift für H. W. Hertzberg* (Göttingen, 1965), pp. 21 ff. W. Richter, *Recht und Ethos* (Munich, 1966), p. 117, prefers "Gruppenethos" to Gerstenberger's "Sippenethos." A. Jepsen, "Beiträge zur Auslegung und Geschichte des Dekalogs," *ZAW* 79 (1967), pp. 302-303, refers both the Decalogue and Sinaitic tradition back to the clans and the elders.

[1]) *Wesen und Herkunft*, p. 115.

[2]) Cazelles, *Études*, p. 113. Kornfeld, *Studien zum Heiligkeitsgesetz*, pp. 59-60, shares this opinion and adds that apodictic law also differs from wisdom literature in that it is addressed to a real rather than to a fictitious individual ("my son"). Cf. also Kilian, "Apodiktisches und kasuistisches Recht," *BZ* 7 (1963) p. 195, who finds much in common between the two, but classifies wisdom literature as a separate literary genre.

[3]) Y. Kaufmann, *The Religion of Israel*, trans. M. Greenberg (Chicago, 1960), pp. 316-317, in his discussion of Torah and wisdom literature makes the following distinctions: "For Torah and prophecy, the source of morality is the will of God, and the basis of moral obligation is the command of God communicated through prophecy. . . . Biblical wisdom literature is pervaded with the idea that morality stems from wisdom. Its source is not prophetic revelation, but understanding and discernment. . . . The one speaks in categorical imperatives; the other appeals to prudence and utilitarian considerations. One is based on faith and trust; the other—on observation and experience." (This last sentence, omitted in the original translation, is to be found in Vol. V, p. 559 of the Hebrew edition of תולדות האמונה הישראלית [Tel Aviv, 1955].) Cf. Kilian, *op. cit.*, p. 195.

[4]) S. Gevirtz, "West Semitic Curses and the Problem of the Origins of Hebrew Law," *VT* 11 (1961), pp. 137-158.

[5]) *Ibid.*, p. 140.

discussion of the nature of apodictic law is in order.[1]) Once again reference is made to Mackenzie's study: "An apodictic article of law lays a command directly on the subject, obliging him to do (or refrain from doing) some particular action judged by the legislator to be desirable (or harmful). It may be identical in form with a precept given by a superior to an individual inferior, but what distinguishes law from precept, at least in intention, is the universalized character of the former. In time, its validity is unlimited; it is intended to be always in force, 'until further notice.' In extent, it is equally unrestricted (apart, of course, from express limitations); all those are bound by it who are responsible for the action or omission prescribed and who come under the authority of its author. In its pure form, apodictic law does not contemplate the hypothesis of disobedience or contumacy. Its enunciation, unlike that of casuistic law, makes no provision for the statement of a penalty." [2])

Now this type of formulation—whatever its ultimate origin may be—is found in the wisdom, curse, and treaty genres of extra-biblical literature. We thus are in full agreement with Gerstenberger, who states: "Im Alten Orient existierte eine Gattung von überwiegend negativ, in der 2. Person Singular formulierten Regeln, die sich in mancherlei Literaturgattungen erhalten hat und deren Urform völlig mit der Form der aus dem Alten Testament bekannten Prohibitive übereinstimmt." [3]) Hence, wisdom literature employs this style to express moral and ethical exhortations for the benefit of the individual; inscriptional curses direct prohibitionary warnings (without any moral content) against the individual; treaties, in turn, stipulate vassal obligations of fealty on the part of the inferior (individual or realm) to the superior power.

However, this direct address formulation, while found in several

---

[1]) For studies of biblical legal formulations, see Cazelles, *loc. cit.*; Mackenzie, "The Forms of Israelite Law;" and Kornfeld, *loc. cit.* Cf. also Gese, "Beobachtungen zum Stil alttestamentlicher Rechtssätze," *ThLZ* 85 (1960), pp.147-150. Other studies of apodictic law have been made by Rabast, *Das apodiktische Recht im Deuteronomium und im Heiligkeitsgesetz*, and H. Schmökel, "Biblische 'Du-Sollst' Gebote und ihr historischer Ort," *ZSS*, *kanon.*, Abt. 36 (1950), pp. 365-390 ("Tempelbelehrung"). For Mesopotamian law, see p. 113, n. 2.

[2]) Mackenzie, "Formal Aspect," *Meek Vol.*, p. 39. Cf. Gerstenberger, *Wesen und Herkunft*, pp. 26-27.

[1]) Gerstenberger, *op. cit.*, p. 137. For the possibility of an independent development of the same forms, cf. Stamm, "Dreissig Jahre Dekalogforschung," *ThR* 27 (1961), p. 215. For the difference between *form* and *intent*, however, see Stamm and M. E. Andrew, *The Ten Commandments in Recent Research* (Naperville, 1967), pp. 62, 67. See also pp. 44-75, for a review of the problem of apodictic law.

literary genres, is not present in any of the cuneiform juridical corpora, but is unique to biblical legal compilations. Though these apodictic formulations deal primarily with moral and religious commandments,[1] the question still remains as to why they are part and parcel of biblical jurisprudence and are noticeably absent from all Mesopotamian corpora. Once again a unique aspect of a society is explicable only in terms of its entire complex.[2] The Israelite society was founded on a convenantal agreement based on the will of God, who expressed his demands in covenant law declared publicly to the entire community. By making his will personally and directly known to man, an I-Thou relationship is established which characterizes the unique feature of this newly founded nation. Moral and religious prescriptions are directed to each and every member of this nation in categorical imperatives.[3] The constitution for this new polity (i.e., covenant law) incorporates and emphasizes both customary civil law (i.e., casuistic formulations) and moral-ethical admonitions together with religious-cultic obligations (i.e., apodictic formulations). However, whereas casuistic law deals with precedent and what is, apodictic commandments express what must and ought to be.[4] It addresses man a priori as to what is right or wrong.[5] It is prescriptive not descriptive, prospective not retrospective, absolute not relative, categorically imperative and obligatory not conditional, subjective and personal ("Thou shalt [not]," i.e., I-Thou) not objective and impersonal ("If a man...") [6]—God's will not man's. Its purpose is to shape and form a society, not to state cases and provide remedies. No time limit is placed on its demands. Sanctions are absent; yet it appeals to the conscience of the individual for constant obedience and fidelity. It is preventive and precautionary, obliging the responsibility of every member of the community. Hence, to impersonal legislation is added personal obligation and commandment; to the formula is added feeling; to the intellect, the heart; and to the letter of the law is added

---

1) Their primary non-juristic character has been emphasized by Cazelles, *op. cit.*, p. 125; Gerstenberger, *loc. cit.*; and Fohrer, *loc. cit.* The juridical aspect, of course, is not absent from many of these commands, e.g., Ex. 23:1-3, 6 ff.

2) See above, p. 1.

3) Kornfeld, *Heiligkeitsgesetz*, pp. 56, 61.

4) Gerstenberger, *op. cit.*, pp. 25-26.

5) Cf. Fohrer, *op. cit.*, p. 52.

6) The only apodictic regulations found in Mesopotamian corpora—all of which are of an amoral, strictly legal nature—are those of the impersonal third-person jussive formulation. See above, p. 119, n. 5. Cf. Kornfeld, *op. cit.*, p. 58, and Gerstenberger, *op. cit.*, pp. 66-70.

the spirit and values of metajuristic principles—together they constitute the charter of the people of Israel.

The apodictic commandment, the I-Thou relationship found only in biblical legal corpora, would seem to be Israel's contribution to the "theology of jurisprudence." [1])

---

[1]) This choice phrase was coined by W. Seagle, *History of Law* (New York, 1946), p. 24.

For a discussion of this problem, see now S. M. Paul, "Types of Formulation in Biblical and Mesopotamian Law," (Heb.), *Leshonenu* 34 (1970), pp. 257-266.

BIBLIOGRAPHY

ABARBANEL, D. I., *Commentary to the Torah.* (Heb.). Tel-Aviv, 1960.

ALBRIGHT, W. F., *History, Archaeology and Christian Humanism.* New York, 1964.

——, *Yahweh and the Gods of Canaan.* New York, 1968.

ALT, A., *Die Ursprünge des israelitischen Rechts.* Leipzig, 1934 = *Kleine Schriften zur Geschichte des Volkes Israel.* Vol. I. Munich, 1959, pp. 278-332.

——, "Das Verbot des Diebstahls im Dekalog," *Kleine Schriften.* Vol. I, pp. 333-340.

——, "Zur Talionsformel," *ZAW*, N.F. 11 (1934), pp. 303-305 = *Kleine Schriften.* Vol. I, pp. 341-344.

——, "Eine neue Provinz des Keilschriftrechts," *WO* 1 (1947), pp. 78-92 = *Kleine Schriften.* Vol. III. Munich, 1959, pp. 141-157.

——, *Essays on Old Testament History and Religion.* Trans. R. A. Wilson. New York, 1967.

The Ancient Near East in Pictures Relating to the Old Testament (= *ANEP*). Ed. J. Pritchard. Princeton, 1954.

Ancient Near Eastern Texts Relating to the Old Testament (= *ANET*). Ed. J. Pritchard. Second edition. Princeton, 1955.

ARTZI, P., "Two Pre-Hammurabi Codes Newly Discovered," (Heb.). *BIES* 16, 1/2 (1951), pp. 30-37; *ibid.*, 16, 3/4, pp. 69-70.

——, "The Laws of Ur-Nammu", (Heb.). *Beth Mikra* 13 (1962), pp. 68-77.

——, "Law," (Heb.). *Lexicon Miqrai.* Vol. II. Tel Aviv, 1965, pp. 581-610.

BAENTSCH, B., *Das Bundesbuch.* Halle, 1892.

——, *Exodus-Leviticus-Numeri.* (*Handkommentar zum Alten Testament*). Göttingen, 1903.

BALTZER, K., *Das Bundesformular.* 2. Auflage. Neukirchen, 1964.

BARTON, G. A., *The Royal Inscriptions of Sumer and Akkad.* New Haven, 1929.

BAUER, J. B., "Könige und Priester, ein heiliges Volk (Exodus XIX, 6)," *BZ* 2 (1958), pp. 283-286.

BEER, G., *Exodus.* (*Handbuch zum Alten Testament*). Tübingen, 1939.

BEGRICH, J., "*Berit*," *ZAW* 60 (1944), pp. 1-11 = *Gesammelte Studien zum Alten Testament.* Munich, 1964 (= *Theologische Bücherei* 21), pp. 55-66.

BENEDICT, R., *Patterns of Culture.* New York, 1960.

BEYERLIN, W., *Herkunft und Geschichte der ältesten Sinaitraditionen.* Tübingen, 1961.

——, *Origins and History of the Oldest Sinaitic Traditions.* Trans. S. Rudman. Oxford, 1965.

——, "Die Paränese im Bundesbuch und ihre Herkunft," *Gottes Wort und Gottes Land: Festschrift für H. W. Hertzberg zum 70. Geburtstag.* Göttingen, 1965, pp. 9-29.

BICKERMAN, E. J., "Couper une alliance," *AHDO* 5 (1950), pp. 133-156.

——, "Two Legal Interpretations of the Septuagint," *RIDA*, 3e série, 3 (1956), pp. 81-104.

DE BOER, P. A. H., "Some Remarks on Exodus XXI:7-11," *Orientalia Neerlandica.* Leiden, 1948, pp. 162-166.

BOISSIER, A., "Lipit Ishtar législateur," *Babyloniaca* 9 (1926), pp. 19-22.

BORGER, R., "*niṣirti bārûti*, Geheimlehre der Haruspizin," *BiOr* 14 (1957), pp. 190-195.

——, "Das Problem der *ʿapiru* ('Habiru')," *ZDPV* 74 (1958), pp. 121-132.

——, "Kleinigkeiten zur Textkritik des Kodex Ḫammurapi," *Or* 31 (1962), pp. 364-366.

——, *Babylonisch-Assyrische Lesestücke*. 3 Vols. Rome, 1963.

——, "Marduk-zākir-šumi I und der Kodex Ḫammurapi," *Or* 34 (1965), pp. 168-169.

BOTTÉRO, J., *Le problème des Ḫabiru à la 4e rencontre assyriologique internationale* (= *Cahiers de la société asiatique* 12). Paris, 1954.

BOYER, G., "*Ṣupur X kīma kunukkišu*," *Symbolae ad iura orientis antiqui pertinentes Paulo Koschaker dedicatae*. Leiden, 1938 (= *Studia et Documenta* 2), pp. 208-218 = *Mélanges* (Paris, 1965), pp. 3-13.

——, "Les articles 7 et 12 du code de Ḫammurabi," *Publications de l'institut de droit romain* 6 (1950), pp. 155-171 = *Mélanges*, pp. 15-28.

——, "De la science juridique et de sa méthode dans l'ancienne mésopotamie," *Semitica* 4 (1951-1952), pp. 5-11 = *Mélanges*, pp. 45-51.

——, "Sur quelques emplois de la fiction dans l'ancien droit oriental, *RIDA*, 3e série, 1 (1954), pp. 73-100 = *Mélanges*, pp. 87-109.

——, *Archives royales de Mari* (= *ARM*). Vol. 8: *Textes juridiques*. Paris, 1958.

——, "Introduction bibliographique à l'histoire du droit suméro-akkadien," *AHDO* 2 (1938), pp. 63-110.

——, and Szlechter, E., "Introduction bibliographique à l'histoire du droit suméro-akkadien II," *RIDA*, 3e série, 3 (1956), pp. 41-79.

BRICHTO, H. C., *The Problem of "Curse" in the Hebrew Bible* = (*Journal of Biblical Literature Monograph Series*, Vol. 13). Philadelphia, 1963.

VAN BUREN, E. D., "The *ṣalmê* in Mesopotamian Art and Religion," *Or* 10 (1941), pp. 65-92.

——, "The Rod and Ring," *ArOr* 17^2 (1949), pp. 434-450.

CARDASCIA, G., "Les droits cunéiformes," *Histoire des institutions et des faits sociaux des origines à l'aube du Moyen Age*. Paris, 1956, pp. 17-68.

——, "La codification en Assyrie," *RIDA*, 3e série, 4 (1957), pp. 53-71.

——, "La transmission des sources juridiques cunéiformes," *RIDA*, 3e série, 7 (1960), pp. 31-50.

——, "Bibliography of Biblical Law," *RHD* 41 (1963), pp. 504-511; 42 (1964), pp. 506-511; 43 (1965), pp. 512-516; 44 (1966), pp. 507-513. (For continuation of series, see M. H. Prévost.)

——, *Les lois assyriennes*. Paris, 1969.

——, Review of R. Yaron, *The Laws of Eshnunna* in *RHD* 47 (1969), pp. 474-478.

CASPARI, W., "Heimat und soziale Wirkung des alttestamentlichen Bundesbuchs," *ZDMG* 83 (1929), pp. 97-120.

CASSUTO, U., *A Commentary on the Book of Exodus*. (Heb.). Jerusalem, 1951.

CAZELLES, H., *Études sur le code d'alliance*. Paris, 1946.

——, "Loi israélite," *Supplément au dictionnaire de la Bible* (= *SDB*). Vol. V. Ed. Pirot. Paris, 1952-1953, pp. 497-530.

——, "Hébreu, Ubru, Ḫapiru," *Syria* 35 (1958), pp. 198-217.

——, "Pentateuque," *SDB*. Fascicules 38 (1963) and 39 (1964), pp. 708-858.

——, "Les origines du Décalogue," *Eretz Israel*. Vol.9 = *W. F. Albright Volume*. Jerusalem, 1969, pp. 14-19.

CHAVEL, C. B., *Commentary on the Torah by Moshe ben Nachman* (*Nachmanides*). Vol. I. Jerusalem, 1959.

Chicago Assyrian Dictionary (= *CAD*).

CHIERA, E., *Old Babylonian Contracts* = *University Museum Publication of the Babylonian Section*. Vol. VIII/2. Philadelphia, 1922.

——, *Joint Expedition with the Iraq Museum at Nuzi*. Vol. III: *Exchange and Security Documents*. Paris, 1931.

——, *Joint Expedition with the Iraq Museum at Nuzi.* Vol. IV: *Proceedings in Court.* Philadelphia, 1934.

——, *Joint Expedition with the Iraq Museum at Nuzi.* Vol. V: *Mixed Texts.* Philadelphia, 1934.

The City Invincible: A Symposium on Urbanization and Cultural Development in the Ancient Near East Held at the Oriental Institute of the University of Chicago. December 4-7, 1958. Eds. C. H. Kraeling and R. M. Adams. Chicago, 1960.

Civil, M., "New Sumerian Law Fragments," *Studies in Honor of Benno Landsberger on His Seventy Fifth Birthday, April 21, 1965.* Chicago, 1965, pp. 1-12.

Clay, A. T., *Miscellaneous Inscriptions in the Yale Babylonian Collection. Yale Oriental Series: Babylonian Texts.* Vol. I. New Haven, 1915.

Cody, A., "When is the Chosen People Called a *Gôy*," *VT* 14 (1964), pp. 1-6.

Cohen, B., *Jewish and Roman Law.* 2 Vols. New York, 1966.

Cowley, A., *The Aramaic Papyri of the Fifth Century B.C.* Oxford, 1923.

Cruveilhier, P., *Introduction au code d'Hammourabi.* Paris, 1937.

——, *Commentaire du code d'Hammourabi.* Paris, 1938.

Daube, D., *Codes and Codas in the Pentateuch.* Edinburgh, 1941 = *Studies in Biblical Law.* Cambridge, 1947, pp. 74-101.

——, "*Lex Talionis,*" *Studies in Biblical Law.* Cambridge, 1947, pp. 102-153.

——, "Direct and Indirect Causation in Biblical Law," *VT* 11 (1961), pp. 246-269.

David, M., *Der Rechtshistoriker und seine Aufgabe.* Leiden, 1937.

——, "The Manumission of Slaves under Zedekiah," *OTS* 5 (1948), pp. 63-79.

——, "The Codex Hammurabi and its Relation to the Provisions of the Law in Exodus," *OTS* 7 (1950), pp. 149-178.

——, and Ebeling, E., "Assyrische Rechtsurkunden," *ZVRW* 44 (1929), pp. 305-381.

Deimel, P., "Die Reformtexte Urukaginas," *Or* 2 (1920), pp. 3-31.

Diamond, A. S., "An Eye for an Eye," *Iraq* 19 (1957), pp. 151-155.

van Dijk, J., "L'hymne à Marduk avec intercession pour le roi Abīʾešuḫ," *MIO* 12 (1966), pp. 57-74.

Dinur, B., "The Religious Character of the Cities of Refuge and the Ceremony of Admission into Them," (Heb.). *Eretz-Israel* 3 (1954), pp. 135-146.

Dossin, G., "L'inscription de fondation de Iaḫdun-Lim, roi de Mari," *Syria* 32 (1955), pp. 1-28.

Draffkorn, A. E., "*Ilāni/Elohim,*" *JBL* 76 (1957), pp. 216-224.

Driver, G. R. and Miles, J. C., *The Assyrian Laws.* Oxford, 1935.

——, *The Babylonian Laws.* Vol. I: *Legal Commentary.* Oxford, 1960. Vol. II: *Text and Transliteration.* Oxford, 1960.

Driver, S. R., *The Book of Exodus.* Cambridge, 1918.

Ebeling, E., "*Talīm,*" *AfO* 5 (1928-1929), pp. 218-219.

Edzard, D. O., *Die "zweite Zwischenzeit" Babyloniens.* Wiesbaden, 1957.

Eerdmans, B. D., *The Religion of Israel.* Leiden, 1947.

Ehrlich, A. B., *Randglossen zur hebräischen Bibel.* Vol. I. Leipzig, 1908.

——, *Miqrah KiFshuto.* (Heb.). Vol. 1. Berlin, 1898.

Eichrodt, W., *Theology of the Old Testament.* Vol. I. Trans. J. A. Baker. Philadelphia, 1961.

——, "Bund und Gesetz," *Gottes Wort und Gottes Land: Festschrift für H. W. Hertzberg zum 70. Geburtstag.* Göttingen, 1965, pp. 30-49.

Eilers, W., "Die Gesetzesstele Chammurabis," *AO* 31, 3/4. Leipzig, 1932.

Eissfeldt, O., *The Old Testament: An Introduction.* Trans. P. R. Ackroyd. New York, 1965.

——, "Das Gesetz ist zwischeneingekommen. Ein Beitrag zur Analyse der Sinai-Erzählung, Ex. 19-34," *ThLZ* 91 (1966) pp. 1-6 = *Kleine Schriften.* Vol. 4. Tübingen, 1968, pp. 209-214.

——, "Die Komposition der Sinai-Erzählung Ex. 19-34," *FF* 40 (1966), pp. 213-215 = *Kleine Schriften*. Vol. 4. Tübingen, 1968, pp. 231-237.

ELLIGER, K., "Das Gesetz Leviticus 18," *ZAW* 67 (1955), pp. 1-25 = *Kleine Schriften zum Alten Testament. Zu seinem 65. Geburtstag am 7. März 1966*. Munich, 1966, pp. 232-259.

FALK, Z. W., "Exodus XXI:6," *VT* 9 (1959), pp. 86-88.

——, *Hebrew Law in Biblical Times*. Jerusalem, 1964.

——, "Law," (Heb.). *Lexicon Miqrai*. Vol. II. Tel Aviv, 1965, pp. 610-625.

——, *Current Bibliography of Hebrew Law*. Nos. 1-8. Tel-Aviv, 1966-1969.

FALKENSTEIN, A., "Philologisches zum Gesetzbuch Lipit Ishtar von Isin," *Or* 19 (1950), pp. 103-111.

——, "Ur Nammu Law Code," *Or* 23 (1954), pp. 49-51.

——, *Die neusumerischen Gerichtsurkunden*. Three Vols. *Abhandlungen der Bayerischen Akademie der Wissenschaften. Phil.-Hist. Klasse*. N.F. 39, 40, 44. Munich, 1956-1957.

——, and VON SODEN, W., *Sumerische und akkadische Hymnen und Gebete*. Zurich, 1953.

FEIGIN, S. J., "The Law Book of Yitro," (Heb.). *Sefer Hashanah* 7 (1944), pp. 89-125.

——, "Homicide in the Ancient Oriental Law and in Babylonian-Assyrian Contracts," (Heb.). *Hatekufa* 32-33 (1947), pp. 740-765.

FENSHAM, F. C., "New Light on Exodus 21:6 and 22:7 from the Laws of Eshnunna," *JBL* 78 (1959), pp. 160-161.

——, "The *Mišpāṭîm* in the Covenant Code." Unpublished dissertation. John Hopkins, 1960.

——, "Ex. XXI:18-19 in the Light of Hittite Law 10," *VT* 10 (1960), pp. 333-335.

——, "The Possibility of the Presence of Casuistic Legal Material at the Making of the Covenant at Sinai," *PEQ* 93 (1961), pp. 143-146.

——, "Widow, Orphan, and the Poor in Ancient Near Eastern Legal and Wisdom Literature," *JNES* 21 (1962), pp. 129-139.

——, "*ʿD* in Ex. XXII:12," *VT* 12 (1962), pp. 337-339.

——, "Maledictions and Benedictions in Ancient Near Eastern Vassal-Treaties and the Old Testament," *ZAW* 74 (1962), pp. 1-9.

——, "Common Trends in Curses of the Near Eastern Treaties and *Kudurru*-Inscriptions with Maledictions of Amos and Isaiah," *ZAW* 75 (1963), pp. 155-175.

——, "Clauses of Protection in Hittite Vassal-Treaties and the Old Testament," *VT* 13 (1963), pp. 133-143.

——, "Aspects of Family Law in the Covenant Code in Light of Ancient Near Eastern Parallels," *Dine Israel*. Ed. Z. W. Falk. Vol. 1. Jerusalem, 1969, pp. V-XIX.

FINKELSTEIN, J. J., "Ammiṣaduqa's Edict and the Babylonian 'Law Codes'," *JCS* 15 (1961), pp. 91-104.

——, "Some New *Misharum* Material and its Implications," *Studies in Honor of Benno Landsberger on His Seventy-Fifth Birthday, April 21, 1965*. Chicago, 1965, pp. 233-246.

——, "Sex Offenses in Sumerian Laws," *JAOS* 86 (1966), pp. 355-372.

——, Unpublished paper on the "Goring Ox."

——, "An Old Babylonian Herding Contract and Genesis 31:38 f.," *JAOS* 88 (1968), pp. 30-36.

——, "Ancient Near Eastern Law," (Heb.). *Encyclopaedia Biblica*. Vol. 5. Jerusalem, 1968, pp. 588-614, 1138-1140.

——, "A Late Old Babylonian Copy of the Laws of Hammurapi," *JCS* 21 (1967), pp. 39-48.

——, "The Laws of Ur Nammu," *JCS* 22 (1968-1969), pp. 66-82.

FISH, T., "Law and Religion in Babylonia and Assyria," *Judaism and Christianity*. Vol. III. Ed. E. J. J. Rosenthal. London, 1938, pp. 29-44.

FOHRER, G., "Das sogenannte apodiktisch formulierte Recht und der Dekalog," *KuD* 11 (1965), pp. 49-74.

FORBES, R., *Studies in Ancient Technology*. Vol. III. Leiden, 1965.

FRANKENA, R., "The Vassal-Treaties of Esarhaddon and the Dating of Deuteronomy," *OTS* 14 (1965), pp. 122-154.

FRANKFORT, H., *Kingship and the Gods. A Study of Ancient Near Eastern Religion as Integration of Society and Nature*. Chicago, 1948.

——, *The Problem of Similarity in Ancient Near Eastern Religions*. Oxford, 1951.

——, *The Art and Architecture of the Ancient Orient*. Baltimore, 1955.

FREEDMAN, D. N., "Divine Commitment and Human Obligation: The Covenant Theme," *Interpretation* 1964, pp. 3-15.

FRIEDRICH, J., *Die hethitischen Gesetze*. Leiden, 1959.

GADD, C. J., *Ideas of Divine Rule in the Ancient East*. London, 1948.

GELB, I. J., Review of *Die hethitischen Gesetze* by J. Friedrich. *JSS* 7 (1962), pp. 98-100.

——, "The Ancient Mesopotamian Ration System," *JNES* 24 (1965), pp. 230-243.

GEMSER, B., "The Importance of the Motive Clause in Old Testament Law," *Supplements to VT* 1 (1953), pp. 50-66.

GERSTENBERGER, E., Review of *Treaty and Covenant* by D. J. McCarthy. *JBL* 83 (1964), pp. 198-199.

——, *Wesen und Herkunft des "apodiktischen Rechts"*. Neukirchen, 1965.

——, "Covenant and Commandment," *JBL* 84 (1965), pp. 38-51.

GESE, H., "Beobachtungen zum Stil alttestamentlicher Rechtssätze," *ThLZ* 85 (1960), pp. 147-150.

——, "The Structure of the Decalogue," *Fourth World Congress of Jewish Studies*. Vol. 1. Jerusalem, 1967, pp. 155-159.

——, "Der Dekalog als Ganzheit betrachtet," *ZTK* 64 (1967), pp. 121-138.

GEVIRTZ, S., "West Semitic Curses and the Problem of the Origins of Hebrew Law," *VT* 11 (1961), pp. 137-158.

GINSBERG, H. L., "The Brooklyn Museum Aramaic Documents," *JAOS* 74 (1954), pp. 153-162.

GOETZE, A., "The *t*-Form of the Old Babylonian Verb," *JAOS* 56 (1936), pp. 297-334.

——, "Mesopotamian Laws and the Historian," *JAOS* 69 (1949), pp. 115-120.

——, Translation of the Laws of Eshnunna. *ANET*, pp. 161-163.

——, Translation of the Hittite Laws. *ANET*, pp. 188-197.

——, *The Laws of Eshnunna*. New Haven, 1956.

——, "On § 163, 164/5 and 176 of the Hittite Code," *JCS* 20 (1966), pp. 128-132.

——, and Levy, S., "Fragment of the Gilgamesh Epic from Megiddo," *ʿAtiqot* 2, (1959), pp. 121-128.

GOLDMAN, S., *From Slavery to Freedom*. London, 1958.

GORDON, C., "אלהים in its Reputed Meaning of *Rulers, Judges*," *JBL* 54 (1935), pp. 134-144.

——, "Hos. 2:4-5 in the Light of New Semitic Inscriptions," *ZAW* 54 (1936), pp. 277-280.

——, "The Status of Women Reflected in the Nuzi Tablets," *ZA* 43 (1936), pp. 146-169.

——, "Strata of Society in CH," *Joshua Starr Memorial Volume. Studies in History and Philology = Jewish Social Studies. Publications* No. 5. New York, 1953, pp. 17-28.

——, *Ugaritic Textbook*. 3 Vols. Rome, 1965.

Gottstein, M. H., "Du sollst nicht stehlen," *ThZ* 9 (1953), pp. 394-395.

Gray, M. P., "The Ḫâbirū-Hebrew Problem," *HUCA* 29 (1958), pp. 135-202.

Greenberg, M., "Hebrew *s^egullā*: Akkadian *sikiltu*," *JAOS* 71 (1951), pp.172-174.

——, *The Ḫab/piru*. New Haven, 1955.

——, "The Biblical Conception of Asylum," *JBL* 78 (1959), pp. 125-132.

——, "נסה in Exodus 20:20 and the Purpose of the Sinaitic Theophany," *JBL* 79 (1960), pp. 273-276.

——, "Some Postulates of Biblical Criminal Law," *Yehezkel Kaufmann Jubilee Volume*. Ed. M. Haran. Jerusalem, 1960, pp. 5-28.

——, "Another Look at Rachel's Theft of the Teraphim," *JBL* 81 (1962), pp. 239-248.

——, "Avenger of Blood," *IDB*. Vol. I, p. 321.

——, "Banishment," *IDB*. Vol. I, p. 346.

——, "Blood Guilt," *IDB*. Vol. I, pp. 449-450.

——, "City of Refuge," *IDB*. Vol. I, pp. 638-639.

——, "Crimes and Punishments," *IDB*. Vol. I, pp. 733-744.

——, "Lecture Notes to Exodus."

Gurney, O. R., *The Hittites*. Baltimore, 1962.

——, and S. N. Kramer.,"Two Fragments of Sumerian Laws," *Studies in Honor of Benno Landsberger on His Seventy-Fifth Birthday, April 21, 1965*. Chicago, 1965, pp. 13-19.

Güterbock, H. G., "Authority and Law in the Hittite Kingdom," *JAOS*, Supplement 17 (1954), pp. 16-24.

Haase, R., "Zur Systematik der zweiten Tafel der hethitischen Gesetze," *RIDA*, 3e série, 7 (1960), pp. 51-54.

——, "Körperliche Strafen im altorientalischen Recht," *RIDA*, 3e série, 10 (1963), pp. 55-75.

——, *Einführung in das Studium keilschriftlicher Rechtsquellen*. Wiesbaden, 1965.

——, "Die Behandlung von Tierschäden in den Keilschriftrechten," *RIDA*, 3e série, 14 (1967), pp. 11-65.

Haelvoet, M., "La théophanie du Sinai. Analyse littéraire des récits d'Ex. XIX-XXIV," *Ephemerides Theologicae Lovanienses* 29 (1953), pp. 374-397.

Hahn, E. A., "Some Hittite Words in *ta-*," *Language* 12 (1936), pp. 108-120.

——, "The Shift of a Hittite Conjunction from the Temporal to the Conditional Sphere," *Language* 20 (1944), pp. 91-107.

Halivni (Weiss), D., *Sources and Traditions*. (Heb.). Tel Aviv, 1968.

Hallo, W. W , "The Royal Inscriptions of Ur: A Typology," *HUCA* 33 (1962), pp. 1-43.

——, "Royal Hymns and Mesopotamian Unity," *JCS* 17 (1963), pp. 112-118.

Haran, M., "The Book of the Covenant," (Heb.). *Encyclopaedia Biblica*. Vol. 5. Jerusalem, 1968, pp. 1087-1091.

Harner, P. B., "Exodus, Sinai, and Hittite Prologues," *JBL* 85 (1966), pp. 233-236.

Harrelson, W. J., "Law in the Old Testament," *IDB*. Vol. III, pp. 77-89.

——, "Ten Commandments," *IDB*. Vol. IV, pp. 569-573.

Harris, R., "The *nadītu* Laws of the Code of Hammurapi in Praxis," *Or* 30 (1961), pp. 163-169.

Hawkes J. and Wooley, L., *Prehistory and the Beginnings of Civilization = History of Mankind*. Vol. I. New York, 1963.

Heinemann, G., *Untersuchungen zum apodiktischen Recht*. Hamburg, 1958.

Heinisch, P., *Das Buch Exodus*. Bonn, 1934.

Held, M., "A Faithful Lover in an Old Babylonian Dialogue," *JCS* 15 (1961), pp. 1-26.

Hempel, J., "Gottesgedanke und Rechtsgestaltung in Altisrael," *ZST* 8 (1931), pp. 377-395.

Hillers, D. R., *Treaty Curses and the Old Testament Prophets* (= *Biblica et Orientalia* 16). Rome, 1964.

Hoftijzer, J., "Ex. XXI:18," *VT* 7 (1957), pp. 388-391.

Horst, F., "Der Diebstahl im Alten Testament," *Studien zur Geschichte und Kultur des nahen und fernen Ostens: Paul Kahle zur 60. Geburtstag.* Leiden, 1935, pp. 19-28 = *Gottes Recht*, pp. 167-175.

——, "Recht und Religion im Bereich des Alten Testaments," *EvTh* 16 (1956), pp. 49-75 = *Gottes Recht: Gesammelte Studien zum Recht im AT.* Munich, 1961, pp. 260-291.

Huffmond, H. B. and Parker, S. B., "A Further Note on the Treaty Background of Hebrew *Yāda*ʿ," *BASOR* 184 (1966), pp. 36-38.

Humbert, P., "Étendre la main," *VT* 12 (1962), pp. 383-395.

ibn Ezra, A., see *Miqraoth Gᵉdoloth.*

ibn Ganah, Y., see M. Wilensky, *Sefer Hariqma ab Jona ibn Ganah.* (Heb.). Vol. 1. Jerusalem, 1964.

van Imschoot, P., "L'alliance dans l'ancien Testament," *NRTh* 75 (1952), pp. 785-805.

The Interpreter's Dictionary of the Bible (= *IDB*). 4 Vols. Ed. G. A. Buttrick. New York, 1962.

Iwry, S., "והנמצא—A Striking Variant Reading in 1QIsª," *Textus* 5 (1966), pp. 34-43.

Jacob, E., "Die altassyrischen Gesetze und ihr Verhältnis zu den Gesetzen des Pentateuch," *ZVRW* 41 (1925), pp. 319-387.

Jacobsen, T., "Early Political Development in Mesopotamia," *ZA* 52 (1957), pp. 91-140.

——, "An Ancient Mesopotamian Trial for Homicide," *Studia Biblica et Orientalia.* Vol. III. *Oriens Antiquus.* Rome, 1959 = *Analecta Biblica* 12, pp. 130-150.

Jean, C. F., "Nouveaux contrats de Larsa," *RA* 26 (1929), pp. 104-107.

Jepsen, A., *Untersuchungen zum Bundesbuch.* Stuttgart, 1927.

——, "Die 'Hebräer' und ihr Recht," *AfO* 15 (1945-1951), pp. 55-68.

——, "*Amaʰ* und *Schiphchaʰ*," *VT* 8 (1958), pp. 293-297, 425.

——, "Berith. Ein Beitrag zur Theologie der Exilzeit," *Verbannung und Heimkehr. W. Rudolph zum 70. Geburtstag.* Tübingen, 1961, pp. 161-179.

——, "Beiträge zur Auslegung und Geschichte des Dekalogs," *ZAW* 79 (1967), pp. 277-304.

——, "Israel und das Gesetz," *ThLZ* 93 (1968), pp. 85-94.

Jirku, A., *Das weltliche Recht im Alten Testament.* Gütersloh 1927.

Kapah, D., *Rabbenu Saadia Gaon's Commentary to the Pentateuch.* (Heb.). Jerusalem. 1963.

Kaufmann, Y., *Toldoth Haʾ Emunah HaYisreʾelith.* (Heb.). Vols. 2, 3, 6. Tel Aviv, 1955.

——, *Sefer Yehoshua*ʿ. (Heb.). Jerusalem, 1959.

——, *The Religion of Israel.* Trans. M. Greenberg. Chicago 1960.

Kilian, R. "Apodiktisches und kasuistisches Recht im Licht ägyptischer Analogien," *BZ* 7 (1963), pp. 185-202.

——, *Literarkritische und Formgeschichtliche Untersuchungen des Heiligkeitsgesetzes.* Bonn, 1963.

Klíma, J., "Au sujet de nouveaux textes juridiques de l'epoque prehammurapienne," *ArOr* 16 (1947-1949), pp. 326-333.

——, "La base religieuse et éthique de l'ordre social dans l'orient ancien," *ArOr* 16 (1947-1949), pp. 334-356.

——, "Einige Bemerkungen zur Bedeutung der 'nicht juristischen' Bestandteile der altbabylonischen Gesetzeswerke," *JJP* 5 (1951), pp. 161-186.

——, "New Discoveries of Legal Documents from Pre-Hammurapian Times," *ArOr* 19^{1-2} (1951), pp. 37-59.

——, "Zu den neuentdeckten Gesetzesfragmenten von Ur-Nammu," *ArOr* 21 (1953), pp. 442-447.

——, Review of *The Babylonian Laws* by G. R. Driver and J. C. Miles. *BiOr* 11 (1954), pp. 107-112.

——, "Über neuere Studien auf dem Gebiete des Keilschriftrechtes I," *ArOr* 18^{1-2} (1950), pp. 525-538.

——, "Über neuere Studien auf dem Gebiete des Keilschriftrechtes II," *ArOr* 18^{4} (1950), pp. 351-353.

——, "Über neuere Studien auf dem Gebiete des Keilschriftrechtes III," *ArOr* 20 (1952), pp. 539-571.

——, "Über neuere Studien auf dem Gebiete des Keilschriftrechtes IV," *ArOr* 21 (1953), pp. 604-640.

——, "Über neure Studien auf dem Gebiete des Keilschriftrechtes V," *ArOr* 26 (1958), pp. 224-242.

——, "Bibliographisches zum Keilschriftrecht I," *JJP* 6 (1952), pp. 153-184.

——, "Bibliographisches zum Keilschriftrecht II," *JJP* 7-8 (1953-54), pp. 295-356.

——, "Bibliographisches zum Keilschriftrecht III," *JJP* 9-10 (1955-56), pp. 431-475.

——, "Bibliographisches zum Keilschriftrecht IV," *JJP* 11-12 (1957-58), pp. 194-261.

——, "Bibliographisches zum Keilschriftrecht V," *JJP* 13 (1961), pp. 269-290.

——, "Zur Bibliographie der Keilschriftrechtsforschung," *BiOr* 13, 3/4 (1956), pp. 106-108.

——, Review of "Keilschriftrecht" by V. Korošec. *BiOr* 22 (1965), pp. 284-287.

——, "Bibliographisches zu dem Keilschriftrechten VI," *JJP* 15 (1965), pp. 367-396.

——, "Zu einigen Problemen der altmesopotamischen Gesetzgebung," *Festschrift für Wilhelm Eilers*. Wiesbaden, 1967, pp. 107-121.

——, "Quelques reflexions sur les droits de l'antiquité," *ArOr* 37 (1969), pp. 76-81.

KNUDTZON, J. A., *Die El-Amarna-Tafeln*. Vol. I. Leipzig, 1907.

KORNFELD, W., *Studien zum Heiligkeitsgesetz*. Wien, 1952.

KOROŠEC, V., *Hethitische Staatsverträge. Ein Beitrag zu ihrer juristischen Wertung*. Leipzig, 1931.

——, "Das Eigentum an Haustieren nach dem hethitischen Gesetzbuch," *Symbolae ad iura orientis antiqui pertinentes Paulo Koschaker dedicatae*. Leiden, 1939 (= *Studia et Documenta* 2), pp. 37-49.

——, "Le problème de la codification dans le domaine du droit hittite," *RIDA*, 3e série, 4 (1957), pp. 93-105.

——, "Le code de Hammurabi et les droits antérieurs," *RIDA*, 3e série, 8 (1961), pp. 12-27.

——, "Keilschriftrecht," *Handbuch der Orientalistik*, 1. Abt. Ergänzungsband 3: *Orientalisches Recht*. Leiden, 1964, pp. 49-219, 466-478.

——, "Gesetze," *Reallexikon der Assyriologie*. Vol. 3. Berlin, 1966, pp. 243-297.

——, "Ueber die neuesten sumerischen Gesetzesfragmente aus Ur," *BiOr* 25 (1968) pp. 286-289.

KOSCHAKER, P., *Rechtsvergleichende Studien zur Gesetzgebung Ḫammurapis, Königs von Babylon*. Leipzig, 1917.

——, "Neue babylonisch-assyrische Rechtsdenkmäler," *ZSS* 41 (1920), pp. 278-296.

——, *Quellenkritische Untersuchungen zu den "altassyrischen Gesetzen"*. Leipzig, 1921 = *MVAG* 26, Vol. 3.

——, *Neue keilschriftliche Rechtsurkunden aus der el-Amarna-Zeit* (= *NKRA*). *Abhandlungen der Sächsischen Akademie der Wissenschaften. Philologisch-Historische Klasse* 39. Nr. 5. Leipzig, 1928.

——, "Forschungen und Ergebnisse in den keilschriftlichen Rechtsquellen," *ZSS* 49 (1929), pp. 188-201.

——, *Über einige griechische Rechtsurkunden aus den östlichen Randgebieten des Hellenismus. Abhandlungen der Sächsischen Akademie der Wissenschaften. Philologisch-Historische Klasse* 42, Nr. 1. Leipzig, 1931.

——, "Cuneiform Law," *Encyclopedia of the Social Sciences*. Vol. 9. New York, 1932, pp. 211-219, 263-264.

——, "Fratriarchat in Keilschriftrechten," *ZA* 41 (1933), pp. 1-89.

——, Review of *Die Gesetzesstele Chammurabis* by W. Eilers. *ZSS* 53 (1933), pp. 605-607.

——, "Keilschriftrecht," *ZDMG* 89 (1935), pp. 1-39.

——, "Göttliches und weltliches Recht nach den Urkunden aus Susa. Zugleich ein Beitrag zu ihrer Chronologie," *Or* 4 (1935), pp. 38-80.

——, "Was vermag die vergleichende Rechtswissenschaft zur Indogermanenfrage beizusteuern," *Germanen und Indogermanen: Volkstum, Sprache, Heimat, Kultur. Festschrift für Hermann Hirt*. Ed. Helmuth Arntz. Vol. I. Heidelberg, 1936, pp. 145-153.

——, and Ungnad, A., *Hammurabi's Gesetz*. Vol. VI. Leipzig, 1923.

Kraeling, E. G., *The Brooklyn Museum Aramaic Papyri*. New Haven, 1953.

Kramer, S. N., "Ur Nammu Law Code," *Or* 23 (1954), pp. 40-48.

——, Translation of Lipit-Ishtar Lawcode. *ANET*, pp. 159-161.

——, "Sumerian Theology and Ethics," *HTR* 49 (1956), pp. 45-61.

——, *The Sumerians*, Chicago, 1963.

Kraus, F. R., "Ein Sittenkanon in Omenform," *ZA* 43 (1936), pp. 77-113.

——, "Codex Ḫammurabi IV:32-44," *WZKM* 51 (1948-1952), pp. 173-177.

——, *Ein Edikt des Königs Ammi-Ṣaduqa von Babylon*. Leiden, 1958 (= *Studia et Documenta ad Iura Orientis Antiqui Pertinentia* 5).

——, "Ein zentrales Problem des altmesopotamischen Rechts: Was ist der Codex Ḫammu-rabi," *Genava* 8 (1960), pp. 283-296.

——, "Altmesopotamisches Lebensgefühl," *JNES* 19 (1960), pp. 117-132.

——, "Ein Edikt des Königs Samsu-Iluna von Babylon," *Studies in Honor of Benno Landsberger on His Seventy-Fifth Birthday, April 21, 1965*. Chicago, 1965, pp. 225-231.

——, Review of *Baghdader Mitteilungen*. Vol. 2. Berlin, 1963. *BiOr* 22 (1965), pp. 287-293.

Kuhl, C., "Neue Dokumente zum Verständnis von Hos. 2:4-15," *ZAW* 52 (1934), pp. 102-109.

Kutsch, E., *Salbung als Rechtsakt im alten Testament und im alten Orient* (= *BZAW* 87). Berlin, 1963.

——, "Gesetz und Gnade," *ZAW* 79 (1967), pp. 18-35.

Labat, R., *Le caractère religieux de la royauté assyro-babylonienne*. Paris, 1939.

Lacheman, E. R., *Harvard Semitic Series* (= *HSS*). Vol. 19: *Family Law Documents*. Cambridge, 1962.

Lacquer, R., "Formen geschichtlichen Denkens im alten Orient und Okzident," *Neue Jahrbücher für Wissenschaft und Jugendbildung* 7 (1931), pp. 489-505.

Laessøe, J., "On the Fragments of the Hammurabi Code," *JCS* 4 (1950), pp. 173-187.

——, "Literacy and Oral Tradition in Ancient Mesopotamia," *Studia Orientalia Ioanni Pedersen Septuagenario*. Copenhagen, 1953, pp. 205-218.

LAMBERT, M., "Les 'réformes' d'Urukagina," *RA* 50 (1956), pp. 169-184.

——, Review of "Les anciennes codifications en Mésopotamie" by E. Szlechter. *RA* 53 (1959), pp. 42-47.

——, and TOURNAY, R.-J., "La statue B de Gudéa," *RA* 45 (1951), pp. 49-66.

LAMBERT, W. G., "Morals in Ancient Mesopotamia," *JEOL* 15 (1957-1958), pp. 184-196.

——, "Nebuchadnezzar King of Justice," *Iraq* 27 (1965), pp. 1-11.

——, "A New Look at the Babylonian Background of Genesis," *JTS* 16 (1965), pp. 288-300.

LANDSBERGER, B., "Die Eigenbegrifflichkeit der babylonischen Welt," *Islamica* 2 (1926), pp. 355-372.

——, *Die Serie ana ittišu. Materialien zum sumerischen Lexicon.* Vol. I. Rome, 1937.

——, "Die babylonischen Termini für Gesetz und Recht," *Symbolae ad iura orientis antiqui pertinentes Paulo Koschaker dedicatae.* Leiden, 1939 (= *Studia et Documenta* 2), pp. 219-234.

——, "Gerichtsprotokoll über einen Mordprozess," *ZA* 43 (1936), pp. 315-316.

——, "Jungfräulichkeit: Ein Beitrag zum Thema 'Beilager und Eheschliessung' (mit einem Anhang: Neue Lesungen und Deutungen im Gesetzbuch von Ešnunna)," *Symbolae Juridicae et Historicae Martino David Dedicatae.* Vol. 2. Leiden, 1968, pp. 41-105.

LAUTERBACH, J. Z., *Mekilta de-Rabbi Ishmael.* Vol. III. Philadelphia, 1949.

LEEMANS, W. F., "*Kidinnu*: Un symbole de droit divin babylonien," *Symbolae ad jus et historiam antiquitatis pertinentes Julio Christiano van Oven dedicatae.* Leiden, 1946, pp. 36-61.

——, "Some Aspects of Theft and Robbery in Old Babylonian Documents," *Rivista degli Studi Orientali* 32 (1957) = *Scritti in Onore di Giuseppi Furlani,* pp. 661-666.

——, "King Ḫammurapi as Judge," *Symbolae Juridicae et Historicae Martino David Dedicatae.* Vol. 2. Leiden, 1968, pp. 107-129.

LEROY, J., *Introduction à l'étude des anciens codes orientaux.* Paris, 1944.

LETTINGA, J. P., "Het sumerische Wetboek van Lipitistar Koning van Isin," *JEOL* 12 (1951/52), pp. 249-263.

LEVY, H., "Gleanings From a New Volume of Nuzi Texts," *Or* 10 (1941), pp. 205-230.

LEWY, I., "Dating of Covenant Code Sections on Humaneness and Righteousness," *VT* 7 (1957), pp. 322-326.

LEWY, J., "Ḫābirū and Hebrews," *HUCA* 14 (1939), pp. 587-623.

——, "New Parallels between Ḫābirū and Hebrews," *HUCA* 15 (1940), pp. 47-58.

——, "Origin and Significance of the Biblical Term 'Hebrew'," *HUCA* 28 (1952), pp. 1-13.

L'HOUR, J., "L'alliance de Sichem," *RB* 69 (1962), pp. 5-36, 161-184, 350-368.

——, *La morale de l'alliance.* Paris, 1966 = *Cahiers de la Revue Biblique* 5.

LIEBESNY, H., "Evidence in Nuzi Legal Procedure," *JAOS* 61 (1941), pp. 130-142.

LORETZ, O., "Ex. 21, 6; 22, 8 und angebliche Nuzi-Parallelen," *Biblica* 41 (1960), pp. 167-175.

——, "ברית 'Band-Bund'," *VT* 16 (1966), pp. 239-241.

LOEWENSTAMM, S. E., Review of *The Laws of Eshnunna* by A. Goetze. *IEJ* 7 (1957), pp. 192-198.

——, "מהר," *Encyclopaedia Biblica.* Vol. 4. Jerusalem, 1962, pp. 702-706.

——, "מדה כנגד מדה," *Encyclopaedia Biblica.* Vol. 4. Jerusalem, 1962, pp. 840-846.

——, "The Laws of Adultery and Homicide in Biblical and Mesopotamian Law Corpora," (Heb.). *Beth Mikra* 13 (1962), pp. 55-59; *ibid.*, 19 (1964), pp. 77-78.

——, "Biblical Law," (Heb.). *Encyclopaedia Biblica*. Vol. 5. Jerusalem, 1968, pp. 614-637.

LÜDDECKENS, E., *Ägyptische Eheverträge*. Wiesbaden, 1960.

LUZATTO, S. D., *Commentary to the Pentateuch*. (Heb.). Tel Aviv, 1965.

MCCARTHY, D. J., *Treaty and Covenant* (= *Analecta Biblica* 21). Rome, 1963.

——, "Covenant in the Old Testament: The Present State of Inquiry," *CBQ* 27 (1965), pp. 217-240.

MACKENZIE, R. A. F., "The Forms of Israelite Law." Unpublished Ph.D. dissertation. Rome, 1949.

——, "The Formal Aspect of Ancient Near Eastern Law," *The Seed of Wisdom: Essays in Honour of T. J. Meek*. Ed. W. S. McCullough. Toronto, 1964, pp. 31-44.

MECHILTA, see J. Z. Lauterbach, *Mekilta de-Rabbi Ishmael*. Vol. III. Philadelphia, 1949.

MEEK, T. J., "The Asyndeton Clause in the Code of Hammurabi," *JNES* 5 (1946), pp. 64-72.

——, *Hebrew Origins*. New York, 1960.

——, Translation of The Code of Hammurabi. *ANET*, pp. 163-180.

——, Translation of The Middle Assyrian Laws. *ANET*, pp. 180-188.

——, Translation of the Neo-Babylonian Laws. *ANET*, pp. 197-198.

MEISSNER, B. *Die babylonisch-assyrische Literatur*. Wildpark-Potsdam, 1928.

MENDELSOHN, I., *Legal Aspects of Slavery in Babylonia, Assyria and Palestine*. Williamsport, 1932.

——, "The Conditional Sale into Slavery of Free Born Daughters in Nuzi and the Law of Ex. 21:7-11," *JAOS* 55 (1935), pp. 190-195.

——, "The Canaanite Term for Free Proletarian," *BASOR* 83 (1941), pp. 36-39.

——, *Slavery in the Ancient Near East*. New York, 1949.

——, "Authority and Law in Canaan and Israel," *JAOS*, Supplement 17 (1954), pp. 25-33.

——, "New Light on the *Ḫupšu*," *BASOR* 139 (1955), pp. 9-11.

——, "On Slavery in Alalakh," *IEJ* 5 (1955), pp. 65-72.

——, "On Marriage in Alalakh," *Essays on Jewish Life and Thought Presented in Honor of S. W. Baron*. New York, 1959, pp. 351-357.

MENDENHALL, G. E., *Law and Covenant in Israel and the Ancient Near East*. Pittsburgh, 1955 = *BA* 17 (1954), pp. 26-46, 50-76.

——, "Covenant," *IDB*. Vol. 1, pp. 714-723.

MENES, A., *Die vorexilischen Gesetze Israels im Zusammenhang seiner kulturgeschichtlichen Entwicklung* =*BZAW* 50. Giessen, 1928.

MERCER, S. A., *The Oath in Babylonian and Assyrian Literature*. Paris, 1912.

MERZ, E., *Die Blutrache bei den Israeliten* = *BWAT* 20. Leipzig, 1916.

MILES, J. C. and GURNEY, O. R., "The Laws of Eshnunna," *ArOr* 17^2 (1949), pp. 174-188.

Miqraoth Gᵉdoloth. (Heb.). Vol. II. Pardes. New York, 1951 (for the commentaries of Rashi, ibn Ezra, and Nahmanides).

MORAN W. L., Review of *The Laws of Eshnunna* by A. Goetze. *Biblica* 38 (1957), pp. 216-221.

——, "Moses und der Bundesschluss am Sinai," *Stimmen der Zeit* 1962, pp.120-133.

——, "De Foederis Mosaici Traditione," *VD* 40 (1962), pp. 3-17.

——, "A Kingdom of Priests," *The Bible in Current Catholic Thought*. Ed. J. L. McKenzie. New York, 1962, pp. 7-20.

MORGENSTERN, J., "The Book of the Covenant, Part I," *HUCA* 5 (1928), pp. 1-151.

——, "The Book of the Covenant, Part II," *HUCA* 7 (1930), pp. 19-258.

——, "The Book of the Covenant, Part III," *HUCA* 8-9 (1931-1932), pp. 1-150.

——, "The Book of the Covenant, Part IV," *HUCA* 33 (1962), pp. 59-105.

Mørstad, E., *Wenn du der Stimme des Herrn, deines Gottes, gehorchen wirst — Die primären Einführungen zu Dtn. 28, 3-6 und 16-19.* Oslo, 1960.

Mowinckel, S., "Die vorderasiatischen Königs- und Fürsteninschriften — Eine stilistische Studie," *Eucharisterion: Studien zur Religion und Literatur des alten und neuen Testaments. Hermann Gunkel zum 60. Geburtstag.* Göttingen, 1923, pp. 278-322.

——, *Le Décalogue.* Paris, 1927.

——, "Zur Geschichte des Dekalogs," *ZAW* 55 (1937), pp. 218-234.

Muffs, Y., *Studies in Aramaic Legal Papyri from Elephantine = Studia et Documenta ad Iura Orientis Antiqui Pertinentia* 8. Leiden, 1969.

Mühl, M., *Untersuchungen zur altorientalischen und althellenischen Gesetzgebung = Klio: Beiträge zur alten Geschichte.* Vol. 29. Leipzig, 1933.

Muilenburg, J., "The Form and Structure of the Covenantal Formulations," *VT* 9 (1959), pp. 347-365.

——, *The Way of Israel: Biblical Faith and Ethics.* New York, 1961.

——, "The 'Office' of the Prophet in Ancient Israel," *The Bible in Modern Scholarship.* Ed. J. Philip Hyatt. Nashville, 1965, pp. 74-97.

Müller, D. H., *Die Gesetze Ḫammurabis und ihr Verhältnis zur mosaischen Gesetzgebung sowie zu den XII Tafeln.* Wien, 1903.

Nahmanides, M., see *Miqraoth Gᵉdoloth.*

Naveh, J., "A Hebrew Letter from the Seventh Century B.C.," *IEJ* 10 (1960), pp. 129-139.

Neufeld, E., *Ancient Hebrew Marriage Laws.* London, 1944.

——, *The Hittite Laws.* London, 1951.

Nielsen, E., *Die zehn Gebote: Eine traditionsgeschichtliche Skizze.* Copenhagen, 1965.

Noth, M., *Die Gesetze im Pentateuch. Ihre Voraussetzungen und ihr Sinn.* (*Schriften der Königsberger Gelehrten Gesellschaft*). Halle, 1940 = *Gesammelte Studien zum Alten Testament.* Munich, 1960, pp. 9-141.

——, "Das alttestamentliche Bundschliessen im Lichte eines Mari-Textes," *Gesammelte Studien zum Alten Testament,* pp. 142-154.

——, "Die mit des Gesetzes Werken umgehen, die sind unter dem Fluch," *Gesammelte Studien zum Alten Testament,* pp. 151-171.

——, *Exodus.* Trans. J. S. Bowden. Philadelphia, 1962.

——, *The Law in the Pentateuch and Other Studies.* Trans. D. R. Ap-Thomas. Edinburgh, 1966.

Nougaryol, J., "Le prologue du code Hammourabien d'après une tablette inédite du Louvre," *RA* 45 (1951), pp. 66-79.

——, "Les fragments en pierre du code Hammourabien," *JA* 245 (1957), pp. 339-366.

——, "Les fragments en pierre du code Hammourabien II," *JA* 246 (1958), pp. 143-155.

——, *Le palais royal d'Ugarit* (=*PRU*). Vol. IV. Paris, 1956.

O'Connell, M. J., "The Concept of Commandment in the Old Testament," *ThSt* (USA) 21 (1960), pp. 351-403.

Oppenheim, L., *Ancient Mesopotamia: Portrait of a Dead Civilization.* Chicago, 1964.

Oren, E., "Ex. XXII:1-3," (Heb.). *Tarbiz* 32 (1963), pp. 393-394.

——, "Concerning שארה, כסותה, ועונתה, Ex. XXI:10," (Heb.). *Tarbiz* 33 (1964), p. 317.

Parker, B., "Economic Tablets from the Temple of Mamu at Balawat," *Iraq* 25 (1963), pp. 86-100.

Parrot, A., "Les peintures du palais de Mari," *Syria* 18 (1937), pp. 325-354.

PAUL, S. M., "Exod. 21:10 A Threefold Maintenance Clause," *JNES* 28 (1969), pp. 48-53.
——, "Types of Formulation in Biblical and Mesopotamian Law," (Heb.). *Leshonenu* 34 (1970), pp. 257-266.
PEDERSEN, J., *Israel: Its Life and Culture*. Vols. 1-2. London, 1954.
PEISER, F. E., *Texte juristischen und geschäftlichen Inhalts = Keilinschriftliche Bibliothek*. Vol. IV. Berlin, 1896.
——, "Aus Rom," *OLZ* 7 (1904), p. 39.
PETSCHOW, H., *Neubabylonisches Pfandrecht*. Berlin, 1956.
——, Review of "Keilschriftrecht" by V. Korošec. *ZSS* 82 (1965), pp. 341-346.
——, "Zur Systematik und Gesetzestechnik im Codex Hammurabi," *ZA* 23 (1965), pp. 146-172.
——, "Zu den Stilformen antiker Gesetze und Rechtssammlungen," *ZSS* 82 (1965), pp. 24-38.
——, "Zur 'Systematik' in den Gesetzen von Eschunna," *Symbolae Iuridicae et Historicae Martino David Dedicatae*. Vol. 2. Leiden, 1968, pp. 131-143.
PFEIFFER, R. H., "The Transmission of the Book of the Covenant," *HTR* 24 (1931), pp. 99-109.
——, "The Influence of Hammurabi's Code Outside of Babylon," *Akten des XXIV internationalen Orientalisten-Kongresses*. Munich, 1957, pp. 148-149.
PHILO, *On the Special Laws = The Loeb Classical Library*. Vols. 7-8. Trans. F. H. Colson. Cambridge, 1950, 1954.
PIEPKORN, A. C., *Assurbanipal: King of Assyria*. Chicago, 1933.
PIRENNE, J., "La loi et les décrets royaux en Égypte sous l'ancien empire," *RIDA*, 3e série, 4 (1957), pp. 2-31.
VAN DER PLOEG, J., "*Šāpāṭ* et *Mišpāṭ*," *OTS* 2 (1945), pp. 144-155.
——, Review of *Études sur le code de l'alliance* by H. Cazelles. *BiOr* 4 (1947), pp. 118-120.
——, "Studies in Hebrew Law I," *CBQ* 12 (1950), pp. 248-259.
——, "Studies in Hebrew Law II," *CBQ* 12 (1950), pp. 416-427.
——, "Studies in Hebrew Law III," *CBQ* 13 (1951), pp. 28-43.
——, "Studies in Hebrew Law, IV," *CBQ* 13 (1951), pp. 164-171.
——, "Studies in Hebrew Law V," *CBQ* 13 (1951), pp. 296-307.
POEBEL, A., *Babylonian Legal and Business Documents from the Time of the First Dynasty of Babylon = Babylonian Expedition of the University of Pennsylvania. Series A: Cuneiform Texts*. Vol. VI/2. Philadelphia, 1909.
——, *Grundzüge der sumerischen Grammatik*. Rostock, 1923.
VAN PRAAG, A., *Droit matrimonial assyro-babylonien* (= *Archaeologisch-Historische Bijdragen. Allard Pierson Stichting* 12). Amsterdam, 1945.
PREISER, W., "Vergeltung und Sühne im altisraelitischen Strafrecht," *Festschrift für Eberhard Schmidt zum 70. Geburtstag*. Göttingen, 1961, pp. 7-38.
PRESS, R., "Das Ordal im alten Israel," *ZAW* 51 (1933), pp. 121-140, 227-255.
PRÉVOST, M. H., "Bibliography of Biblical Law," *RHD* 45 (1967), pp. 529-532; 46 (1968), pp. 530-535; 47 (1969), pp. 524-534.
PRIEST, J. F., "'*ÓRKIA* in the *Iliad* and Consideration of a Recent Theory," *JCS* 23 (1964), pp. 48-56.
PRINGSHEIM, F., "Some Causes of Codification," *RIDA*, 3e série, 4 (1951), pp. 301-311.
VAN PRÔOSDIJ, B. A., "*Šar Mešarim*: Titres des rois babyloniens comme législateurs," *Symbolae ad jus et historiam antiquitatis pertinentes Julio Christiano van Oven dedicatae*. Leiden, 1946, pp. 29-35.
PUKKO, A. F., *Die altassyrischen und hethitischen Gesetze und das Alte Testament = StOr* 1 (1925).

RABAST, K. H., *Das apodiktische Recht im Deuteronomium und im Heiligkeitsgesetz*. Berlin, 1949.

RABINOWITZ, J. J., *Jewish Law*. New York, 1956.

——, "Ex. XXII:4 and the Septuagint Version Thereof," *VT* 9 (1959), pp. 40-46.

——, "The Susa Tablets, the Bible and Aramaic Payri," *VT* 11 (1961), pp. 55-76.

VON RAD, G., *Old Testament Theology*. Trans. D. M. G. Stalker. Vol. 1. Edinburgh, 1962; Vol. 2, 1965.

——, *The Problem of the Hexateuch and Other Essays*. Trans. E. W. Trueman Dicken. New York, 1966.

RAPAPORT, I., "The Origins of Hebrew Law," *PEQ* 73 (1941), pp. 158-167.

RASHBAM, *Rashbam's Commentary to the Torah*. (Heb.). New York, 1949.

RASHI, see *Miqraoth Gedoloth*.

REVENTLOW, H. G., *Gebot und Predigt im Dekalog*. Gütersloh, 1962.

——, "Kultisches Recht im Alten Testament," *ZTK* 60 (1963), pp. 267-304.

RICHTER, W., *Recht und Ethos*. Munich, 1966 = *Studien zum Alten und Neuen Testament* 15.

RIFTIN, A., *Ancient Babylonian Juridical and Administrative Documents in Collections in the USSR*. (Russian). Moscow, 1937.

RING, E., *Israels Rechtsleben im Lichte der neuentdeckten assyrischen und hethitischen Gesetzesurkunden*. Stockholm, 1926.

ROSENZWEIG, F., "Die Einheit der Bibel," *Kleinere Schriften*. Berlin, 1937, pp. 128-133.

ROST, L., "Das Bundesbuch," *ZAW* 77 (1965), pp. 255-259.

ROWLEY, H. H., "Moses and the Decalogue," *BJRL* 34 (1951), pp. 81-118.

RUIZ, V. A., "La codification dans l'Égypte ancienne," *JJP* 11-12 (1957-1958), pp. 25-46.

SAADYAH GAON, see M. Zucker, *Rav Saadya Gaon's Translation of the Torah*. New York, 1959.

SAALSCHÜTZ, J. L., *Das Mosaische Recht*. Berlin, 1848.

SAARISALO, A., "New Kirkuk Documents Relating to Slaves," *StOr* V/3 (1934).

SAN NICOLÒ, M., "Die Stellung der Keilschrifturkunden in der vorderasiatischen Rechtsentwicklung," *ZSS* 48 (1928), pp. 21-50.

——, *Beiträge zur Rechtsgeschichte im Bereiche der keilschriftlichen Rechtsquellen*. Oslo, 1931.

——, "Rechtsgeschichtliches zum Gesetz des Bilalama von Ešnunna," *Or* 18 (1949), pp. 258-262.

——, "Nuove fonte prehammurapiche di diritto," *SDHI* 15 (1949), pp. 24-33.

——, "Rechtsgeschichtliches zum Gesetzbuch Lipit-Ishtar von Isin," *Or* 19 (1950), pp. 111-118.

——, "Rassegna di diritto cuneiforme I," *SDHI* 16 (1950), pp. 419-458.

——, "Rassegna di diritto cuneiforme II," *SDHI* 20 (1954), pp. 485-520.

SARNA, N. M., *Understanding Genesis*. New York, 1966.

SCHEIL, V., *Mémoires de la Mission Archéologique de Perse*. Vol. 24. *Mission en Susiane. Actes Juridiques Susiens*. Paris, 1933.

SCHELBERT, G., "Exodus XXII 4 im palästinischen Targum," *VT* 8 (1958), pp. 253-263.

SCHMÖKEL, H., "Biblische 'Du-Sollst' Gebote und ihr historischer Ort," *ZSS. kanon*. Abt. 36 (1950), pp. 365-390.

——, "Hammurabi und Marduk," *RA* 53 (1959), pp. 183-204.

SCHORR, M., *Urkunden des altbabylonischen Zivil- und Prozessrechts*. Leipzig, 1913.

SCOTT, R. B. Y., "A Kingdom of Priests (Ex. XIX:6)," *OTS* 8 (1950), pp. 213-219.

SEAGLE W. *History of Law*. New York, 1946.

——, *Men of Law from Hammurabi to Holmes*. New York, 1947.

SEDLÁKOVÁ, J., "Bibliographisches zum hebräischen Recht I," *JJP* 11-12 (1957-1958), pp. 263-292.

——, "Bibliographisches zum hebräischen Recht II," *JJP* 14 (1962), pp. 89-107.

SEELIGMANN, I. L., "Zur Terminologie für das Gerichtsverfahren im Wortschatz des biblischen Hebräisch," *Hebräische Wortforschung: Festschrift zum 80. Geburtstag von Walter Baumgartner = Supplements to VT* 16 (1967), pp. 251-278.

VAN SELMS, A., "The Goring Ox in Babylonian and Biblical Law," *ArOr* 18^4 (1950) = *Symbolae Hrozný*, pp. 321-330.

SMEND, R,. *Die Bundesformel = ThSt* [Z] 68 (1963).

VON SODEN, W., "Der hymnisch-epische Dialekt des Akkadischen," *ZA* 40 (1931), pp. 163-227; *ibid.*, 41 (1933), pp. 90-183.

——, "Religion und Sittlichkeit nach den Anschauungen der Babylonier," *ZDMG* 89 (1935), pp. 143-169.

——, "Ein Zwiegespräch Ḫammurabis mit einer Frau," *ZA* 49 (1950), pp. 151-194.

——, *Grundriss der akkadischen Grammatik*. Rome, 1952 (= *Analecta Orientalia* 33).

——, Review of *Les lois d'Eshnunna* by E. Szlechter. *BiOr* 13 (1956), pp. 32-34.

——, *Akkadisches Handwörterbuch*. Vols. 1-8. Wiesbaden, 1959-1967.

SOLLBERGER, E., "A New Fragment of the Code of Hammurapi," *ZA* 56 (1964), pp. 130-132.

SPEISER, E. A., "New Kirkuk Documents Relating to Family Laws," *AASOR* 10 (1928-1929). New Haven, 1930, pp. 1-73.

——, "New Kirkuk Documents Relating to Security Transactions," *JAOS* 52 (1932), pp. 350-367; *ibid.*, 53 (1933), pp. 24-46.

——, "Notes to Recently Published Nuzi Texts," *JAOS* 55 (1935), pp. 432-445.

——, "Some Sources of Intellectual and Social Progress in the Ancient Near East," *Studies in the History of Culture: The Disciplines of the Humanities* (= *W. G. Leland Presentation Volume*). Ed. Percy W. Long. Wisconsin, 1942, pp. 51-62.

——, "A Note on the Derivation of *šumma*," *JCS* 1 (1947), pp. 321-328.

——, "The Ancient Near East and Modern Philosophies of History," *PAPS* 95 (1951), pp. 583-588.

——, "Early Law and Civilization," *CBR* 31 (1953), pp. 863-877.

——, "Authority and Law in Mesopotamia," *JAOS*, Supplement 17 (1954), pp. 8-15.

——, "Ancient Mesopotamia," *The Idea of History in the Ancient Near East*. Ed. R. C. Dentan. New Haven, 1955, pp. 35-73.

——, "The Durative *Hithpaʿel*: A *tan*-Form," *JAOS* 75 (1955), pp. 118-121.

——, "Nuzi Marginalia," *Or* 25 (1956), pp. 1-23.

——, *Government and Religion in the Near East*. New York, 1956.

——, "*ṬWṬPT*," *JQR* 48 (1957-1958), pp. 208-217.

——, "The Biblical Idea of History in its Common Near Eastern Setting," *IEJ* 7 (1957), pp. 201-216.

——, "Three Thousand Years of Bible Study," *Centennial Review* 4 (1960), pp. 206-222.

——, " 'People' and 'Nation' of Israel," *JBL* 79 (1960), pp. 157-163.

——, "An Angelic 'Curse': Exodus 14:20," *JAOS* 80 (1960), pp. 198-200.

——, "Leviticus and the Critics," *Yehezkel Kaufmann Jubilee Volume*. Jerusalem, 1960, pp. 29-45.

——, "Cuneiform Law and the History of Civilization," *PAPS* 107 (1963), pp. 536-541.

——, "The Stem *PLL* in Hebrew," *JBL* 82 (1963), pp. 301-306.

——, "Background and Function of the Biblical *Nāśīʾ*," *CBQ* 25 (1963), pp. 111-117.

——, *Genesis*. New York, 1964.

——, Translation of "The Epic of Gilgamesh". *ANET*, pp. 72-99.

——, *Oriental and Biblical Studies*. Eds. J. J. Finkelstein and M. Greenberg. Philadelphia, 1967.

——, and PFEIFFER, R. H., *One Hundred New Selected Nuzi Texts* (= *AASOR* 16). New Haven, 1936.

SPIES O. and PRITSCH, E., "Klassisches Islamisches Recht," *Handbuch der Orientalistik* 111/1. *Orientalisches Recht*. Leiden, 1964, pp. 220-343.

STAMM, J. J., *Der Dekalog im Lichte der neueren Forschung*. Bern, 1958.

——, "Dreissig Jahre Dekalogforschung," *ThR* (27) 1961, pp. 189-239, 281-305.

——, and M. E. ANDREW., *The Ten Commandments in Recent Research*. Naperville, 1967.

STEELE, F. R., "Lipit-Ishtar Law Code," *AJA* 51 (1947), pp. 138-164; *ibid.*, 52 (1948), pp. 425-450.

——, "An Additional Fragment of the Lipit-Ishtar Code Tablet from Nippur," *ArOr* 18^{1-2} (1950), pp. 489-493.

SZLECHTER, E., "L'affranchissement en droit suméro-akkadien," *AHDO-RIDA* 1 (1952), pp. 125-195.

——, "À propos du code d'Ur Nammu," *RA* 47 (1953), pp. 1-10.

——, *Les lois d'Eshnunna*. Paris, 1954.

——, "Le code d'Ur Nammu," *RA* 49 (1955), pp. 169-177.

——, "Les anciennes codifications en Mésopotamie," *RIDA*, 3e série, 4 (1957), pp. 73-92.

——, "Le code de Lipit Ishtar," *RA* 51 (1957), pp. 57-82, 177-196; *ibid.*, 52 (1958), pp. 74-90.

——, "Revue critique des droits cunéiformes III," *SDHI* 22 (1956), pp. 478-499. (This and the ensuing articles are a continuation of the series started by M. San Nicolò in the same journal.)

——, "Revue critique des droits cunéiformes IV," *SDHI* 25 (1959), pp. 485-514.

——, "Revue critique des droits cunéiformes V," *SDHI* 27 (1962), pp. 470-497.

——, "La loi et la coutume, manifestations d'autorité et sources d'enseignement dans l'antiquité orientale," *Travaux et recherches d'institut de l'université de Paris* 23 (1962), pp. 5-11.

——, "La 'loi' dans la Mésopotamie ancienne," *RIDA*, 3e série, 12 (1965), pp. 55-77.

——, "La procédure accusatoire en droit suméro-babylonien," *RIDA*, 3e série, 1968, pp. 73-102.

——, „Droit cunéiformes," *RHD* 39 (1961), pp. 159-161; 40 (1962); pp. 92-96; 41 (1963), pp. 123-129; 42 (1964), pp. 139-147; 43 (1965), pp. 121-129; 44 (1966), pp. 118-127; 45 (1967), pp. 145-153; 46 (1968), pp. 142-150; 47 (1969), pp. 121-130.

TADMOR, H., "Hammurabi and His Period," (Heb.). *Ha'Ishiyut WeDorah*. Jerusalem, 1963, pp. 39-56.

TALMON, S., "The New Hebrew Letter from the Seventh Century B.C. in Historical Perspective," *BASOR* 176 (1964), pp. 29-38.

TEICHER, J., "A Sixth Century Fragment of the Palestinian Targum?" *VT* 1 (1951), pp. 125-129.

THUREAU-DANGIN, F., *Die sumerischen und akkadischen Königsinschriften*. Leipzig, 1907.

——, *Lettres et contrats de l'époque de la première dynastie babylonienne*. Paris, 1910.

——, "Trois contrats de Ras Shamra," *Syria* 18 (1937), pp. 245-255.

TOEG, A., "Exodus XXII, 4: The Text and the Law in the Light of the Ancient Sources," (Heb.). *Tarbiz* 39 (1970), pp. 223-231.

The Torah: *The Five Books of Moses*. Jewish Publication Society. Philadelphia, 1967.

TUCKER, G. M., "Covenant Forms and Contract Forms," *VT* 15 (1965), pp. 487-503.

TUR-SINAI, N. H., "שארה,כסותה,ועונתה," (Heb.). *The Language and the Book*. Vol. 2. Jerusalem, 1950, pp. 215-218.

——, *Peshuto Shel Miqra*. (Heb.). Vol. 1. Jerusalem, 1962.

UNGNAD, A., *Babylonische Briefe aus der Zeit der Hammurapi Dynastie* (= *Vorderasiatische Bibliothek*, Vol. 14). Leipzig, 1914.

DE VAUX, R., Review of *Études sur le code de l'alliance* by H. Cazelles. *RB* 54 (1947), pp. 434-435.

——, "Les patriarches hébreux et les découverts modernes," *RB* 55 (1948), pp. 321-347.

——, *Ancient Israel*: *Its Life and Institutions*. Trans. J. McHugh. New York, 1961.

——, "Le problème des Ḫapiru après quinze années," *JNES* 27 (1968), pp. 221-228.

VIROLLEAUD, C., "Sur le nom de Ḫammurabi," *JA* 243 (1955), pp. 133-134.

WAGNER, V., "Zur Systematik in dem Codex Ex. 21:2—22:16," *ZAW* 81 (1969), pp. 176-182.

WATERMAN, L., "Pre-Israelite Laws in the Book of the Covenant," *AJSL* 38 (1921), pp. 36-54.

WEINBERG, J. J., *Meḥqarīm beTalmud*. (Heb.). Vol. I. Berlin, 1937-1938.

WEINFELD, M., "Israelite and Non-Israelite Concepts of Law," (Heb.). *Beth Mikra* 17 (1964), pp. 58-63.

——, "Traces of Assyrian Treaty Formulae in Deuteronomy," *Biblica* 46 (1965), pp. 417-427.

——, "נכרי," *Encyclopaedia Biblica*. Vol. 5. Jerusalem, 1968, pp. 866-867.

——, *Deuteronomy and the Deuteronomic School*. Oxford, 1970.

WEISMANN, J., "Talion und öffentliche Strafe im Mosaischen Rechte," *Festschrift für Adolf Wach*. Vol. I. Leipzig, 1913, pp. 1-102.

WEISS (HALIVNI), D., "Notes on the Mishna and Baraita," (Heb.). *Tarbiẓ* 27 (1957), pp. 17-30.

——, "A Note on אשר לא ארשה," *JBL* 81 (1962), pp. 67-69.

WHITLEY, C. F., "Covenant and Commandment in Israel," *JCS* 22 (1963), pp. 37-48.

WILENSKY, M., *Sefer Hariqma ab Jona ibn Ganah*. (Heb.). Vol. 1, Jerusalem, 1965.

WILLIAMS, J. G., "Concerning One of the Apodictic Formulas," *VT* 14 (1964), pp. 484-489.

——, "Addenda to 'Concerning One of the Apodictic Formulas'," *VT* 15 (1965) pp. 113-115.

WILSON, J. A., *The Culture of Ancient Egypt*. Chicago, 1956.

——, Translation of "The Instruction of the Vizier Ptah-Hotep." *ANET*, pp. 412-414.

——, Translation of "A Song of the Harper." *ANET*, p. 467.

WISEMAN, D. J., *The Alalakh Tablets*. London, 1953.

——, "The Goddess Lama at Ur," *Iraq* 22 (1960), pp. 166-171.

——, "The Laws of Hammurabi Again," *JSS* 7 (1962), pp. 161-172.

WRIGHT, G. E., *The Old Testament Against Its Environment* = *Studies in Biblical Theology* No. 2. Naperville, 1957.

WÜRTHWEIN, D. E., "Der Sinn des Gesetzes im Alten Testament," *ZTK* 55 (1958), pp. 255-270.

YARON, R., "Forms in the Laws of Eshnunna," *RIDA*, 3e série, 9 (1962), pp. 137-153.

——, "Varia on Adoption," *JJP* 15 (1965), pp. 171-183.

——, "The Goring Ox in Near Eastern Laws," *ILR* 1 (1966), pp. 396-406.

——, *The Laws of Eshnunna.* Jerusalem, 1969.
ZENGER, E., "Eine Wende in der Dekalogforschung?" *ThRe* 3 (1968), pp. 189-198.
ZIMMERLI, W., "Das Gesetz im Alten Testament," *ThLZ* 85 (1960), pp. 482-498.
——, *The Laws and the Prophets: A Study of the Meaning of the Old Testament.* Trans. R. E. Clements. Oxford, 1965.
——, "Ich bin Jaweh," *Geschichte und Altes Testament. Albrecht Alt zum 70. Geburtstag.* Tübingen, 1953, pp. 179-209.
ZUCKER, M., *Rav Saadya Gaon's Translation of the Torah.* New York, 1959.

INDEX OF SOURCES

A. BIBLICAL SOURCES

Genesis

4:23 76
9:5 83
5-6 79
6 61
12:2 31
26:20-22 67
28:8 53
31:15 54
39 94
33:14 89
42:38 72

Exodus

2:13 74
12:48 91
18:16 89
22 89
19 28
3b 30
3b-6 29, 30, 101
4 32
5-6 30, 41
7-25 29, 32
18-19 34
19—24 27, 28, 35, 101
20:2 32
2-17 28, 29
3-6 33
12 64, 65, 103
13-16 108
15 65
18-21 28, 29, 33
22-26 28, 34
20:22—23:19 29, 34
20:22—23:30 28
21:1 38, 46
2 46, 47, 64
2-6 40, 45-46, 102
2-11 106
2—22:16 2, 28, 43, 101
3 47, 48
4 47, 48, 49
5 49, 50
6 49, 50, 51, 90, 91

Exodus

7 53
7-8 102-103
7-11 52-53
8 53, 54
9 53, 55, 82
10 53, 59, 103, 104
10-11 56-61
11 53
12 28, 37, 61-62, 70, 74 ,81, 104, 107, 108, 109
12-17 107-108
12-27 107-109
12—22:16 106
13 64, 107, 115
13-14 62-64
14 63, 108
15 64-65, 66, 79, 108
15-16 108
15-17 28, 108
16 65-66, 82, 108
17 65, 66-67, 79, 103, 108
18-19 67-69, 73, 74, 103, 108
18-27 108-109
19 73
20 40, 70, 78
20-21 52, 69-70, 75, 83, 108
22 108, 109
22-23 70-73
22 ff 104
23 64
23 ff. 67
23-25 40, 73-77, 103
26 69
26-27 40, 52, 75, 78, 109
27 69, 78
28 79, 81, 84, 109
28-29 109
28-32 78-79, 107, 109
28-34 89
29 79, 84, 109

Exodus

29-30 80-82, 104
30 109
31 55, 73, 79, 82-83, 84, 109, 117
32 69, 78, 83, 84, 109
33 109
33-34 83-84, 109
33-36 107, 109
34 84, 85, 109
35 80, 84, 109
35-36 84-85, 103, 109
36 80, 84, 85, 109, 117
37 65, 85-86, 109, 110
21:37—22:2-3 110
21:37—22:16 107, 109-111
22:1 66, 110
1:2a 86-87, 110
2 109, 110
2a 86
2b 86
2b-3 85, 110
3 65, 66, 85, 86, 91, 109, 110, 111
4 88-89, 109, 110
4-5 73, 87-89, 104, 110
5 88, 109, 110
6 85, 90, 92, 104, 109, 110, 111
6-8 89, 92, 93
7 90, 91, 92, 93, 101, 111
22:7-8 90-91, 93, 102
7-10 50
8 85, 90, 91, 92, 109, 110
9 92, 95, 110, 111
9-12 92, 93, 94, 110
10 90, 93, 109, 110, 111
11 109, 110, 111

Exodus

12 94, 109
13 92, 94, 104, 109
13-14a 94, 96, 111
14 109
14b 95-96
15 54, 97, 109
15-16 44, 96-98, 103, 111
16 83, 97, 109
16-17 43
22:17—23:13 28
22:17—23:19 43, 101
19 28
27 44
28-30 28
23:1-3 123
3 110
4-5 110
6 110
6 ff. 123
10-13 28
10-19 34, 35
10-33 35
14-19 28
20-25 28, 35
20-33 28, 29, 34, 35, 102
22 35
24 34, 35
26-33 28, 35
31 35
32-33 35
24 29
24:7 28
25:11 74
34:9-13 28
11-17 35
11-16 35
12 35
14-26 28
18-28 35

Leviticus

5:1 93
17:1 ff. 34
1-6 34
7 ff. 34
18 119, 120
1-5 27
3 34
24-30 37
26 34
19:3 65
19:20 54
37 27
20:9 65, 66
10 37
26 27
21:17-18 91
22:22 92
24:10 74
19-20 74
26 27
1-2 34

Numbers

16:3 31
35:9-15 63
11 62
15 62
16-18 63
20 62
20-21 63
22 62
22-23 62
22-28 63
27 86
31 37, 62, 77, 82

Deuteronomy

1—11 27
1:1—4:40 27
4:41-43 63
4:44—11:32 27
5:20 ff. 34
7:6 31
12—26:15 27
12:1 ff. 34
1-3 34
4-28 34
29-30 35
29-31 34
31 34
14:2 31
21 31
15:12 ff. 45, 46
12-18 47, 50
15 52
17 50
17:6 119
19:1-10 63
4-5 62
6 62, 63
11 63
19-21 74
21:15-17 49
18 ff. 66
18-19 65
22:23 54
23-24 37
23-27 98
25 54
22:27-28 54
28-29 97
29 83
24:7 65
25:1 90
11-12 40, 77
26 34
26:16—31:30 27
19 31
27 118
15-26 119
16 65, 66
28:9 31
31:10-13 38

Joshua

20 63
24 33

Judges

9:23 55
15:5 88
19:12 54

I Samuel

15:9 89
18:27 73
24:11 62

II Samuel

12:6 85
20 61
14:6 74
24:24 83

I Kings

1:50 ff. 63
2:28 ff. 63
8:32 90
13:28 92

Isaiah

58:4 74
61:3 61
62:12 31

Jeremiah

1:5 54
2:34 87
34:8 ff. 45
9 46
14 46
35:6-7 120

Ezekiel

16:18-19 61
34:4 92
16 92

Hosea

2:7 61
10 61
11 61
6:7 55

Amos

3:2 54
12 94

Micah

3:2 59
3 59

Zechariah

11:16 92

Malachi

2:10-11 55
14-15 55

Psalms

6:10 92
21:3 97
23:5 61
45:8 61
49:8-9 82
69:9 54
78:20 59

Proverbs

6:31 85
10:13 69
13:24 69
30:17 77

Ruth

3:3 61

Ecclesiastes

6:2 54
9:7-9 61

Esther

9:15 89

Nehemiah

5:15 83
8:18 38
13:11 67
17 67

II Chronicles

17:13 89
28:15 61

B. CUNEIFORM SOURCES

LU

1-30 17
43-72 17
73-86 18
97-103 18
104-116 18
112-113 18
117-123 18
143-149 18
162-165 18
166-167 19

LI

I:1-19 13-14
20-37 14-15
22 15
25-26 15
32 15
38 13
38-51 15-16
52-55 16
27 56-57
27-28 103
28 56
34-37 95
XIX:6-8 16
9-17 16
17 16
36-37 16
38 16-17
39-48 17
XIX:49-XX:51 17

LE

1 114
4 114
9 58, 114
12 87, 115
12-13 86
13 87, 115
15 115
16 115
17 114
19 115
26 65
27 65
28 65
32 57-58
36 104
36:14-15 92
37 91
37:18 91
37:20 92
42 ff. 75
43 114
51 115
51-52 115
52 115
53 84-85, 103
54 80, 81, 104
54-55 78
56 81

LH

I:1-26 13-14
27 13
27-49 14-15
32-34 15
32-39 12
37-39 19
47-48 15
50-53 14-15
51 15
I:50-V:13 15-16
II:24-25 19
32-33 19
37-38 19
49-51 19
56-65 19

LH

IV:11-16 19
29-30 19
V:14-24 12, 16
6 86
6-11 39, 65, 86, 90
6-13 65
8 85, 86
9:4-5 66
14 65
15 ff. 65
19:1-2 66
21 39, 86, 87
22 39, 86
25 39, 86
36 113, 115
38 113, 115
39 113, 115
40 113, 115
42:3 89
43:8 89
55:37 89
57:52-53 88
58:71-74 88
60:25-26 49
62:43 89
116 40, 73, 77, 83
116:40-42 62
117 47
120 85, 90, 92
124 85, 90, 104
124:53-59 92
125 90, 91, 92
125:75 92
125:79 ff. 84
126 85, 90, 92, 117
129 37, 98
132 117
138 117
148 56
170:58-59 49
178 58
187 113, 115
192 65, 66
192-195 40, 77
193 65
195 64
196-197 74, 75
196-205 68, 74
198 75
199 78
200 74, 75
201 75
202 77
203 77
205 40
206 68, 74
206:10-11 63
206-208 74
207 77, 104
207:14-15 62
207-208 63
209 72
209-214 71, 74, 104
210 40, 72, 73, 75, 77, 83
211 72
212 72, 75
214 72
218 40, 77
226 40, 77
227:52-53 63
230 40, 73, 77, 83
241 ff. 82
242-249 95
244 94, 95
244:5 95
249 95
249:38 93
249:39 64
250 79
250-252 78
251 79, 80-81, 104
252 83
253 40, 77
253:80-81 66
266 93, 94
266:77 64, 93
267 93
278-282 52
282 40, 52
XXIVb:8-58 16
33-34 16
53-54 16
59-62 12, 19
70-78 13
74-75 8, 16-17
81 8
84-88 16
XXIVb:93-XXVb:2 22
XXVb:3-19 13, 22, 38
12 ff. 8
41-47 22
48-58 22-23
59-94 22
64 ff. 8
78 ff. 8
95-98 6, 13
99 8
XXVIb:2-17 17, 22
3 ff. 8
11-17 13
19 8
XXVIb:18-XXVIIIb:91 17, 22

MAL A

3 65, 86, 90
4 39, 40
5 40
7 39
8 40
9 39, 40
10 62, 72, 82
14-16 37
15 40, 98
18-21 39
20 40
21 71, 73
23 37
24 40
36 58
40 39, 40, 113, 114, 115
40:42-45 115
58-60 115
61-62 115
63-65 115
68-76 115
84-86 51
89-93 115
101-103 51
41 114
41:6-10 115
42:17 54
42-43 60
43:20 54
43:21-22 54
44 39
44:45 51
46:99 56
47 114
47:7-13 115
50 40, 71, 72, 73, 77
69 73
71 73
73 73

MAL A

75-79 73
80-81 73
50-52 71
52 71
52:91 73
55 40, 77, 97
55:33-37 97
56 96-97, 103
57 ff. 85
57-59 114

B

2 62, 72, 82
6 114

F

2 114, 115

HL

1 66
1-2 64
1-4 37, 61
1-5 61, 71
3:6-7 64
3-4 62, 63-64, 104
4:8 64
5 62
7-16 73
7 ff. 75
8 78
10 68-69, 103
12 78
14 78
16 78
17 72, 73
17-18 71
18 72
19 66
28 65
29 65
48 114, 115
50-51 115
50-52 114, 115
54-56 114
56 115
57 85
57-59 85
63 85
67 85
69 85
70 85
75 93, 94

HL

75:75 93
76 95, 96
78 95
92 40
93 87
93-95 87
96-97 87
105 88
105-106 88
105-107 104
107 88
126 65
166 40
167 114
178 114
178-183 114
181-186 114
185A 114
185:15 115
186 115
197 62, 98
198 37, 62, 98

NB

2:31 89
2:34 89
3:40 89
6:21 116

AASOR 10

4 66

AAṢOR 16

23 49, 53
23:12-13 53
29 49
30 49, 53
33 53
42 49, 53
42:21-22 55

Alalakh

7:20-23 49

ana ittišu

3, III, 47-50 57
VII 114

ARM II

24:9 64

ARM III

61:10 64

Chiera, *UM* VIII/2

116:8-9 58
153:19-20 58, 60

Civil, *Sumerian Laws*

55-21-71, iii, 2′-13′ 71
7′-8′ 72
9′-11′ 94
I′, 2′, iii, 11′ 95
9′ 95

el-Amarna

27:17 97
29:17 97
29:19 97
29:21 97

David-Ebeling, *ZVRW* 44 (1929)

5 65

Ebeling, *AFO* 5 (1928-1929), pp. 218-219. 51

Falkenstein, *UR* III

6 56
8:4-10 57
178:15 55

Greenberg, *Ḫāpiru*

38 48
38:2 49
39 48
41 46
42 46
43 46
44 46
45 46
48 46
49:10 48
58 46, 48
58:3 49
59 46
59:19 48
60 46
60:4 48
60:16 48
61 46
62 46
63 46, 48

Greenberg, *Ḫāpiru*

64:15-23 48
64:16 48
64:17 49
65:4 48
65:5-7 48
65:8 48

Gudea B

VII: 42-43 19

HG VI

1752 51

HSS V

73:27-28 54

HSS IX

10 70

HSS XIX

1:14 67
10:38-39 67

Jean, *RA* 26 (29), pp. 104-107 58

JEN IV

341:4-9 85

JEN V

299 48
437 48-49

KAR III

298:43 ff. 51

KB IV

44:7, 11 59

Koschaker, *NKRA*

p. 83 49

Kültepe

31:5 51

Peiser, *OLZ* 7 (1904), p. 39 58

Petschow, *NB Pfandrecht* 83

Poebel, *Babylonian Documents*

28 58, 60
48 58
48:31 60

PRU IV

17:128:9-10 71
17:251:14-15 72
17:230:9 73
17:230:14 73

PRU V

60:12 30

Riftin

46 66

Scheil, *MDP*

332:17-18 60-61
333:13-15 60-61

Schorr, *Urkunden*

19:33-34 59
19:35 59
65:15 59
78:7 59
125:12 59
223:7 59
242:6 59

Speiser, *JAOS* 53 (1933), pp. 36-37

lines 6-10 48

Thureau-Dangin, *Syria* (18), 1937, pp. 245-255 67, 103

Urukagina, Cones B and C

XII:23-25 19

VAB VI

245:7 ff. 66

Yaḫdun-Lim 6

C. RABBINIC SOURCES

Mishnah

Ohiloth 7:6 71

Tosefta

Terumoth 9:14 60

Mechilta

Ex. 20:15 65
21:6 50, 51-52

Mechilta

21:10 59
16 65
22-23 71, 72, 73
23-25 74
26-27 78
31 82
37 85
22: 6-8 92, 93
22:7 91
9-12 93, 94
14b 95
15-16 96

Talmud Bavli

Kethubboth 47b-48a 59
Qiddushin 22a 52
Baba Qamma 83b-84a 72
Sanhedrin 72b 71

D. VARIA

II Aqht

6:26-27 97

Cowley, *Aramaic Papyri*

10:16-17 54

Gordon, *Ugaritic Textbook*

67:II:12, 20 49

Kraeling, *Aramaic Papyri*
7:32 55
34 55
38 55
38-40 60
39 55
40 55
Naveh, *IEJ* 10 (1960), p. 134
line 12 37

Neofiti
Ex. 22:4 88

Philo, *On the Special Laws*
II:248 66
III:104-107 68, 74
108-109 72
140-141 70
195-197 74, 78
201 78
IV:35 93

Twelve Tables
VIII:2 77